AF740825

across media and disciplines

Edited by Sarah Huber

the purpose

Students are often overwhelmed by the volume of information they must navigate in today's academic landscape. Part of the challenge is that many instructors continue to guide their students with "decades-old approaches to teaching research-based writing, as there is little else available" (Bungert et al. 2022, 28). These traditional approaches tend to privilege the essay as the primary means of demonstrating understanding, narrowing the range of ways students can process and communicate what they learn.

In The Extended Mind, Annie Murphy Paul (2021) argues that our society places too much emphasis on the brain as the sole source of cognition. She explains that the brain alone lacks the biological capacity to manage complex information and instead relies on extensions such as bodily movement, physical environments, and collaboration with others. As Paul notes, "the lack of physical movement in our society is due in large part to academic learning and to knowledge work" (46). Libraries have traditionally supported access to and creation of knowledge primarily through text—a format that often keeps bodies still and cognition narrowly focused. Yet libraries are uniquely positioned to expand beyond this tradition by experimenting with information formats that activate embodied, spatial, and social ways of thinking. For example, a podcast interview can surface relationships, emphasis, and meaning through voice, timing, and interaction—dimensions that may remain implicit or invisible in an essay—demonstrating how format itself extends thinking.

Working as a librarian across educational settings, I have supported students creating knowledge beyond the traditional essay—through podcasts, videos, prototypes, textiles, and infographics. Across disciplines, however, I consistently observe uneven preparation and expectations for this work. Students in the liberal arts are often more familiar with art, design, and material principles that support work across varied formats, while students in other fields frequently select formats outside their disciplines without understanding how form conveys meaning or how to work within it intentionally. Many have never been taught foundational concepts such as material properties, visual hierarchy, or color theory. This gap across disciplines leaves students without shared language, tools, or consistent expectations as creators.

There are historical models for treating such principles as common intellectual groundwork rather than specialized or aesthetic concerns. At the Bauhaus, art, craft, and technology were positioned as equal forms of knowledge, united by purpose (Gropius 1965). This approach was extended at the Hochschule für Gestaltung Ulm, where design was taught as a systematic methodology for thinking, problem-solving, and communication (Hochschule für Gestaltung Ulm n.d.; HfG-Archiv Ulm n.d.). Drawing on these models, this book treats format knowledge as a shared, teachable foundation—supporting instructors in helping students use diverse formats not simply to present ideas, but to think through them.

Formats as Pedagogy

Throughout this book, I use *format* to describe how content is structured and presented—such as a podcast, dance, or essay—while *media* refers to the sensory channels through which a format is experienced (audio, visual, kinesthetic, or textual). These terms often overlap: a podcast is a format experienced through audio, and a dance is a performance format that engages both kinesthetic and visual media. While disciplines may use different terms—such as medium, mode, or genre—there is broad agreement that the form of communication shapes meaning. This shared understanding is captured by Marshall McLuhan's well-known assertion in *Understanding Media: The Extensions of Man* that "the medium is the message": the characteristics of how information is expressed influence what is understood, not just what is said.

This edited volume is a hands-on resource for instructors designing assignments that ask students to think and work creatively through and with different formats. Each chapter focuses on a specific format and includes an adaptable lesson plan written by an expert in that discipline, designed to help students understand the nature of the format—how it is constructed, what it affords, and how it shapes meaning—along with resources instructors can use to design related assignments. While formats function differently across disciplines, the book emphasizes shared art and design practices—such as visual hierarchy, color, perspective, and timing—that shape meaning across contexts. In this way, format creation becomes a pedagogical method for teaching how information is organized, interpreted, and communicated. Although the contributors write from higher education contexts, the approaches and lessons are adaptable for use across K–12 settings.

Drawing on research with faculty and students, I argue that intentional format choice—and the quality of work within a format—is part of the content itself. In a study of visual assignments in engineering and business courses, participants valued multimodal work but claimed that content mattered more than its expression. When asked about support to create multimodal work, they described assignment expectations and resource finding as a "Wild West" (Huber et al. 2024, 12). In a study of student podcasters, this same assumption about format versus content shifted when students examined how pacing, timing, and sound shaped understanding—revealing that quality within a format is not separate from content but integral to its meaning, as uninformed choices can distract from the message itself (Bochenek et al. 2025). For example, an abruptly cut interview or music that lingers too long can pull attention away from an idea, while the same choices, made intentionally, can add emphasis, tension, or clarity.

This approach aligns with librarians Silke Higgins and Ngoc-Yen Tran's work on "alternative assignments," which notes that "a growing number of students no longer believed that traditional research assignments aligned with the goals and outcomes they had set for their academic journey" (Higgins and Tran 2022, ix).

It also reflects evidence that "when instructional style matches the nature of the content, all learners learn better, regardless of their differences" (Brown et al. 2014). While students regularly create meaning across modes in everyday digital contexts, effective communication beyond familiar classroom audiences requires shared language and expectations that allow varied meaning-making practices to be recognized, discussed, and assessed. This book begins a shared conversation by offering format entry points that help students communicate clearly across academic and public contexts.

Knowledge Organization Through Formats

I first encountered the idea that reorganizing informational systems could reshape how we think through the Sitterwerk Foundation, as described in *The Dynamic Library.* Sitterwerk's dynamic, nonhierarchical library prioritizes discovery, embodied interaction, and associative thinking over linear retrieval. When I visited in 2023, its catalog, smart tables, and material archives revealed cross-disciplinary connections that emerged through movement, making, and annotation rather than text alone.

This experience led me to consider how external systems of organization shape internal cognition. As Anthon Åström, Fabian Wegmüller, and Lukas Zimmer (2015) argue, our systems of organization remain "heavily based on the physical world," privileging linear and hierarchical structures; challenging these systems can "lead to fundamental changes in our ideas, how we organize things, and our sense of knowledge itself" (93). Just as the Sitterwerk challenged linear systems through its library organization, regular engagement with varied information formats can challenge the primarily linear nature of text. Is this another way of looking at what Paul (2021) discusses in *The Extended Mind*—that working with information in diverse ways extends our minds' capabilities? While research explicitly connecting format, cognition, and internal knowledge structures remains limited, the Sitterwerk model suggests this relationship merits further investigation.

The Human-Centered Classroom in the Age of AI

Many lesson plans are hands-on and tactile; others focus on visual expression, movement, and interaction. Students design, collage, tell stories, and work collaboratively, using digital tools when needed but not always required. These approaches emphasize active participation and shared meaning-making, in contrast to the increasingly solitary and automated nature of contemporary learning technologies.

Working across material, visual, auditory, and kinesthetic formats brings attention to the decisions through which learning happens. Through making and revising work in different forms, students can actively construct knowledge and gain insight into how disciplines organize information and meaning. This exposure broadens perspectives beyond a single field and supports informed choices about when—and when not—to integrate approaches into their own work.

As AI tools become more embedded in academic contexts, the content provided asks how educators and librarians can design learning experiences that preserve human-centered thinking and sense-making while still helping students use AI intentionally and effectively. Format knowledge, alongside art and design skills, helps students make informed judgments about AI outputs rather than treating them as authoritative or complete.

Building Communities of Practice

When I joined Purdue University as an assistant professor of library science, I was asked to develop STEM-focused makerspace programming. Early attendance was low, prompting a reconsideration of what "making" could mean in a library context. Expanding beyond engineering-centered practices to include craft-based and material forms of making significantly increased student engagement and reshaped the space I now direct, the Knowledge Lab. Through this work, I began to see how a library makerspace could function as a foundation for a multimodal writing center—one where students creatively make and communicate knowledge through a range of formats.

This insight became especially clear through a project with Dr. Pamela Sari, director of Purdue's Asian American and Asian Resource and Cultural Center (AAARCC), in which students transformed archival images into a multimedia quilt combining fabric, narrative, and sound. The project demonstrated how material formats communicate meaning in ways text alone cannot. At the same time, it revealed a familiar challenge: without shared language, documentation, and institutional frameworks, non-textual work is often undervalued or difficult to assess. This aligns with Loveless's (2019) argument that creative practices function as legitimate forms of inquiry but require institutional recognition to be sustained.

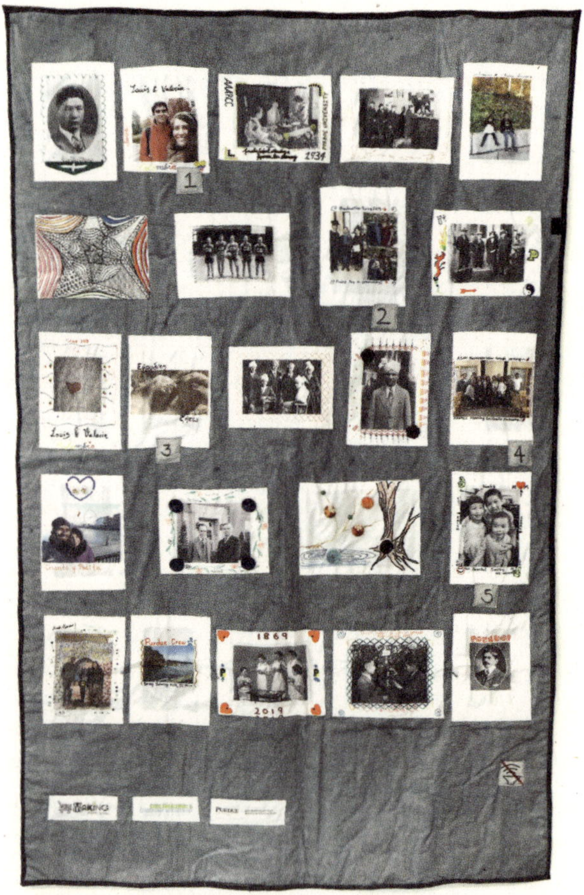

Image: AAARCC quilt
Photo credit: Sarah Huber

These experiences connect directly to the Association of College and Research Libraries' Framework for Information Literacy in Higher Education, particularly the frame "Information Creation as a Process," which emphasizes how meaning is shaped by format as information moves across contexts. Students already live in a media-rich environment where ideas constantly change form, yet academic coursework often remains narrowly text-centered—leaving little room to reflect on how formats shape understanding.

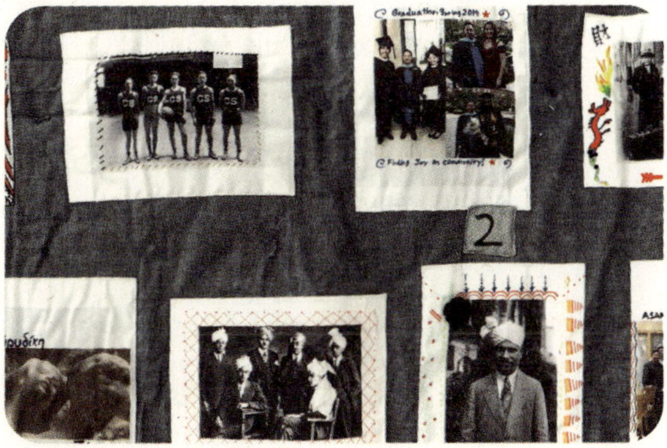

This work offers a practical foundation for building a community of practice around format-based learning and communicating. Echoing Bauhaus and Ulm's emphasis on foundational practices rather than siloed specialization, the book provides accessible points of entry rather than advanced design training. The text is primarily grounded in Western art and design traditions, whose codified principles—such as hierarchy and grid-based composition—provide a structured starting point for exploring diverse approaches. While not everyone will become a designer, shared introductory skills help students work more intentionally with form. Rather than teaching discipline-specific content, these materials treat format creation as pedagogy—supporting students in communicating ideas through diverse forms.

Åström, Anthon, Fabian Wegmüller, and Lukas Zimmer. 2015. "New Orders of Knowledge." In *The Dynamic Library: Organizing Knowledge at the Sitterwerk—Precedents and P Possibilities*, edited by Ariane Roth and Marina Schütz, translated by Alta L. Price, 93-102. Soberscove Press.

Bochenek, Annette, Sarah Huber, and Renusree Varma Mudduluru. 2025. "Libraries Facilitating Knowledge Creation Through Podcasting: Exploring Podcasts as a Form of Scholarship." *The Journal of Academic Librarianship* 51 (3): 103042. https://doi.org/10.1016/j.acalib.2025.103042.

Brown, Peter C., Henry L. Roediger, III, and Mark A McDaniel. 2014. *Make It Stick: The Science of Successful Learning*. Belknap Press.

Bungert, Nicole, Shevaun Ganski, Kate L. Watson, and Kristin M. Woodward. 2022."Thresholds Concepts and Rhetorical Contexts: Looking for Transfer and Letting Go of the Research Paper." In E*mbracing Change: Alternatives to Traditional Research Writing Assignments* edited by Silke Higgins and Ngoc-Yen Tran. Association of College and Research Libraries.

Gropius, Walter. 1965. *The New Architecture and the Bauhaus*. Translated by P. Morton Shand. MIT Press.

HfG-Archiv Ulm. n.d. "History of the HfG Ulm." Museum Ulm. https://bit.ly/4bLueCn.

HfG-Archiv Ulm. n.d. "The HfG Archive." Museum Ulm. https://bit.ly/4pX8okv.

Higgins, Silke, and Ngoc-Yen Tran. 2022. "Introduction." In *Embracing Change: Alternatives to Traditional Research Writing Assignments*, edited by Silke Higgins and Ngoc-Yen Tran. Association of College and Research Libraries.

Hochschule für Gestaltung Ulm. n.d. "HfG Ulm." https://bit.ly/4jPpPjM.

Huber, Sarah, Zoeanna Mayhook, and Wanju Huang. 2024. "Visual Media Assignments: Faculty vs. Student Experiences and Expectations in Engineering and Business." *The Journal of Academic Librarianship* 50 (6): 102971. https://doi.org/10.1016/j.acalib.2024.102971.

Loveless, Natalie. 2019. H*ow to Make Art at the End of the World: A Manifesto for Research-Creation*. Duke University Press.

Paul, Annie Murphy. 2021. *The Extended Mind: The Power of Thinking Outside the Brain*. Houghton Mifflin Harcourt.

Roth, Ariane and Marina Schütz, eds. 2015. *The Dynamic Library: Organizing Knowledge at the Sitterwerk—Precedents and Possibilities*. Translated by Alta L. Price. Soberscove Press.

creative formats

A Set Margins' publication

contents

PART 1:

GETTING STARTED

editorial disclaimer

This book explores creative formats across media—from photography to dance performances and song writing. The materials emphasize how each format carries and communicates information differently, shaping both meaning and understanding. Throughout, I use format to describe how content is structured (a photo, a dance, a song) and media to describe the sensory channels involved (a visual, kinesthetic, audio). I write from a librarian's perspective, where format is a familiar organizing concept, though I use both terms to engage readers from different disciplines. The lesson plans and resources are grounded in art and design practices, incorporating foundational elements—such as color, visual hierarchy, perspective, and composition—to help build understanding and establish a shared language that functions across disciplines.

In Understanding Media: The Extensions of Man (1964), Marshall McLuhan coined the phrase "the medium is the message," arguing that the characteristics of a medium shape what is communicated as much as the content itself. This insight is central here: the formats we choose—and the media through which they work— actively shape how we experience and make meaning from content.

This book is practical and exploratory—a starting point, not a prescription. Use the lesson plans with colleagues, adapt them to your field, and reflect on where different formats help students learn. You don't need to use an entire lesson plan. If one element seems useful—say, filming with shadows in the video lesson—pull just that piece and apply it to your assignment to build proficiency in video. An instructor activity guides you through deciding which skills will benefit your students. I published in print so you can write and take notes.

1.1
How to use this book

The book is organized into the following sections:

Accessibility and Inclusion Guide

This book offers a range of visual, active, and hands-on lesson plans, many of which are analog. While not all lessons include explicit accessibility strategies, this guide provides adaptable tools, standards, and digital options to support inclusive participation and ensure all students can engage with the material. It is tailored to the content of this book and should be seen as a starting point, as accessibility and inclusion are broad, evolving fields with much more to explore.

Information Formats Table

This book includes a table of formats with their qualities, affordances, and constraints, supported by citations. It helps faculty and students intentionally choose formats for specific purposes and communication goals. The list is not exhaustive or prescriptive—it's a starting point for discussion that students can expand through their own research. For example, a student exploring a scientific process might decide that folding the pages of a book or zine in certain ways could help them think through the material and share in that process. The list is composed of the formats included in this book.

Lesson Plan Structure

Each lesson plan serves as a point of entry to trying a new format in your course. You don't need to use an entire lesson plan. If one element seems useful—say, filming with shadows in the video lesson—pull just that piece and apply it to your assignment to build student proficiency in video. An instructor activity guides you through deciding which skills will benefit your student. Each lesson plan across all three lesson plan sections includes:

> Key information qualities

> Intended audience

> Learning outcomes

> Instructional context and materials needed

> An adaptable assignment

> Assessment criteria

> Cross-disciplinary applications

> An instructor activity to help integrate the lesson into your classroom

> Further resources

Lesson Plans: Compositional Principles

The lesson plans in this section highlight compositional principles that support students working thoughtfully and creatively across many other formats included in this book. Even if they are using automated tools, these principles will help them make informed decisions during the creation process.

For visuals, two key design principles are visual hierarchy and the rule of thirds. For stories, students often default to a linear arc, with a beginning, middle, and end; however, a nonlinear composition can sometimes communicate ideas or experiences more effectively across disciplines like science or history. For poetry, the haiku is a common default, but students can benefit from encountering a wider range of poetic forms.

These four lesson plans on compositional principles serve as points of entry. There are, of course, more layers to build upon, discover, and reimagine.

Lesson Plans: Discipline-Specific Formats

The lesson plans in Part 3 focus on formats that are native to and defining of specific disciplines, such as photography as an art form, bookmaking as a craft, dance as embodied expression, and journal essays in technical and professional writing. These are written by experts who teach these formats as the core practice of their respective fields.

Student Stories

This section includes two stories showing how material processes serve as tools for learning and communication. One student uses sewing to explore faith, identity, and style through garments in a fashion show. Another uses knitting as a research method, creating pieces that embody findings through texture and form. Both illustrate how making transforms understanding into tangible expression.

Lesson Plans: Formats Across Disciplines

Unlike disciplines organized around one dominant format, many fields integrate diverse formats as pedagogical tools to create, interpret, and share knowledge. This section shows how instructors adapt formats from outside their disciplines, repurposing them as tools for inquiry and communication rather than teaching the formats themselves as practices to be mastered. Video becomes a research documentation tool in anthropology rather than an exercise in cinematography.

Practical Skills Index

Throughout the book, assignments introduce a range of basic skills and design principles to help students make informed choices when working in different information formats. These foundational elements are not meant to prescribe outcomes but to build awareness and understanding of how visual, material, and auditory design decisions shape meaning. This section supplements the assignments with resources for skills—such as video taking or editing—that are mentioned in the lessons but not fully detailed, supporting students in building informed excellence across various formats.

instructor note

Accessibility is not a one-size-fits-all checklist. Pair these strategies with input from **disability resource centers** or campus accessibility experts for maximum impact, as was done in making this guide

Purpose of This Guide

> Provide a baseline for accessibility in all lesson plans.

> Offer adaptation ideas for tools, visuals, and classroom setups.

> Support Universal Design for Learning (UDL) so all students benefit.

1.2
Accessibility and Inclusion Guide

Adaptive Tools and Equipment

Challenge	Solution Ideas
Fine motor and/or grip	Pencil grips, weighted pens, ergonomic scissors, Velcro tool straps, universal cuffs
Standing, sitting, or bending	Adjustable-height tables, supportive chairs, table risers, accessible seating, such as armless chairs, chairs without wheels, chairs with a stationary backrest.
Equipment access	Offer digital mockups as alternatives to analog creative work (such as collages), pre-cut templates, or assign partners for shared tasks.
Machinery (e.g., button making, sewing machine)	Provide premade samples, digital templates, and short video demonstrations in advance, so students can understand the process, plan their approach, and request support if needed.

Accessibility Strategies

Visual Accessibility

> Use high-contrast, colorblind-friendly palettes (WebAIM Contrast Checker).
> Add patterns or labels—don't rely on color alone.
> Use clear diagrams with descriptive labels.
> Choose sans-serif fonts (Arial, Verdana, Calibri).
> Use bold, headings, and spacing for emphasis; avoid ALL CAPS.
> Aim for 14–18 pt font (this may be difficult for made objects like buttons).
> Provide large-print versions and resizable digital files.

Audio and Multimedia Accessibility

> Provide captions for all videos.
> Ensure transcripts are available in digital, screen-reader-friendly format.
> Use clear diagrams with descriptive labels.
> Allow time to repeat and review instructions or visuals.
> Ensure media players have player controls that allow users to pause and rewatch content as needed.

Instructional Design Tips

> **Multiple formats:** Many lesson plans have students creating physical pieces but offer the choice of digital creation—discuss the benefits of both.

> **Flexible grouping**: Pair students by complementary strengths, with their consent.

> **Scaffolding**: These lesson plans allow instructors to adapt to their class. There may be ambiguity built in to allow variations. Remember to scaffold projects to support understanding and success.

> **Flexible timing:** Build in buffer time or asynchro nous options.

> **Seek learner feedback**: Ask students to share suggestions to make assignments, projects, and lesson plans more inclusive

Accessibility Checklist

> Adaptive tools available

> Accessible tables and seating

> High-contrast colors and clear fonts

> Step-by-step visuals and instructions

> Digital and analog options ready

> Flexible timelines and grouping

Creativity and a Layered Access Approach

Creative expression is part of how meaning is communicated, and students' unique style adds value to their project. This book encourages students to explore creative approaches. Examples of this could include intricate handwriting, unconventional color palettes, layered collages, or nonlinear arrangements. However, these forms of expression may not be accessible to all people. Accessibility ensures the work can be understood by the widest audience. It is recommended that if students' work does not meet accessibility standards, they take a layered access approach. What this would look like:

> Students produce their creative work as they choose in the format they choose.

> Students provide at least one accessible alternative so that all viewers can engage with their work.

Examples of accessible alternatives:
> A transcript or plain-text description of handwritten or collage content
> An alternative color-contrast version or grayscale copy
> Alt-text or a digital narrative description for complex visuals
> A linear, simplified version (e.g., a basic chart or outline) alongside a more expressive piece

Recommended Resources

CAST Universal Design for Learning (UDL):
https://bit.ly/4ovuskL

CAST National Center on Accessible Educational Materials (AEM):
https://bit.ly/4oBTi2j

Colblindor. n.d. "Coblis—Color Blindness Simulator." Accessed March 4, 2026: https://bit.ly/4bnSrOw

National Center on Health, Physical Activity and Disability:
Adapted Physical Education Equipment and Strategies:
https://bit.ly/4hNo5GW

WebAIM Contrast Checker:
https://bit.ly/47YRzoZ

National Center on Accessible Educational Materials:
https://bit.ly/4hILQzM

In these pages, Qualities, Affordances, and Constraints per medium are listed, and referenced.

1.3 Information formats Table

> Orients space

> Often perceived as capturing a moment that cannot be reproduced

> Functions as evidence

> Conveys meaning across languages and cultures, though interpretation and description vary by linguistic and cultural context

> Reproducible and easily distributable

> Subject to manipulation through framing, raising issues of consent, representation, and exploitation

Berger and Ponti 2024, Cleland and MacLeod 2021, Hofer and Swan 2005, Kress 2010, Newman and Kanjanawong 2005, Sontag 1977

> Combines orders of time and space

> Enables multimodal engagement

> Effective for storytelling, demonstration, and education

> Shareable and accessible when captions are provided

> Can be complex to shoot and edit

> Prone to bias through selective framing and editing

> Raises ethical and consent concerns

> Involves framing choices and data-collection complexities when used in research

Bordwell and Thompson 2008, Kress 2010, Luff and Heath 2012, Nichols 2017

Text (reflective writing)

> Precise, structured, and scalable

> Enables detailed explanation, logical and sequential reasoning, and reflective, abstract thought

> Stable, reproducible, and accessible across platforms

> Compatible with text-to-speech tools

> Fixes meaning

> May be misinterpreted without context and requires sustained time and literacy

> Less multisensory, which may be less engaging for some

Chartier 1995, Hall 1976, Johns 1998, Kress 2010, McLuhan 1994, Nielsen 2000, Ong 1982, Sweller et al. 1998, Tufte 1990

> Ideas or narrative rendered in tangible form, often organized in a sequence

> Form can shape the idea or narrative

> Combines material and textual qualities

> Promotes engagement through materiality, facilitating interaction beyond reading

> Labor-intensive, potentially fragile, and not always easily scalable

Drucker 2004, McNeil 2015

> Focuses on independent thought

> Low barrier to entry

> Open to anyone as a publishing format

> Affordable and easily reproduced

> Combines images, text, and Symbolism

> Can be folded and configured in different ways to create different effects

> Immediate production and circulation

> Easily preserved long term

> May have limited distribution or visibility

> Often does not meet accessibility standards, but can be created as an ezine or use tactile elements to be more inclusive

Drucker 2004, Freedman n.d. Terrell 2025

> Landscape and human-designed systems collaborate to express place-based narratives

> Not static--ever-changing, reflecting people, ideas, and impermanence

> The visible is the result of invisible processes

> Connects humans to environment through sensory experience

> Communicates patterned relationships that carry meaning

> Subject to environmental change

Corner 1999, Spirn 1998

> Encodes individual and cultural meaning through sound

> Reinforces memory and recall through rhythm, meter, and song

> Can transcend language barriers

> Abstract and interpretive, requiring time and context for comprehension

Frith 1996, Sacks 2007

> Embodied thought as kinetic

> Movement functions as a cognitive tool

> The body as a place of inquiry

> Expressive in nature

> Communicates through gesture, rhythm, and spatial form

> Ephemeral; insight can be difficult to document or trace

> Dependent on bodily literacy or instruction for those untrained

Foster 2011, Paul 2021, Sheets-Johnstone 2011, Snowber 2016

> Multimodal and contextual

> Integrates objects, media, and narrative to support interactive meaning-making and learning

> Creates contextual understanding through space and sensory cues

> Curatorial choices can shape perception in unintended or unethical ways

Hein 1998, Hooper-Greenhill 2000, May et al. 2021

> Immersive and portable

> Conveys tone, rhythm, and emotion

> Builds connection through voice, conversation, and storytelling

> Fosters deep listening

> Serves to disseminate scholarly work and research

> Can be produced with minimal equipment

> Can be time-consuming to produce

> Difficult to search without robust metadata

Carterette et al. 2021, Clarke and Bjork 2023, Cook 2023, The Podcast Consultant 2025, Sterne 2003

> Transforms numerical or complex data into visual form to support exploration and reveal patterns, trends, relationships, and anomalies

> Used during analysis to ask questions, test assumptions, and inform decision-making, rather than just to present finalized conclusions

> Meaning is not always fixed; multiple interpretations and insights may emerge

> Can surface uncertainty, variability, and gaps in the data

> Automated software may not select the most appropriate chart or encoding for the data or the analytical task

> Requires design and data literacy to avoid misleading representations

Cairo 2016, Evergreen 2020, Few 2009, Midway 2020, Nguyen et al. 2021, Tufte 1990

> Visual, concise, and integrative

> Designed to communicate synthesized insights rather than explore raw data

> Combines text, image, and selected data to support rapid

> Comprehension and pattern recognition

> Often narrative or persuasive, guiding the viewer toward specific interpretations

> Can transcend language barriers and enhance memory

> Effective for public-facing communication, education, and advocacy

> Risks oversimplification, distortion, or aesthetic bias

> Requires design and data literacy

> Requires careful attention to source credibility

Cairo 2016, Lankow et al. 2012, Midway 2020
Nguyen et al. 2021, Tufte 1990, Veszelszki 2014

> Tactile, symbolic, and participatory

> Merges art and communication for advocacy and identity formation

> Low-cost

> Limited in physical space

Busy Beaver Button Museum n.d.
Carter and Hake 2020, Duncombe and Lambert 2021

> Tactile

> Communicates information through sight and touch

> Merges craft, symbolism, and storytelling

> Reflects culture and identity

> Respond to the environment through programming (computational textiles)

> Reveals complexities of co-produced knowledge in collaborative textile projects

> Time-intensive, requires a set of skills, not easily reproduced

> May rely on cultural literacy for interpretation

Davis 2019, König 2013, Shercliff and Twigger Holroyd 2020

References

Berger, Uri, and Edouardo M. Ponti. 2024. "Cross-Lingual and Cross-Cultural Variation in Image Descriptions." In *Proceedings of the 2024 Conference of the North American Chapter of the Association for Computational Linguistics: Human Language Technologies*. 9447–9454. Association for Computational Linguistics. https://bit.ly/43hMVZz.

Bordwell, David, and Kristin Thompson. 2008. F*ilm Art: An Introduction*. 8th ed. McGraw-Hill.

Busy Beaver Button Company. n.d. "The History of Protest Buttons." Accessed August 22, 2025. https://bit.ly/3LcBBIm.

Cairo, Alberto. 2016. *The Truthful Art: Data, Charts, and Maps for Communication*. New Riders.

Carter, Christian, and Ted Hake. 2020. "The Pin-Back Button Was a Place for Self-Expression Before Social Media." *AIGA Eye on Design*, June 1, 2020. https://bit.ly/3LNHJGD.

Carterette, Ben, Rosie Jones, Gareth F. Jones, Maria Eskevich, Sravana Reddy, Ann Clifton, Yongze Yu, Jussi Karlgren, and Ian Soboroff. 2021. "Podcast Metadata and Content: Episode Relevance and Attractiveness in Ad Hoc Search." *arXiv*. https://bit.ly/4qMy2Iw.

Chartier, Roger. 1995. *The Order of Books: Readers, Authors, and Libraries in Europe Between the Fourteenth and Eighteenth Centuries*. Stanford University Press.

Chartier, Roger. 1994. *The Order of Books: Readers, Authors, and Libraries in Europe Between the Fourteenth and Eighteenth Centuries*. Stanford University Press.

Clarke, Kyra, and Collin Bjork. 2023. "'Listening Closely' to Mediated Intimacies and Podcast Intimacies in Song Exploder." *Convergence: The International Journal of Research into New Media Technologies* 29 (4): 818-835. https://doi.org/10.1177/13548565231160886.

Cleland, Jennifer, and Anna MacLeod. 2021. The Visual Vernacular: Embracing Photographs in Research. *Perspectives on Medical Education, Journal of the Netherlands Association of Medical Education* 10 (4): 230-237. DOI: 10.1007/S40037-021-00672-X.

Cook, Ian M. 2023. *Scholarly Podcasting: Why, What, How?* Routledge.

Corner, James, ed. 1999. *Recovering Landscape: Essays in Contemporary Landscape Architecture*. Princeton Architectural Press.

Davis, Felicia. 2019. FELT: *Communicating Emotion Through Textile Expression. Technology | Architecture + Design*. 3 (2): 146–149. https://doi.org/10.1080/24751448.2019.1640524.

Drucker, Joanna. 2004. *The Century of Artists' Books*. Granary Books.

Duncombe, Steve, and Steve Lambert. 2021. *The Art of Activism*. OR Books.

Evergreen, Stephanie D. H. 2020. *Effective Data Visualization: The Right Chart for the Right Data*. 2nd ed. SAGE.

Few, Stephen. 2009. *Now You See It: Simple Visualization Techniques for Quantitative Analysis*. Analytics Press.

Foster, Susan. 2011. *Choreographing Empathy: Kinesthesia in Performanc*e. Routledge.

Freedman, J. (n.d). *Zines Are Not Blogs*. Barnard Zine Library. Accessed January 10, 2026. https://bit.ly/3MG9txx.

Frith, Simon. 1998. *Performing Rites: On the Value of Popular Music*. Harvard University Press.

Hall, Edward T. 1976). *Beyond Culture*. Anchor Books.

Hein, George E. 1998. *Learning in the Museum*. Routledge.

Hofer, Mark, and Kathleen Owings Swan. 2005. "Digital Image Manipulation: A Compelling

Hooper-Greenhill, Eilean. 2000. *Museums and the Interpretation of Visual Culture*. Routledge. Means to Engage Students in Discussion of Point of View and *Perspective. Contemporary Issues in Technology and Teacher Education* 5 (3/4): 290–299. https://bit.ly/4oWKHXR.

Johns, Adrian. 1998. *The Nature of the Book: Print and Knowledge in the Making*. University of Chicago Press.

König, Anna. 2013. *A Stitch in Time: Changing Cultural Constructions of Craft and M ending. Culture Unbound: Journal of Current Cultural Research* 5: 569-585. https://bit.ly/4qLwNt7.

Kress, Gunther. 2010. *Multimodality: A Social Semiotic Approach to Contemporary Communication*. Routledge.

Lankow, Jason, Josh Ritchie, and Ross Crooks. 2012. I*nfographics: The Power of Visual Storytelling*. Wiley.

Luff, Paul, and Christian Heath. 2012. "Some 'Technical Challenges' of Video Analysis: Social Actions, Objects, Material Realities and the Problems of Perspective. *Qualitative Research* 12(3): 255–279. DOI:10.1177/1468794112436655.

May, Sarah, Katie Todd, Samantha G. Daley, and Gabrielle Rappolt-Schlichtmann. 2021. "Measurement of Science Museum Visitors' Emotional Experiences at Exhibits Designed to Encourage Productive Struggle." *Curator: The Museum Journal*, 64 (4): 1–25. https://bit.ly/3WHNSqg.

McLuhan, Marshal. 1994. *Understanding Media: The Extensions of Man.* MIT Press.

McNeil, Brian. 2015. "More than Words: 16 of the Most Interesting and Unusual Items in VCU's Book Art Collection." *VCU News*. May 22. https://bit.ly/47uWzKI.

Midway, Stephen R. 2020. "Principles of Effective Data Visualization." *Patterns*, 1 (9): 100141. DOI: 10.1016/j.patter.2020.100141.

Newman, Ian M., and Supannee Kanjanawong. 2005. "Using Photography to Cross Generational, Linguistic, and Cultural Barriers to Develop Useful Survey Instruments." *Health Promotion Practice* 6 (1): 53–56. DOI:10.1177/1524839903259307.

Nguyen, Vinh T., Kwanghee Jung, and Vibhuti Gupta. 2021. "Examining Data Visualization Pitfalls in Scientific Publications." *Visual Computing for Industry, Biomedicine, and Art* 4 (1): 27. DOI: 10.1186/s42492-021-00092-y.

Nichols, Bill. 2017. *Introduction to Documentary*. 3rd ed. Indiana University Press.

Nielsen, Jakob. 2000. Designing Web Usability: *The Practice of Simplicity*. New Riders Publisher.

Ong, Walter J. 1982. *Orality and Literacy: The Technologizing of the Word*. Methuen.

Paul, Annie Murphy. 2021. *The Extended Mind: The Power of Thinking Outside the Brain.* Houghton Mifflin Harcourt.

Sacks, Oliver. 2007. *Musicophilia: Tales of Music and the Brain*. Knopf.

Sheets-Johnstone, Maxine. 2011. *The Primacy of Movement.* John Benjamins Publishing.

Shercliff, Emma, and Amy Twigger Holroyd. 2020. "Stitching Together: Participatory Textile Making as an Emerging Methodological Approach to Research." *Qualitative Research Journal* 20(3): 233–245.

Snowber, Celeste. 2016. *Embodied Inquiry: Writing, Living and Being through the Body.* Sense Publishers.

Sontag, Susan. 1977. *On Photography.* Farrar, Straus and Giroux.

Spirn, Anne Winston. 1998. *The Language of Landscape.* Yale University Press.

Sterne, Jonathan. 2003. *The Audible Past: Cultural Origins of Sound Reproduction.* Duke University Press.

Sweller, John, Jeroen J. G. van Merriënboer, and Fred G. W. C. Paas. 1998. "Cognitive Architecture and Instructional Design." *Educational Psychology Review* 10 (3): 251–296. https://doi.org/10.1023/A:1022193728205.

Terrell, Katharine. 2025. "Balancing Accessibility and Creativity in the Classroom: The Case of Zines." *Journal of Perspectives in Applied Academic Practic*e 13 (1). https://doi.org/10.56433/tz36p460.

The Podcast Consultant. April 24, 2025. "Ultimate Guide to Podcast Equipment in 2025." https://bit.ly/3JFTyOC.

Tufte, Edward R. 1990. *Envisioning Information.* Graphics Press.

Veszelszki, Ágnes. 2014. "Information Visualization: Infographics from a Linguistic Point of View." In *The Power of the Image*, edited by András Benedek and Kristóf Nyíri, 99–109. Visual Learning Series, 4. Frankfurt: Peter Lang.

PART 2:

LESSON PLAN

Compositional Principles

LOGICS OF SPACE: THE RULE OF THIRDS IN PHOTOGRAPHY AND VIDEO

By: Sarah Huber

Discipline: Visual Literacy and Library Science

Subject: Photography and Video Composition

Information Qualities of the Compositional Principle

Gunther Kress (2010) describes still images as organized by "logics of space," while moving images combine a "logic of sequence in time" with an underlying "logic of space" (81). The rule of thirds is a visual system that organizes "logics of space." It uses a grid of nine rectangles over a still image or video viewing area to create interest and balance. By dividing an image or video into a 3×3 grid, it helps direct the viewers' attention (Gitner 2023). Therefore, space is organized to communicate meaning.

Who This Is For

Faculty across disciplines can incorporate this simple exercise to help students make informed compositional choices in photography or video. Whether documenting fieldwork, creating how-to tutorials, or telling visual stories, learning the rule of thirds helps students organize space.

Learning Outcomes

> **Identify** how the rule of thirds organizes visual information in still images and video.

> **Analyze** how placement directs viewer's attention and creates narrative.
> **Apply** the rule of thirds to frame balanced and purposeful compositions.
> **Evaluate** when to use or break the rule for creative effect.
> **Reflect** on how composition choices guide viewer attention and communicate meaning.

Instructional Context

> Studio-style or makerspace classroom with tables for collaboration
> Small to medium class (10–20 students)
> One or two 50-minute sessions
> Could be presented as a workshop within disciplines

Materials and Equipment

> Cameras, smartphones, or tablets with camera function
> Grid overlays enabled (camera setting)
> Tracing paper with grid drawn on it
> Access to editing tools (Photoshop, Lightroom, Canva, Premiere, or CapCut)
> Paper, glue, and writing tools
> Example photographs and video clips illustrating rule of thirds vs. centered compositions

Note: In this mix of photos, include photos that are taken from a distance, at medium range, and close up.

Part 1: Introduction and Observation (In-Class Activity)

Assignment: The instructor introduces the idea of rule of thirds. There are many online resources, but here is one from the BBC that explains how the grid produces focal points to direct the viewer's attention in a painting: https://bit.ly/49mytDt

Materials Provided

> Printed photographs (varied subjects) laid out on a table by the instructor
> Tracing paper overlays with the nine-rectangle grid (rule of thirds)

Process and Steps

1. Students work in pairs, overlaying the grid on different photographs.

2. Ask students to move the grid around and notice where the main subject (person, plant, building, etc.) falls and what the focal point(s) is.

3. Discuss the following with partners:
> What draws your attention first?
> How does placement affect the story or feeling?
> What kinds of balance or tension do you notice?

Part 2: Image Creation

Materials Provided

> A box of assorted objects (tools, household items, fruit, etc.)
> Cameras or smartphones

Instructions

Each pair selects one object as their subject.

Round 1: Capture a short video sequence (series of clips) or use several photographs. Work intuitively, without thinking about the rule of thirds. Treat the object as a character; experiment with angles, movement, light, and shadow.

Round 2: Repeat the process intentionally applying the rule of thirds. Use your camera's grid feature to guide composition.

> Decide whether the photos should be from far away, medium, or close.

Part 3: Production and Assembly

Option A: Video Format

1. Edit your clips into a short (one or two minute) sequence that either tells a story or demonstrates a process ("How-to").
2. Create two versions: *Intuitive* (no rule of thirds) and *Intentional* (with rule of thirds).

Option B: Booklet Format (Analog or Digital)

Print and arrange your photographs into two small

booklets or digital slideshows:
Booklet 1: Intuitive compositions
Booklet 2: Intentional compositions using the rule of thirds

Part 4: Reflection and Peer Review

1. Present both versions in class or online.
2. Peers view and comment on the following:
> Which compositions communicated a stronger message and how?
> How did visual placement influence mood, focus, or narrative clarity?
3. Reflect (individually or as pairs) on what you learned about framing, attention, and visual storytelling.

Deliverables

> Two visual works (videos or booklets): *Before* and *After* applying the rule of thirds
> Short written or verbal reflection (150–200 words or two minutes) on what changed in your approach and audience perception

Assessment

The project can be graded on five areas. **Composition** looks at how effectively the rule of thirds was used or how intentionally students chose to break it. **Visual Communication** focuses on how clearly the message or story comes through and how well their framing directs attention. **Creativity** considers originality and willingness to experiment with framing and subject matter. **Reflection** assesses how thoughtfully the student described what they learned about composition, storytelling, and design choices. Finally, **Technical Quality** looks at the clarity of your images or video, including lighting, focus, and editing.

Examples

Both photos show Patricia crocheting; the right image more clearly conveys engagement. Converting to black and white helps isolate the focal point.

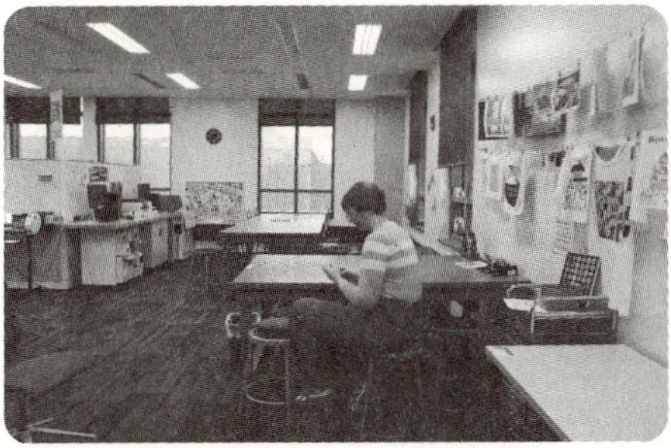

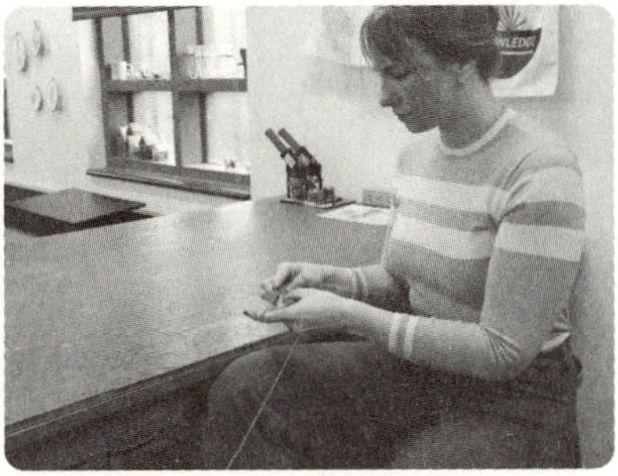

Image 1: Center Photo credit: Sarah Huber

Image 2: Right 3rd Photo Credit: Sarah Huber

Cross-Disciplinary Adaptation

> Business: Apply composition to marketing visuals or product photography to create emphasis and appeal.

> Anthropology: Document artifacts or fieldwork sites, highlighting relationships between subjects and sur roundings.

> Dance or Theater: Frame movement or performance to emphasize body position and spatial awareness.

> Political Science / Law: Compose visual evidence or campaign imagery to analyze framing and persuasion.

Instructor Try-It Activity

Take three quick photos or record a five-second video clip of an everyday object (e.g., a mug, plant, or desk item).

1. First, center the subject.
2. Then, shift it to align with a grid intersection.
3. Compare the emotional or narrative difference.
4. Reflect briefly on the following:

> How does shifting the subject change the story or the viewer's attention?

> Does one version stand out to you over another? Why?

> Finally, in what ways could an activity like this better equip you to create meaningful coursework for your students to support their learning?

Additional Resources/ References

Gitner, Seth. 2022. *Multimedia Storytelling for Digital Communicators in a Multiplatform World.* 2nd ed. Routledge.

Kress, Gunther. 2010. *Multimodality: A Social Semiotic Approach to Contemporary Communication*. Routledge.

HANDS-ON HIERARCHY: DESIGNING A CONCERT POSTER

By: Sarah Huber

Discipline: Photography and Video Composition

Subject: Visual Literacy: Visual Hierarchy for Visual Information

Information Qualities of the Structure

The visual literacy course I teach emphasizes creating, not just reading, visual information. I've learned most students lack familiarity with visual hierarchy, which I see as an essential starting point for creating visuals. Visual hierarchy is like a map, guiding viewers through a design. Without it, a block of information has no clear point of entry. By arranging elements—size, color, typography, alignment, and whitespace—designers lead the viewer's eye from the main point to supporting details. This assignment teaches students how to structure visual content, so audiences have direction on how to navigate the visual information.

Who This Is For

Faculty without visual literacy training can adapt this introductory visual hierarchy activity across visual formats to support their students. As visual information becomes more common in academia, understanding these principles benefits students across fields. Learning visual hierarchy takes time to develop. This is a quick introduction, intended as a starting point for experimentation.

Learning Outcomes

> **Identify** key elements of visual hierarchy.
> **Analyze** concert posters for clarity and readability.
> **Create** clearly understood posters by applying visual hierarchy principles.
> **Demonstrate** design decisions during peer critique using correct terminology.
> **Evaluate** how design choices impact information understanding.

Instructional Context

> Studio-style or makerspace classroom with tables for collaboration
> Small to medium class (10–20 students)
> One or two 50-minute sessions
> Could be presented as a workshop within disciplines

Materials and Equipment

> Scrabble tiles, Bananagrams tiles, or printed letter tiles used for concert details (artist, date, time, venue, ticket price); ChatGPT can be used to generate scrabble tile numbers 0.75 × 0.75 inches.
> Felt squares in a variety of colors
> Precut felt shapes or enough felt squares for students to cut them into shapes
> Scissors
> 12 X 18 felt triangles for organizing concert details on
> Markers, colored pencils, pens
> Rulers, stencils, glue sticks, tape
> Magazines, discarded visual books, etc.
> Optional: Laptops with Canva, Adobe Express, or similar design tools

> Example posters (good and bad) printed or projected for discussion.

Resources Students Should Review for the Assignment

Students can look up posters of their favorite band(s) or search the following:

> Stax Museum of American Soul Music: Promotional and Concert posters: https://bit.ly/47Dp87v
> The Rock Poster Society: https://trps.org/
> Center for the Study of Political Graphics https://www.politicalgraphics.org/
> Canva: The Ultimate Guide to Visual Hierarchy: https://bit.ly/47rcKZw
> W3 Schools Color Schemes: https://bit.ly/43YcTRV

Assignment
Session 1
Opening Exercise Process and Steps

1. Students use letter tiles to arrange concert information.

Image 1:
No hierarchy
Photo credit: Sarah Huber

2. Class discusses how the tiles read when all words and lines have equal value.

> Discuss how it would read differently if some words were larger and highlighted with color.

> Discuss how it would read differently if lines were aligned differently.

> Instructor introduces the elements of visual hierarchy with examples.

Hands-On Felt Activity Process and Steps

1. Students use precut or cut felt into various shapes (circles, rectangles, triangles) in multiple sizes and colors.
2. Individually or in small groups, they arrange and rearrange felt shapes on felt rectangle to experiment with the different effects placement of the following has on visual navigation of information:

> Size contrast (large vs. small)

> Color combinations (analogous vs. complementary)

> Alignment (left or right adjusted)

> Whitespace (crowded vs. open layouts)

3. Students present their layouts and discuss.

> Identify where the eye is drawn first (the focal point) and explain why.

> Analyze how colors, sizes, and placement create visual tension or flow.

> Examine how alignment—or the lack of it—guides the viewer's eye.

> Discuss how whitespace influences flow and clarity.

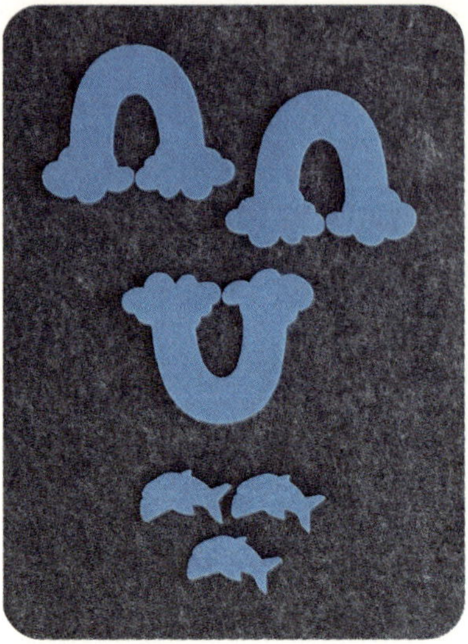

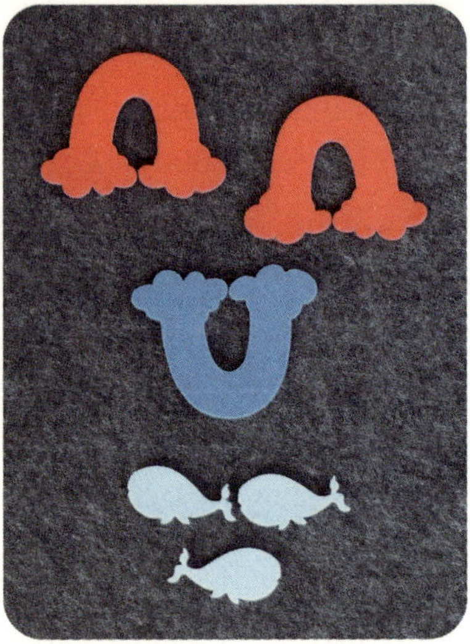

Image 2: Layout

Image 3: Color

Photo credit: Sarah Huber

Session 2
Design
Process and Steps

1. Using drawing materials (or laptops for a digital version), students create a concert poster employing visual hierarchy.
2. Encourage iteration: rough sketch first, then refine.
3. Posters should have a clear focal point, visual flow, and distinct levels of information (most important to least).

> Emphasize keeping it simple: Use just one or two types of fonts and two or three colors. Use the W3 Schools site to find color schemes.

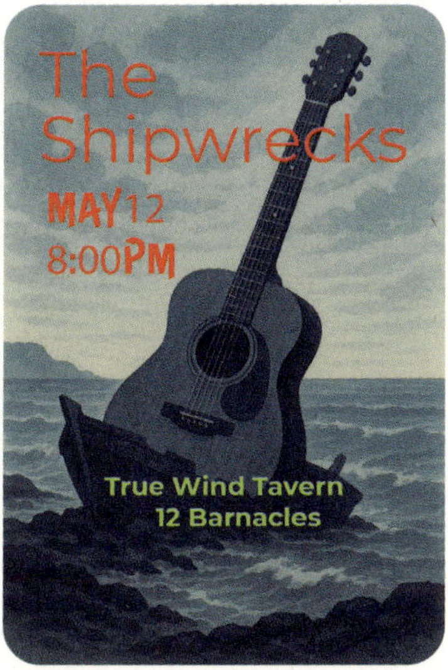

Image 4: Concert poster

Image credit: ChatGPT and Photoshop

Critique and Reflection

1. Display completed posters.
2. Peers provide constructive feedback using the following prompts:

> What path does your eye take?
> What works and what causes visual tension?
> How does color, size, alignment, and whitespace influence understanding?

3. Students write a brief paragraph reflecting on their design choices and areas for improvement.

Assessment

> **Clear Focal Point**: Main idea or message stands out.
> **Organized Information**: Supporting details are grouped logically under the main idea.
> **Effective Visual Hierarchy**: Size, color, alignment,

and spacing guide the viewer's eye.
> **Readable**: Text and visuals are easy to see and understand.
> **Creative Effort**: Shows experimentation and thoughtful design choices.
> **Reflection and Feedback**: Participates in critique and considers improvements.

Cross-Disciplinary Adaptation

In these examples, focal points are suggested, but students ultimately decide what to highlight.

> **STEM**: Students design a poster advertising a research symposium or engineering showcase. Emphasis is placed on the overall theme.
> **Business/Marketing**: Students create a promotional flyer for a product launch event. Emphasis is placed on why the audience would be interested in the product.
> **Public Health**: Students design an informative flyer about a health campaign. Emphasis is placed on the urgency of the situation.
> **Performing Arts**: Students design playbills or performance posters. Emphasis is placed on who is performing.

Instructor Try-It Activity

Before teaching, create your own tile layout and poster, using the following steps:

1. Arrange tiles haphazardly.
2. Redesign into a poster emphasizing:

> Headline prominence (or what you think is most important as the visual entry point).
> Supporting details, such as a clear date and time.

3. Reflect on which choices made the biggest difference. This will help model the design process for students.

Additional Resources/References

Lupton, Ellen, ed. 2014. *Graphic Design Thinking: Beyond Brainstorming*. Princeton Architectural Press.

Tondreau, Beth. 2019. *Layout Essentials: 100 Design Principles for Using Grids. Revised ed.* Rockport Publishers.

INDIGENOUS KNOWLEDGE: LEARNING TO TELL STORIES FROM NATIVE AMERICANS AND FIRST NATIONS PEOPLES

By: Alyssa A. Nez, Diné (Navajo)

Discipline: Endangered Indigenous Languages

Subject: Nonlinear Storytelling

Information Qualities of the Compositional Principle

Everyone knows a linear story structure. It has a beginning, middle, and end. But not all stories fit this structure. Since time immemorial, Indigenous Peoples have told stories in a nonlinear structure. This way of storytelling embodies traditions, beliefs, values, and cultures, instilling a strong sense of identity.

It speaks to relationships of time, cycles, and seasons. Relationships between the young and old. Relationships among generations, seven generations behind and seven generations forward. It teaches us to laugh, to show humility, to be kind, and to commit. Commit to land, traditions, alternate ways of knowing, and most importantly, to our futures.

Storytelling across disciplines often assumes a linear path, though some stories reveal more when told nonlinearly. For example, Stephen Graham Jones uses nonlinear storytelling in *Ledfeather*, not just to show how the choices of a 19th-century Indian Agent affect the life of a 20th-century Blackfeet teen, but to collapse the distance between past and present. The novel loops between eras, allowing actions and identities to echo across generations, highlighting that time is relational rather than chronological. The structure emphasizes continuity over finality, creating a cyclical pattern in which stories, and their consequences, never truly end but continue to shape what comes next.

> **Linear storytelling**, as modeled by Freytag's Pyramid (Freytag 1900), emphasizes sequence, causality, and progression—a clear beginning, rising action, climax, falling action, and end.
> **Nonlinear storytelling** highlights cycles, relationships, iterations, seasons, and perspective shifts.

Who This Is For

Faculty who want their students to tell a story. Students are regularly asked to tell a story—whether about themselves, others, processes, or products—oftentimes without direction on the different ways a narrative can be structured. This activity helps students decide if a nonlinear structure would better represent their story and then what format to deliver it in. For example, a student might use the cyclical rhythm of Midwestern seasons to frame a podcast episode about family music traditions during the holidays and birthdays. The story might loop through recurring songs and family interviews, inviting listeners to experience a sense of continuity rather than a beginning, middle, and end.

Learning Outcomes

> **Define and compare** linear and nonlinear storytelling structures.
> **Analyze** how Indigenous narratives model cyclical, relational approaches.

> **Recognize** how narrative structure impacts format choices in their field.
> **Reflect** on how story structure influences meaning, interpretation, and audience engagement.

Instructional Context

> Two 50-minute sessions
> Comparative analysis of storytelling structures
> Works well in seminar, discussion-based, or interdisciplinary classrooms

Materials and Equipment

Prepare the below for the first session:

> Linear visuals: Freytag's Pyramid, timelines, scientific method diagrams, sequential algorithms
> Nonlinear visuals: Feedback loops (expression of cycles), ecosystem maps, fractals, collage, montage, pictograph winter count log
> Materials: Story mapping templates (timelines, spirals, winter count log), paper, markers, scissors, or digital platforms (Canva, Twine, Miro)

Resources Students Should Review for the Assignment

These resources introduce students to nonlinear storytelling and how Indigenous oral traditions have used cyclical, relational ways of sharing knowledge since the beginning and continuing today.

Readings and Videos

> *Art of Storytelling*: Gene Tagaban (Tlingit),

(YouTube) http://bit.ly/3LlVR9R
Experience storytelling with Robert Lewis (Cherokee Nation), who shares stories of his people and culture. Lewis engages audiences of all ages with witty and amusing personal stories and Cherokee tales of language, history, and the value of shared knowledge.

> *Our Breath of Being: Indigenous Living through Storying Traditions* by Dr. Doreen E. Martinez (Mescalero Apache) http://bit.ly/4ov9ZvZ
Dr. Martinez argues that storytelling in Indigenous Nations and societies isn't merely about narration, but about living, breathing traditions where time, cycles, and connection replace linear sequence, and the act of sharing becomes a form of being.

> *Lone Dog's Winter Count: Keeping History Alive* from the National Museum of the American Indian http://bit.ly/43lCPqm
Native Americans of the Northern Great Plains region recorded their histories through pictographic paintings on bison hides called winter counts. The Lone Dog Winter Count, covered 70 years of Yanktonais Nakota history, demonstrating how generations used visual storytelling to connect identity, land, and time in a cycle rather than a linear sequence. Lone Dog was the last known keeper of this count that included important events, encounters with other Native American tribes, non-Native people, disease epidemics, and times of war.

> *Welcome to Indigenous Foundations* from the First Nations Studies Program, University of British

Columbia Nations http://bit.ly/3WSbick
Throughout history, Aboriginal societies in North America have relied on the oral transmission of stories, histories, lessons and other knowledge to maintain a historical record and sustain their cultures and identities. According to scholars Renée Hulan and Renate Eigenbrod, oral traditions are "the means by which knowledge is reproduced, preserved and conveyed from generation to generation. Oral traditions form the foundation of Aboriginal societies, connecting speaker and listener in communal experience and uniting past and present in memory."

Consider the following after reading or watching:

> How does sharing (or not sharing) knowledge create ongoing cycles rather than closed endings?
> How does collective memory and storytelling strengthen the individual and community?

STEM Parallels

> Withheld data or closed research can stall progress
> Open-source collaboration and mentorship sustain innovation
> Systems—ecological or informational—collapse when feedback is ignored

Assignment

Purpose

To analyze how story structure shapes meaning, representation, and understanding across disciplines, with attention to Indigenous, relational, and cyclical models of storytelling.

Opening Discussion

Share the linear and nonlinear prepared visuals to discuss how stories are presented throughout disciplines in these different ways even though we often think most stories fall into a beginning, middle, and end structure.

Session 1: Comparative Analysis (Individual or with a Partner) Task

Choose one linear and one nonlinear story to compare. Students may select from:

> Linear examples: Freytag's Pyramid, scientific method, timelines, or a favorite film/novel that follows a clear sequence
> Nonlinear examples: Ledfeather, winter counts, stories from Robert Lewis, or favorite film/novel that follows a nonlinear structure (further resources below)

Prompts

In a short presentation (three to five minutes), analyze the following:

> How does each story organize time and causality?
> What does each structure emphasize or hide (e.g., closure vs. continuity, individual vs. community)?
> How does knowledge, relationships, or cycles function within the story?
> Which structure (linear or nonlinear) better communicates interconnectedness or identity and why?

Session 2: Creative Story Reconstruction Task

Reimagine a short story, research process, or personal experience in the opposite structure.

> If it's linear, retell it nonlinearly (cyclical, relational, or looping).

> If it's nonlinear, retell it linearly using Freytag's Pyramid.

Process

Use the provided story mapping templates (timelines, spirals, or winter counts) and available materials (paper, markers, scissors) or digital platforms (Canva, Twine, Miro) to sketch and plan your story in class.

Format Options

Submit your story in one of the following formats:

> Podcast episode

> Infographic

> Short video

> Digital or analog collage

> Cyclical winter log

> Written narrative (350–500 words)

Deliverables

> Final story (in chosen format)

> Reflection (150–250 words)

  o Explain how changing the structure changed the story's meaning (what became more visible or was lost).

Assessment

> Shows a clear understanding of linear vs. nonlinear storytelling.
> Uses content from your field effectively in both versions.
> Thoughtfully includes Indigenous (cyclical, spiral, nonlinear) storytelling ideas.
> Demonstrates understanding of how story structure informs format choice.
> Reflects on how structure changes the meaning and message.

Cross-Disciplinary Adaptation

> **Engineering**: Based on the iterative nature of Design Thinking, create a podcast or flow diagram showing how feedback and user interaction continually reshape a product.
> **Water Resource Management**: Collaborate with peers from different areas of water management to tell a collective story of how human activity disrupts and restores balance in the water cycle.
> **History**: Create a pictographic timeline of key events in a community, nation, or social movement, arranging symbols in a circle or spiral to show how struggles, progress, and renewal repeat through time.

Instructor Try-it Activity
Spiral Story Activity

1. **Review the Example**
   Look at Lone Dog's *Winter Count: Keeping History Alive (page 8) and find the Personal Pictograph Calendar Planning Handout.*

> **Choose Your Time Frame**
Pick a block of time from this academic year. For example, a semester, a project period, or a specific month.

> **Record Events**
Note key moments during that time — student presentations, publications, collaborations, or meaningful conversations.

> **Create Symbols**
Draw simple pictographs or icons to represent each important event.

> **Arrange Your Story**
Place the symbols in a spiral (your "winter count log") that represents the flow of that time period.

2. **Reflect Visually**

> How do the events connect on the spiral?
> Does the ending lead back to the beginning?
> Where do you see continuity vs. closure?

3. **Reflect Conceptually**

> Ask yourself: H*ow might this cyclical way of storytelling help students better understand processes, patterns, and cycles in your discipline?*

Additional Resources/ References

Freytag, Gustav. 1900. F*reytag's Technique of the Drama: An Exposition of Dramatic Composition and Art.* Translated by E. J. MacEwan. Scott, Foresman and Company.

Nonlinear Movies:

Burton, Kevin Lee. 2007. "Nikamowin" (song). Vimeo. http://bit.ly/3WPSevo.

Latimer, Michelle, dir. 2020. *Inconvenient Indian.* Internet Archive. http://bit.ly/3Jloaoe.

Nonlinear Books:

Orange, Tommy. 2018. *There There: A Novel.* Knopf Silko, Leslie Marmon. 1977. Ceremony. Penguin.

Nonlinear Book Recommended for STEM:

Kimmerer, Robin Wall. 2015. *Braiding Sweetgrass.* Milkweed Editions.

MAKING POEMS: EXPLORING EKPHRASIS AND TEXT/IMAGE POETICS

By: Sara Veglahn

Discipline: English, Creative Writing, and Literary Studies

Subject: Poetry and Poetics

Information Qualities of the Compositional Principle

Ekphrasis, from the Greek meaning "to explain," is a literary device that incorporates the use of description. Ekphrastic writing can take the form of poetry or prose and typically provides a written depiction of a work of visual art, either real or imagined. Ekphrasis can also be extended to include **text/image poetics**, a blending of both writing and visual image(s).

Poetics is a theoretical lens through which texts (poetry and prose) can be studied. Poetics is derived from the Greek word *poiesis* meaning "making" and can be understood as being concerned with how poetry/literature is *made*.

Who This Is For

Faculty who want students to exercise their observation and reflection skills from a different lens than typically taught in the discipline. It can be an accessible way into poetry for students because it doesn't require advanced literary or art training. For example, science students can make text/image poems to reinforce the idea that attentive seeing is both a scientific method and artistic practice that supports insight and communication.

Learning Outcomes

> **Analyze** how poetry communicates through descriptive, sensory, and metaphorical language.
> **Experiment** with ekphrastic writing to link visual and textual modes of meaning.
> **Create** original works of poetry inspired by visual art and collage.
> **Reflect** on poetics as the study of "making"—how form, process, and ideology shape artistic practice.
> **Synthesize** word and image to explore text/image poetics.

Instructional Context

> Small seminar or workshop (10–25 students)
> One or two 50-minute sessions
> Classroom with tables to spread out materials

Materials and Equipment

> Heavy paper, scissors, glue/tape (for collage activity)
> Magazines or printed images with text and visuals
> Optional art materials: colored pencils, markers, paints, washi tape, stencils
> Access to open-access museum collections online (NGA, Met, Art Institute of Chicago, Getty)

Assignment

Below are two prompts that can be seen as individual assignments or as a single assignment that investigates text/image poetics from different approaches.

Prompt 1—Collage: Found Art/ Found Language

Visual artist, Kurt Schwitters, developed the concept of Merz—the use of found/scavenged materials to create collages and assemblages, often incorporating language/words. Examples of his work can be found below:

> Tate Museum http://bit.ly/3KYv1op

> Art Institute of Chicago http://bit.ly/4ozXMWQ

Process and Steps

1. **Gather Materials**
   You'll need at least one sheet of heavy paper, some type of fixative (glue, paste, rubber cement, or tape), scissors, and at least one magazine that contains both images and text.
2. **Optional additions**
   You may also want to collect other materials: tissue paper, tracing paper, newspaper, old postage stamps, letters, postcards, markers, paints, or colored pencils.
3. **Find and Cut**
   Go through your magazine and select images that interest you. Cut them out and begin arranging them on your paper.
4. **Affix Your Collage**
   Glue or tape the images (and any optional materials you've chosen) onto your heavy paper.
5. **Add Language**
   As you work, also search for words and phrases that catch your attention. Cut them out and use them to create a poem—this is your "found language."
6. **Expand or Revise**
   You can present the text/image collage as it is, or you may expand/revise by pulling the words and phrases into another poem or even a series of poems.

Optional Framing

Some students have taken this further by using altered or collaged family photos and handwriting—poignant, beautiful work that also reimagines narrative and memoir. This may be another way for you to frame your project, through linear or nonlinear storytelling.

Prompt 2—The Lyric: Writing the Self through Ekphrasis

Lyric poems go back to ancient Greece, where they were accompanied by music and tended to be shorter, personal reflections rather than providing a story. In contemporary lyric poetry, there is still a focus on the personal and shorter forms, such as the sonnet, a fourteen-line poem. Often, these poems are in the first person (using "I"), emphasizing both the personal nature as well as highlighting emotions.

In this exercise, you'll incorporate both ekphrasis and the lyric.

Process and Steps

1. **Choose an Artwork**

> If possible, visit a museum or gallery in person. If not, select from open-access collections online:
o National Gallery of Art: http://bit.ly/47DMMSt
o The Met: http://bit.ly/4qsoWxt
o Art Institute of Chicago: http://bit.ly/4hukqOo
o Getty: http://bit.ly/4ozcJbw

2. **Observe**

> Spend at least 15 minutes examining the work.
> Take five to ten minutes making notes on what you see.
> Return to the artwork at least two more times and repeat this process.
> (Optional) Print out the image or set it as your phone/computer wallpaper so you can encounter it throughout the day.

3. **Free Write**

- For 10–15 minutes, alternate between describing the artwork (using all five senses when possible) and recording your memories, emotions, or associations that the artwork evokes.
- Your writing should move between outer description and inner reflection.

4. **Make a Poem**

- From your freewriting, circle descriptions that feel surprising, unique, or resonant, and copy these onto another sheet of paper as individual lines.
- Arrange these into a poem, aiming for at least 14 lines.
- If the artwork inspires extended exploration, feel free to make a longer poem.

5. **Study an Example of a Poem that Reflects on the Visual**

- Read Rainer Maria Rilke's "Archaic Torso of Apollo": http://bit.ly/4nZIXNk

Assessment

- **Collage Poem (Prompt 1)**: Creativity, integration of found language and images, ability to communicate meaning
- **Ekphrastic Poem (Prompt 2)**: Depth of engagement with artwork, use of sensory detail, integration of self-reflection
- **Reflection Component**: Brief artist statement explaining how text and image informed one another in their creative process

Cross-Disciplinary Adaptation

- **Art History**: Compare student ekphrastic works with historical examples of art criticism in poetic form.
- **Philosophy**: Explore the aesthetics of representation—how words can "translate" or "transform" visual art.
- **Media and Communication**: Examine contemporary forms of text/image hybrids (memes, zines, graphic poetry).

Instructor Try-It Activity

Process and Steps

1. **Select a Visual**

> Choose a painting, sculpture, or photograph from the open-access collections provided above.

2. **Describe What You See**

> Spend 10 minutes writing only about the visual details: colors, shapes, textures, gestures, or expressions.

3. **Reflect on Associations**

> Spend the next 10 minutes freewriting about the memories, feelings, or questions the artwork evokes for you.

4. **Draft a Short Poem**

> Write a six- to eight-line poem that alternates between **description of the artwork** and **personal reflection or association**.

5. **Take Notes**

> Consider how this activity could apply to your discipline.

> For example:

- Science—practicing close observation of natural or microscopic images
- Geography—describing and reflecting on landscapes or maps
- History—engaging with artifacts or photographs to explore cultural meaning

> Consider how this process strengthens both **observation skills** and **reflective thinking** for your discipline-specific learning.

Additional Resources/ References

Fischer, Barbara K. 2006. *Museum Meditations: Reframing Ekphrasis in Contemporary American Poetry*. Routledge.

Vicuña, Cecilia. 2024 [1973]. *Saborami: Expanded Facsimile Edition*. Book Works. http://bit.ly/4o79ybv

A general (but extended) definition of ekphrasis with links to poem examples: http://bit.ly/3WZIBu5

Part 2 Lesson Plan: Compositional Principles

PART 3:

LESSON PLAN

Discipline Specific Formats

MAKING PHOTOGRAPHS VERSUS TAKING PHOTOGRAPHS: FROM OBSERVATION TO VISUAL COMMUNICATION

By: Eli Craven

Discipline: Visual Art and Photography

Subject: Taking an Active Role in Photography and Making a Photograph

Information Qualities of the Format

Photography is a medium enmeshed in contradiction—the camera can document reality, yet the photographer's ability to manipulate the medium can influence perception and interpretation of images. Advances in image-editing and artificial intelligence continue to cast doubt, yet images are still used as evidence. Despite the complicated nature of contemporary photography, the process of creating images can be an effective tool for learning observational and analytical skills. In this exercise, we will focus on the role of the photographer as an observer, and how individuals can control and manipulate their subjects and compositions to "make" rather than "take" images.

Who This Is For

Faculty interested in having their students explore observational and analytical skills through image making and interpreting visual media. The context and function of images in our society can be utilized through multiple educational approaches. There will be opportunities to discuss the inherent trust in images and the growing skepticism of the photographic image as a visual communication tool while applying these skills to a broad range of disciplines.

Learning Outcomes

> **Create** images using cameras or smartphones.
> **Analyze** photographic compositions.
> **Communicate** visual messages through photography.
> **Critique** images constructively.
> **Demonstrate** understanding of the image as a tool in visual communication.

Instructional Context

This activity is intended for individuals or small groups, but class size is scalable. It's a two-part exercise that can be integrated into a variety of course designs.

It is estimated that 5.3 billion images are captured daily. Smartphones, social media, and AI image generation are saturating the average visual media experience with new images constantly. The ease at which images are created, and the vast number of images people experience, provides a context in which the care and attention given to the creation of an image is increasingly passive. Many image-makers record their experiences and observations with little thought to the composition and subject.

With this context in mind, we will be paying extra attention to the creation of images, and the students will be asked to participate, consider, and interact with their compositions, taking responsibility for their creative choices and developing an understanding of how to read images, and interpret their meaning.

Materials and Equipment

> Camera: Students and groups will need access to a camera of any design (professional, digital, film, cell phone, or any device that can create or record an image).

> Software: Students will have access to image editing software in the classroom, but use of these applications is optional.

Assignment

This assignment is intended to introduce your students to creative ways they can interact with the image making process and reconsider the context in which images and objects function in society. Through the generation of two images, students will create a diptych (pair of two images) that illustrate a scene, subject, composition, etc. that is first captured in its natural state through observation, and then a second photograph, changing the context and meaning of the original through an active, creative reinterpretation of the subject.

Prep Work

In preparation for exercise part 1, students will be required to keep a journal of observations as they commute in their daily life. We will discuss acts of looking and observing in our environments and we will study photographers that observe and record "reality" through their photography. We will also look to photographers that take an active role in planning, manipulating, and designing their photographs. Students will look for objects, scenes, locations, lighting, scenarios, etc. that they find interesting, attractive, or exciting. We will meet to discuss their observations.

Questions and topics for discussion include:
> What locations interest you?
> What about it interests you? (The architecture, landscape, light, the activity?)
> What objects or subjects did you find interesting in your notes?
> Were they large or small? Do humans interact with these subjects?
> Please share items from your notes, including colors, scale, function, and relationships between people, your locations, and

subjects.

Part 1: Observing and Capturing Image 1

Students will be asked to carry their camera with them, observing and capturing the objects, people, and scenes discussed in our journaling. The initial images should be unaltered, depicting the subjects and scenes as they appear. The images captured in the observation portion of the assignment will be critiqued in a peer review addressing the context and function of the images.

Part 2: Rephotograph the Subject in a New Context to Create Image 2

Following the peer critique of image 1, students should select an image to recreate applying a series of purposeful creative choices. Considering the meaning and context of the original, how can we change the image or subject to create new meaning and prompt questions?

Some possibilities include:

> Change composition (zoom in, rotate your camera, etc.).

> Photograph a small or movable subject in a new location. Consider moving a small subject to an environment that seems out of place, prompting questions. (Example: If you photographed an object such as litter on the ground, maybe a discarded water bottle, could you move the subject to the lighting studio to allow us to look at the object differently?)

> Photograph a large subject or location from an alternate location. Can you photograph the scene from a unique angle (Example: If you created the first image at eye level, could you get on the ground, or move to the top of a building nearby to change your vantage point?)

> If your scene was full of human activity, can you return when the location is empty? (or vice versa: photograph an empty space later

full of activity).

> Does your subject exist in different forms? (If your original image was of a public fountain, could you then photograph a water fountain? Think of alternatives, objects or subjects, that take different forms. Think creatively.)

Cross-Disciplinary Adaptation

> **History**: Document historical sites versus curate archival scenes to visually communicate historical narratives.
> **Social Sciences**: Capture spontaneous cultural behaviors through observation versus construct visual scenes that explore responses and reveal patterns.
> **Psychology**: Observe natural emotional expressions versus staged scenarios to investigate perception and psychological responses.
> **Environmental Science**: Document natural ecosystems and environmental conditions versus stage comparisons and simulations to illustrate ecological change and impact.

Examples:

Part 1: Observation Image **Part 2**: Creative Reinterpretation

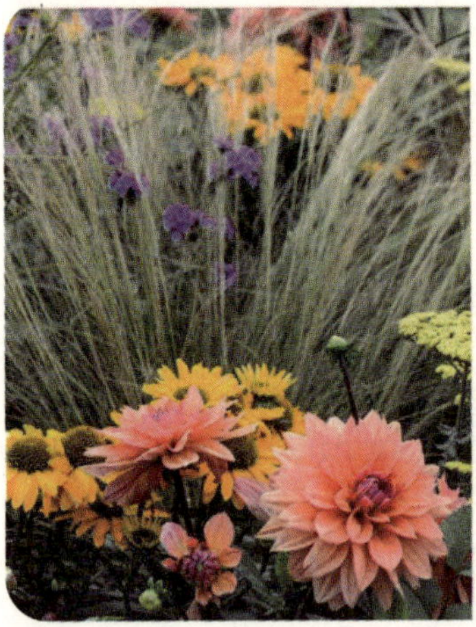

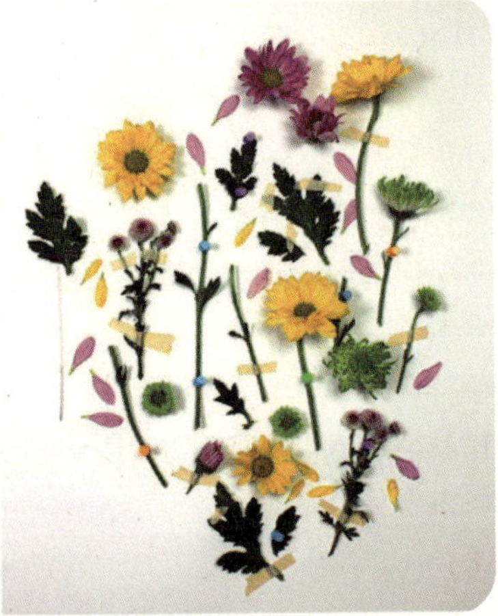

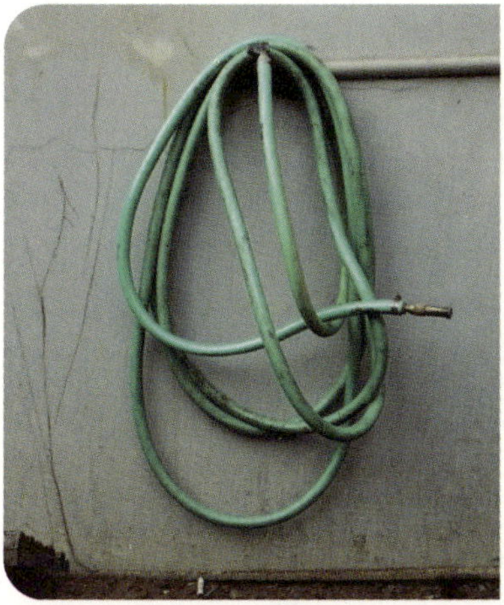

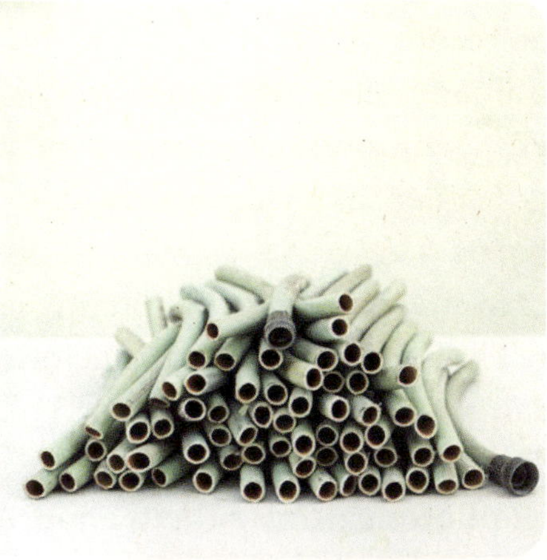

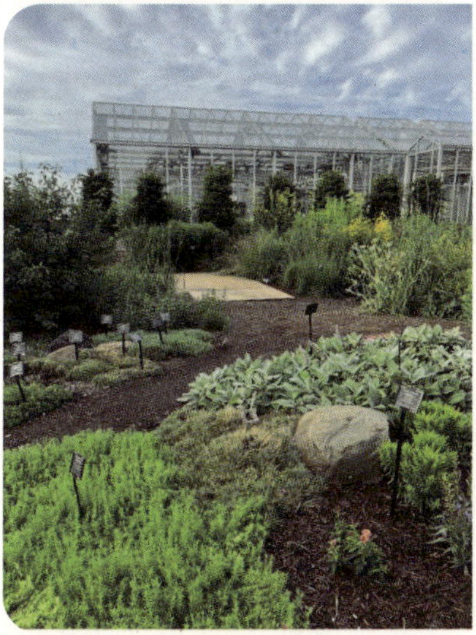

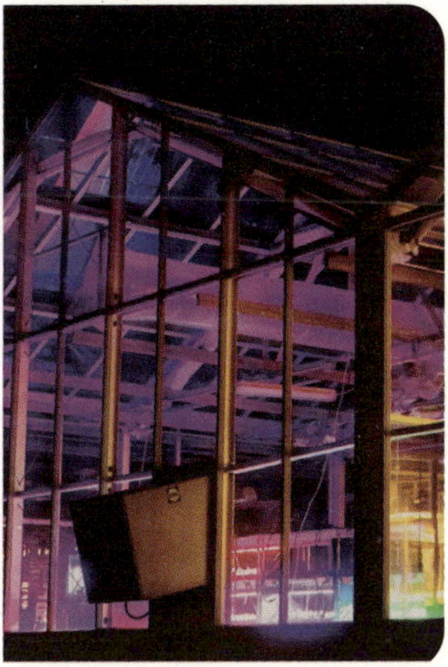

Images 1–6: Making Versus Taking
Photo credit: Eli Craven

Instructor Try-It Activity

Reflect on how students' roles as *creators* versus *observers* shape learning.

Making Photographs Versus Taking Photographs: From Observation to Visual Communication

Process and Steps

1. **Choose a Topic**
   Pick a course concept where this contrast applies.
   Examples: posting versus scrolling on social media; conducting fieldwork versus analyzing others' data.
2. **Take Photos**
   Capture two to four images showing each role—creator and observer. Think about angle, focus, or composition to express each role visually.
3. **Arrange and Label**
   Place the photos side by side in a journal or digital tool (like Canva or PowerPoint). Label each "Creator" or "Observer."
4. **Reflect**
   Write a short paragraph describing:

> The story your images tell
> What you learned through the process
> How this could help students reflect on where learning happens in each role/perspective

Additional Resources/ References

Berger, John. 1980. *About Looking*. Pantheon Books.

Jeffreys, Tom, ed. 2024. *Walking*. MIT Press.

Sontag, Susan. 2001. *On Photography*. Picador.

Wall, Jeff. 2007. *Selected Essays and Interviews*. Museum of Modern Art.

VISUAL ESSAY: CAPTURING VIDEO FOR NARRATIVE COMMUNICATION

By: Liz Evans

Discipline: Media and Mass Communication

Subject: Narrative Video: Filming

Information Qualities of the Format

Video communicates meaning through visual, auditory, spatial, and temporal elements. In this lesson, students explore how camera work, including composition, movement, perspective, the use of natural light, and pacing, can communicate stories and ideas in ways text or static images cannot always accomplish.

Who This Is For

For faculty introducing video as an information communication format in any discipline. Works for any class size with smartphones or cameras. Covers introductory techniques for experimenting to support student video projects across topics. Meant to be paired with the video editing lesson plan.

Learning Outcomes

> **Create** video sequences using selected video capture elements, such as rule of thirds, perspective, pacing, and natural lighting.

> **Construct** a clear, visual narrative through captured video sequences without using text or sound.

> **Demonstrate** understanding of how video capture techniques convey information to an audience.

Instructional Context

This lesson plan is based on the first project in an undergraduate video production course, where the focus is solely on capturing footage that conveys meaning without words. There is no editing yet. This is intended for student experimentation, not mastery.

> Works best in class sessions with flexible time for exploration
> Two 50-minute sessions

Materials and Equipment

> Video camera or smartphone
> Tripod or stabilizer (optional but recommended)
> A storyboard template, such as Canva Storyboard Templates: https://bit.ly/4qMOJDG

Resources Students Should Review for the Assignment

Create a checklist for students to explore. Provide or direct them to find the techniques listed below online (many are listed in the Practical Skills Index section and many are easily found online). Below is an introduction to techniques—a place to begin experimenting. Students can be encouraged to dig deeper into the effects of these approaches.

> Rule of thirds to provide composition structure for visual interest
> Leading lines and symmetry work together to direct the viewer's attention
> Framing choices—wide or close shots—to shape viewer's connection to the scene
> Movement versus stillness to set mood and energy within a scene
> Natural versus artificial light to shape the atmosphere and emotional tone
> Visual rhythm—shot length and pacing—to control flow or tension

> Visual perspective—POV or subjective/objective shots—as the lens viewers develop meaning through

These are movies students can watch, as a whole or in part, that demonstrate the different techniques.

***The Red Balloon* (1956, dir. Albert Lamorisse)**

> **Why it works**: This short French film tells a story almost entirely without dialogue. It uses camera angles, movement, and lighting to achieve this.

> **Watch for**:

- o Wide versus close shots for emotional shifts
- o Tracking shots that mimic the balloon's gentle drifting
- o Parisian streets' natural light setting the mood and tone

***Koyaanisqatsi* (1982, dir. Godfrey Reggio)**

> **Why it works**: A visual essay that communicates ideas about nature, technology, and modern life without narration. Its time-lapse, scale, and rhythmic editing are examples of visual rhythm, sequencing, and perspective.

> **Watch for:**

- o Movement versus stillness to highlight contrasts between natural landscapes and industrial sprawl.
- o Visual perspective (POV and extreme angles) to shift audience perception.
- o Pacing and musical pairing to evoke emotional responses.

Assignment

Create a two or three minute silent video responding to one of the prompts below. Use only camera techniques, no dialogue, subtitles, or advanced editing beyond trimming or some time-lapse effects. Prompts (Each explores a different aspect of video as an information medium.)

> **The Day (or Month, Year, etc.) in the Life of a Peer**
Show how a peer's understanding in your field evolves over time or in different contexts. Focus on temporal qualities, sequencing that moves the story forward.

o Sociology Example: Show a classmate moving through different social settings (family dinner, workplace, protest), each altering their understanding of privilege or group dynamics.

o Studio Art Example: Show a fellow student believing abstract art is "random." Through clips of sketching, critiques, and gallery visits, they begin to see intention, composition, and emotion.

> **From Below or Above**
Tell a story using extreme perspective shifts.
Focus on spatial awareness, power dynamics, or disorientation through camera angle.

o STEM Example (Engineering): Film a bridge or machine from below and above to highlight its structure or reveal complexity.

o Fashion or Design Example: Capture a garment's details close to the ground, then film it from a balcony or ladder to showcase silhouette and movement.

> **The Hidden Life of Shadows**
Tell a story using only the shadows of people/objects in your discipline.
Focus on contrast, abstraction, and mood using natural light (lighting can be complex, so it's good to see how natural light can be optimized).

o Dance: Film dancers' shadows against a wall so that only movement and rhythm tell the story of emotion or narrative arc.

o Nursing/Healthcare: Project shadows of medical tools—like a stethoscope or IV stand—paired with a caregiver's silhouette to convey patient care's emotional weight.

> **Change Over Time**

Document how something evolves or transforms in your field. Focus on sequencing, visual evidence, and temporal compression (time-lapse, montage).

- History: Use archival photos fading into modern footage to show how a historic district has changed across decades.
- Biology: Create a time-lapse of a seed germinating and growing into a plant, illustrating stages of development.

> **An Emotion**

Use facial expressions or body language to communicate one core emotion in response to something discipline-related. Focus on close-ups, visual rhythm, and empathetic framing.

- Engineering: Frustration and relief shown through a designer's tense posture while troubleshooting a prototype, then relaxed satisfaction when it works.
- Environmental Science: Grief and resolve captured in a conservationist's body language while witnessing deforestation.

Process and Steps

1. Storyboard Development: Sketch key shots and discuss how any of the employed video capturing elements convey meaning.
2. Technique Practice: In pairs, practice different angles and movements. Refer to the above checklist handout.
3. Shoot Footage: Capture all required shots following your storyboard and chosen prompt.
4. Silent Drafting: Share raw clips in class for quick peer feedback on clarity and impact.

Final Class Activity

Watch session of raw clips in class. Students note which shots communicate most effectively and suggest improvements.

Assessment

Criteria

Framing and composition
Use of movement/light/perspective
Viewer engagement and clarity

Cross-Disciplinary Adaptation

> **STEM**: Capture a process (e.g., chemical reaction) to highlight time-based change. Employ techniques such as close-ups to highlight temperature change, and wide angle to record the final state. Different lighting, composition (rule of thirds), and pacing to reflect moments of flow or tension.

> **Education**: Film a classroom interaction from unusual perspectives. Experiment with above and below shots to reveal power dynamics and relationships. Work with leading lines and symmetry to experiment with visual interest.

Instructor Try-It Activity
Process and Steps

1. **Gather Materials**

o Smartphone or camera
o Two small objects (e.g., a book and a coffee mug)
o Desk lamp or window light

2. **Experiment with Composition**

o Leading Lines and Symmetry: Place the objects so lines in the environment (table edges, floor tiles) guide attention. Capture one symmetrical and one asymmetrical shot.

o Scale: Take one close-up and one wide shot to show how size affects emphasis.

3. **Play with Perspective and Framing**
o Film the objects from below and from above.
o Shoot a wide shot and then a close-up of the same scene to compare emotional impact.

4. **Movement Versus Stillness**
o Record one static shot and one with camera movement (pan or tilt). Note how the feeling shifts.

5. **Lighting for Mood**
o Use natural light, then switch to lamp light. Capture how the atmosphere changes.

6. **Visual Rhythm**
o Take three short clips (2–3 seconds, 5–6 seconds, 10+ seconds). Combine them in basic editing software to feel how pacing alters tone.

7. **Reflect**
o Ask yourself the following: Which technique surprised you, which was hardest, and which best reveals video's unique information qualities and/or could support student learning?

Additional Resources/References

Brown, Blain. 2021. *Cinematography: Theory and Practice: For Cinematographers and Directors*. 4th ed. Routledge. https://doi.org/10.4324/9780429353239.

VISUAL ESSAY: CAPTURING VIDEO FOR NARRATIVE COMMUNICATION

By: Liz Evans

Discipline: Media and Mass Communication

Subject: Narrative Video: Editing

Information Qualities of the Format

Editing shapes the temporal, emotional, and structural flow of video. Through sequencing, pacing, and transitions, students learn to refine raw footage (filmed during the Capturing Video lesson) into visual narratives without text or dialogue.

Who This Is For

For faculty guiding students from basic filming to purposeful editing. This works for any class size (but depends on how much one-on-one time you would like to provide). Meant to be paired with the video capturing lesson plan.

Learning Outcomes

> **Create** a clear narrative flow by sequencing raw footage.

> **Demonstrate** engagement through video duration, pacing, and transitions.

> **Demonstrate** understanding of how editing choices alter or clarify meaning compared to raw footage.

Instructional Context

This lesson follows the video capture project. Students will import their raw clips and apply introductory editing techniques to enhance narrative clarity (but still without spoken words, captions, or graphics). This is intended for student experimentation, not mastery.

> Works best in class sessions with flexible time for exploration
> Two 50-minute sessions

Materials and Equipment

> Raw footage from previous shooting lesson
> Editing software (Premiere Pro, CapCut, iMovie, Canva Pro)
> Creative Commons or original music/sounds with creator permission (optional, instrumental only)

Resources Students Should Review for the Assignment

Below is an introduction to techniques (listed in the Practical Skills Index or found online) that can be turned into a checklist for students to begin experimenting with and exploring further.

Editing Techniques Checklist

> **Narrative Flow**
o Sequence clips so the story progresses logically and clearly.
o Trim or reorder shots to maintain continuity and audience orientation.

> **Pacing and Shot Duration**
o Adjust shot lengths to build or release tension.
o Use faster cuts for energy or conflict; slower pacing for reflection or gravity.

> **Visual Rhythm**
o Vary shot lengths and movement to create a visual beat or tempo.
o Match pacing to mood changes or subject matter (e.g., quick montage for excitement, lingering shots for contemplation).

> **Transitions and Emphasis**
o Choose cuts, fades, or dissolves purposefully—only when they enhance perspective or emotion.
o Avoid unnecessary transitions that distract from meaning. Keep it simple.

> **Emotional Impact**
o Revisit your sequence: does the edit clarify the concept compared to raw footage?
o Experiment—small timing changes can dramatically shift audience response.

These are movies students can watch, in whole or in part, that demonstrate the different techniques.
***Whiplash* (2014, dir. Damien Chazelle)**
> **Why it works**: Uses pacing, visual rhythm, and shot duration to generate engagement.
> **Watch for**: Rapid cuts and close-ups during drumming sequences; sudden tempo shifts mirror emotional tension between characters.

***Birdman* (2014, dir. Alejandro G. Iñárritu)**
> **Why it works**: Designed to feel like a single continuous shot, showcasing transitions and perspective.
> **Watch for**: Invisible cuts and long takes that guide perspective and mood, immersing the viewer in the protagonist's world.

Assignment

Edit a two to three-minute silent video using the footage you shot for one of the original prompts (*The Day in the Life of a Peer, From Below or Above, The Hidden Life of Shadows, Change Over Time*, or *An Emotion*).
> Don't include dialogue, captions, or on-screen text.
> Use pacing, shot order, and transitions to emphasize perspective and meaning.
> Optional: Include non-lyrical Creative Commons (https://bit.ly/3OZoMlY) music or ambient sound to enhance mood.

Process and Steps

1. **Footage Review**

o Import clips, flag strongest shots, discard weak ones.

2. **Storyboard/Timeline Planning**

o Sketch or list shot order; decide where pacing should quicken or slow.

3. **Editing Workshop**

o Trim and sequence clips.

o Adjust durations for rhythm and emphasis.

o Add basic fades, cuts, or time-lapse effects to reinforce transitions.

o Optional: Layer ambient sound or music (credit properly).

4. **Peer Review and Reflection**

Export a draft. Swap with a partner to watch silently and note:

o Is the narrative clear?

o Which edit created the strongest emotional shift?

o What could be re-sequenced for clarity or impact?

5. **Final Cut**

o Revise based on peer feedback.

Final Class Activity

Mini Film Festival:

Screen final cuts in class. As a group, discuss the following:

> How did editing alter the meaning or experience of similar prompts?

> Which choices in pacing or transitions were most effective?

> What editing decisions surprised or inspired you?

Cross-Disciplinary Adaptation

> **STEM**: Edit lab footage to emphasize process flow or iterative testing.

> **Education**: Sequence clips of a teaching activity to highlight transformation in understanding.

> **Health Sciences**: Edit patient-care scenarios to emphasize empathy or progression of care.
> **Marketing**: Re-cut product footage to evoke different emotional responses.

Instructor Try-It Activity

Process and Steps

1. Import three unrelated clips (e.g., from your phone or video camera).
2. Create two short edits: one fast-paced montage and one slow.
3. Note how pacing alone changes mood and meaning.
4. Share with a colleague and ask which version feels more emotionally impactful or clear.
5. Reflect on a planned video assignment. Ask: Which editing techniques would best deepen student understanding and communication?

Additional Resources/References

Murch, Walter. 2001. *In the Blink of an Eye: A Perspective on Film Editing*. 2nd ed. Silman-James Press.

WRITING: LEVERAGING AN OLD MEDIUM TO REFLECT ON LEARNING

By: Jennifer Bay

Discipline: Technical and Professional Communication

Subject: Reflection Through Writing

Information Qualities of the Format

Writing is a foundational medium for thinking. We've known this since Plato criticized the idea of writing as being artificial because it externalized thoughts. Writing is a technology that restructures thought; it separates the known from the knower (Ong, 1982). As Ong explains, it allows humans to interpret data, to separate logic from good speaking, and more. As such, writing is as much a technology as other media that allows humans to bring into being different ways of thinking in the world.

Because writing allows us to separate ourselves from our experiences, it is a perfect medium for reflection. Reflection allows humans to express how various life processes, events, and experiences changed or affected us. Reflection has been a foundational aspect of engaged teaching, a high-impact practice that often incorporates service-learning, work-integrated learning, and other experiential learning situations where students "learn by doing." Reflection is important in these contexts because students need to connect their applied experiences to what they have learned in the classroom.

As a medium for reflection, writing allows us to distance ourselves from our experiences, thoughts, and feelings and take a broader, more contextual view. As such, reflection can be seen as a form of critical thinking (Schoen 1987) in which students learn to adapt or modify prior knowledge to a current situation. Students can gain empathy from trying to understand their experiences from a variety of perspectives, not just their own. They can also gain self-efficacy, or confidence in their abilities to succeed because they are able to assess what is needed for success and in what ways they can gain that knowledge or ability.

Who This Is For

This assignment fits any course needing reflection on experiences or processes. While the reflection focus of this lesson is on communication practices in an internship, it offers multiple reflective approaches and resources adaptable to other courses or learning contexts.

Learning Outcomes

> **Analyze** experiences to connect applied learning with theoretical concepts.
> **Evaluate** workplace or project communication practices and propose improvements.
> **Developing** self-efficacy by explaining/expressing what was learned and why it matters.
> **Adapt** prior knowledge to new contexts, demonstrating problem-solving and flexibility.
> **Develop** empathy and emotional intelligence by reflecting on multiple perspectives.

Instructional Context

These reflective writing assignments work well in courses that involve **experiential learning**—where students learn by doing, such as internships, service-learning, lab research, or community engagement.

Materials and Equipment

Pencil and paper or tablets/laptops/computers/phones

Resources Students Should Review for the Assignment

Instructors might provide an example of the kind of reflection they want students to complete. This will help students understand the expectations for formality and depth of thinking that the instructor has.

Assignment

Recommendation for Teaching

Experiment with the different types of reflective writing below to see what resonates with students and fits your assignment. Use a formal reflection for major, long-term projects and a brief, informal piece for a single experience. Reflection can be a quick paragraph, a formal memo, or an ongoing journal.

Reflections on Service-Learning and Engagement Using the DEAL Model

The DEAL model (Ash and Clayton 2009) helps guide reflection, especially for service-learning. **DEAL** stands for **Describe, Examine, and Articulate Learning** https://bit.ly/4nDN9Bh.

1. **Describe**: Outline what happened—where, who was involved, and what took place.
2. **Examine**: Analyze the experience from personal, civic, or academic perspective—your feelings, strengths used, power dynamics, community impact, or course connections.
3. **Articulate Learning**: Explain what you learned, how you learned it, and why it matters.

Reflective Memo

A staple in many writing classrooms in which students reflect on their writing process in a memorandum (or memo) to the instructor. They will provide a detailed account of the steps they completed like idea generating, drafting, revising, and editing; discuss challenges and strategies they took to overcome them; and sometimes be asked to share personal insights or past experiences describing what the impact of writing as reflection had on the process. This can be a quick in-class activity to share with peers or a formal memo submitted with the final assignment.

Journaling

Journaling has a long history in English and writing contexts. Students have often been asked to keep a journal for a class that details their reading responses, personal reflections, creative writing, and more. Journaling has been scientifically proven to help students become more comfortable with writing and to externalize their thoughts and ideas. Journaling is best when it is made consistent and accountable, meaning students are journaling on a schedule and instructors are checking that work. Sometimes, journals are not intended to be read by an audience, meaning the students are writing more for themselves than an instructor or peers. Other times, journals can be used for students to provide responses to readings throughout a semester and thus instructors might read those journals to ensure students comprehend the readings and are building on the ideas throughout the semester.

Prompt

Reflect on How Communication Functions in Your Workplace

> What formal or informal rules guide communication, and how do they relate to the chain of command (who supervises whom)?

> How did you learn these rules, including non-verbal signals?

> Are there broader ethics that shape communication and workflow? How do you connect to them?

> Have you adapted your communication or writing for different audiences? If so, how, and what values or ethics guided you?
> What would you change about the communication or writing practices you've seen so far, and where do you see your role within them?

Assessment

This rubric is for structured reflections in an internship course. Students post reflections and respond to peers on the discussion board. Writing quality can be evaluated, but it isn't always required.

Reflection means to think deeply about a situation, task, or experience from multiple perspectives—personal, academic, social, professional, civic, for example. It means asking questions, considering possible answers and solutions, and thinking about their implications. Reflection also involves looking inside yourself to understand your own reasons and responses to external issues, helping you learn more about yourself, others, your work, and the world.

Articulate means you are trying to get across your ideas in a way people can understand. It doesn't mean your writing is perfect, but it does demonstrate that you, as a writer, are trying to find the best and most appropriate language for describing your topic.

Thoughtful means it's clear you are actively and critically thinking about the discussion topic and exploring the various aspects of it. You're doing more than skimming the surface.

Engaged means you are thoughtfully, respectfully, and actively contributing to a discussion with your peers. It means you ask questions when you are confused, need more information, or want to prompt a classmate to think further about the topic. It means you offer possible solutions, make connections to your own experiences or explore how your experiences are different.

Rubric

Deep engagement:

Original post:

> 400 words. At least 4 responses to discussion posts.
> Posts are thoughtful, detailed, and engaging, with clear examples and full exploration of the topic.
> Demonstrates depth and precision; background information anticipates audience needs.
> May post more than required and shows strong effort to involve others.

Thoughtful engagement:

> Original post and 4 responses meet word counts.
> Reflective and articulate but missing some examples or details.
> Ideas are present but not fully explored, requiring readers to ask for more information.

Limited engagement:

> Meets word counts but posts feel padded or superficial.
> Limited reflection or engagement, with repetitive or off-topic content.
> Frequent errors impede readability.

Incomplete participation:

> Missing word counts or required responses.
> Posts are short, shallow, and fail to engage the prompt.

Cross-Disciplinary Adaptation

> **STEM Fields—Lab or Project Journals**: Use structured lab journals to record procedures, errors, and observations. Incorporate drawings for procedure clarity. Add short reflective notes on teamwork, problem-solving, or ethical questions to connect technical work with broader impacts.

> **Arts and Humanities—Creative Process Journals**: Encourage process journals where students document inspirations, creative decisions, and audience reactions. Encourage drawings, collages, images to support the process.

> **Health Sciences—Clinical Reflection Journals**: Assign clinical journals for students to reflect on patient interactions or community health projects. Prompts might guide them to analyze emotions, ethics, and professional growth.

> **Business and Social Sciences—Professional Practice Journals**: Use professional practice journals for students to evaluate workplace culture, leadership, and communication. They can analyze decision-making, diversity, and ethics, linking theory to real-world practice.

Instructor Try-It Activity
Process and Steps

1. **Spotlight a Teaching Moment**

> Recall a class, project, or interaction—success or disaster—that has stuck with you.

2. **Flash Write for 5 Minutes**

> Capture the moment in a quick paragraph.

> Include what you felt, what succeeded or failed, and what you discovered about yourself or your teaching.

3. **Layer on the DEAL Framework (Optional)**

> Describe: Sketch the event or situation.

> Examine: Dig into what it revealed about your teaching or your students' learning.
> Articulate Learning: Name one takeaway you'll apply in the future.

4. **Connect and Compare (Optional)**

> Trade reflections with a colleague or small group. Look for shared themes, surprises, or new perspectives.

5. **Reimagine for Your Students**

> Think about when this could deepen their learning—after a lab, service activity, field trip, or major project.

Additional Resources/ References

Ash, Sarah L. and Patti H. Clayton. 2009. "Generating, Deepening, and Documenting Learning: The Power of Critical Reflection in Applied Learning." *Journal of Applied Learning in Higher Education* 1: 25–48.

Ong, Walter J. 1982. *Orality and Literacy: The Technologizing of the Word*. Taylor & Francis.

Schön, Donald A. 1987. *Educating the Reflective Practitioner: Toward a New design for Teaching and Learning in the Professions.* Jossey-Bass.

By: Brian Hitselberger

Discipline: Studio Art and Design

Subject: Simple Book Formats

Information Qualities of the Format

How information is structured in books is a familiar organizational system to most. Books are an ideal format to bring together a variety of voices, perspectives, or bodies of knowledge—even, and especially, those in tension with one another. Simple adjustments made to the book design/structure can allow for visual patterns in the information that highlight inter-relationships between elements. Depending on your design, these relationships could be understood as typologies, hierarchies, contradictions, or something else entirely.

Who This Is For

Educators, students, artists, and designers interested in visually organizing a range of information systems into varieties of understanding i.e., how structure within a format communicates meaning.

Learning Outcomes

> **Curate** and **organize** a collection of content into a structured visual system.

> **Construct** a 12-page handmade book whose physical design reinforces or alters the interpretation of its content.

> **Reflect** on how design choices influence reading, meaning making, and information flow.

> **Explore** the expressive potential of structure within a book format as authorship.

Instructional Context

> Individual or small group activity (maximum of 15 students for workshop settings)
> Ideal for project-based, seminar-style, or studio environments
> Can be used as an intro to book arts, or a capstone project in a course on visual thinking, information design, or epistemology

Optional Group Variation:

Begin with shared physical constraints (e.g., decreasing page size or accordion fold) and compare how different participants map radically different content into the same structure.

Materials and Equipment

Essential materials

> Bone folder
> Long-arm stapler
> Heavy books or objects (used as weights)
> A variety of text-weight paper
> Access to design software (e.g., Canva or Adobe InDesign) for digital alternative

Optional materials

> Heavier paper or cardstock for cover
> Scissors, glue sticks, tape for collage
> Pens/colored pencils for drawing
> Printer (for pre-type content)

Resources Students Should Review for the Assignment

Technique and Structure

Smith, Esther K. 2007. *How to Make Books: Fold, Cut & Stitch Your Way to a One-of-a-Kind Book.* Potter Craft.

Todd, Mark and Esther Pearl Watson. 2006. *Whatcha Mean, What's a Zine?: The Art of Making Zines and Minicomics*. Graphia.

Inspiration
Joseph, Brandon W. and Drew Sawyer. 2024. *Copy Machine Manifestos: Artists Who Make Zines.* Phaidon.

Tufte, Edward R. 2006. ***Beautiful Evidence***. Graphics Press.

Design Thinking
Lupton, Ellen. 2024. *Thinking with Type*. Princeton Architectural Press.

Assignment

Guidance for Beginners

Keep things simple—If you introduce any variability into your paper choices (color, for example), consider keeping other aspects consistent (weight and size, for example).

Part 1: Preparatory Phase

1. **Gather Your Content**

> This can be photographs, interview excerpts, opinions, diagrams, notes, tables, or quotes. Consider the significance of each element when gathering material—it should be considered content—not filler—collected with attention to **themes, contrasts, and patterns**.

> Ask yourself : *What do I notice about this material? How can I sort it? Sequence it? Measure it?*

2. **Gather Your Materials**

> The weight, size, or color of your paper can all influence how your finished book will read.

> Based on your content, consider: Will each section be one page? Will page sizes change as content thins or expands? Will colors or textures help distinguish types?

Part 2. Book Construction Phase

1. **Create a "Dummy" or Prototype**

> This is a sketch version of your book, roughly the same size as your intended final piece.

> It should include all planned content (text, images, placeholders, etc.).

> To make one:

o Cut a stack of pages to size.

o Fold them in half.

o Number the lower corner of each page.

> Do not bind the dummy—you'll want to take it apart easily during your design process.

> Your dummy is an opportunity to test different methods or strategies—you may find it helpful to create more than one to compare them. No matter how clearly we feel that we can imagine something, it is always instructive to see and handle a physical version, to better understand its flow.

> *Note*: Consider having each participant create two dummies utilizing different organizational methods and leading an in-process critique among your group discussing the differences between each.

2. **Design and Lay Out Your Content**

> With intention, decide how text and/or visuals will appear on each page.

> Some things to consider:

o Visual hierarchy—What catches the eye first?

o Flow—How do elements compare with one another on the page? Across both pages? From one page to the next?

o Narrative/Absence of narrative

o Use of negative (empty) space

3. **Print, Paste, Draw, or Write Your Content Into Place**
> Using the pages from your dummy, re-create your design. This may be through cut-and-paste collage techniques, digital design software (like InDesign or Canva), direct drawing/painting onto pages, or some combination of these processes.

4. **Bind and Press the Finished Book**
> Fold your finished pages in half, using bone folder to crease the spine sharply, and your long-arm stapler to attach pages together.
> Place your folded/stapled book under a pile of heavy books to flatten it. The longer you can leave it under weight, the better.

5. **Write a Short Reflection or Artist's Statement on Your Finished Piece**
> After you remove your book from the weights, spend some time with it, considering how the sequence of pages and movement through the work *as a whole* alters your understanding of your content.
> What relationships do you observe that you did not before? How does form of a book affect our understanding of the content?

Assessment

When assessing work, consider several aspects of the finished piece both independently and interdependently using a **reflective, process-based rubric**. Consider the following:

> Clarity/structure
> Organization of content
> Craft and assembly
> Short reflection composed after finished

How successful are each of the above, and how do they each contribute to one's understanding of content? Books are simultaneously physical, cognitive and emotional experiences—how do each of the above criteria work together to affect readers?

Cross-Disciplinary Adaptation

> **Sociology**: Voices within a community—use the book format to bring together 12 different interviews asking the same question(s).
> **Education**: Varying Methods—use the book format to contrast different methods of teaching the same subject (for. ex Math). It is possible to design a book that showcases educational methods, or could physically integrated in a lesson with students.
> **Anthropology**: Cultural Analysis—use the book format to bring together many examples of housing, textile design, pottery, or spiritual ritual.

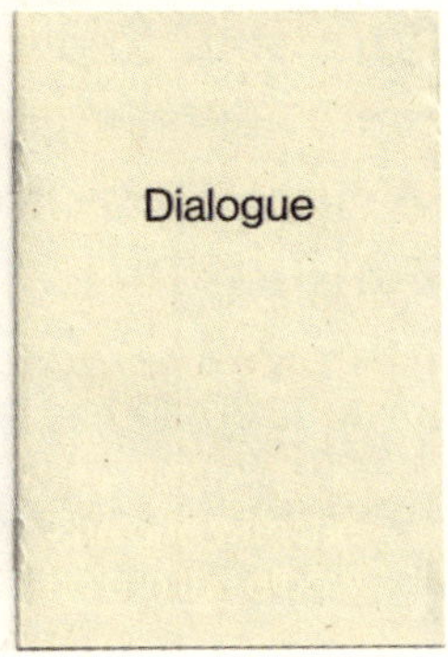

Examples

Sample 1a: Two voices on opposing pages, using "top" and "bottom" margin to denote speaker

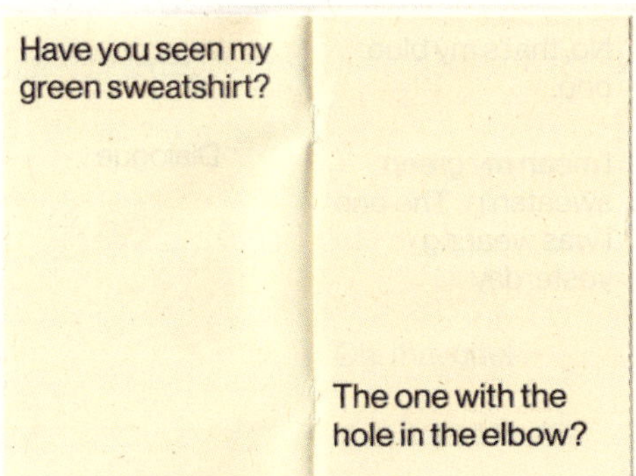

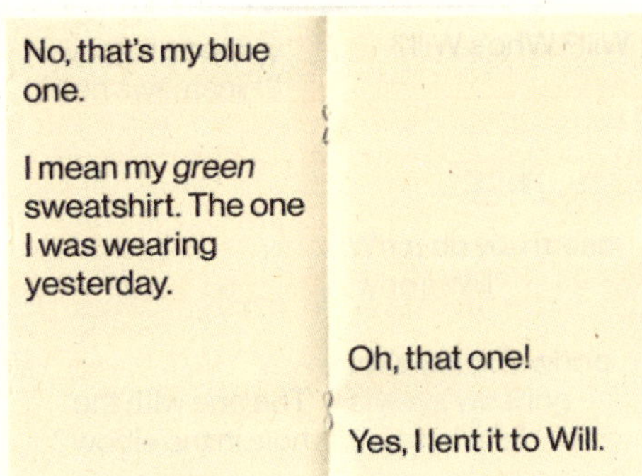

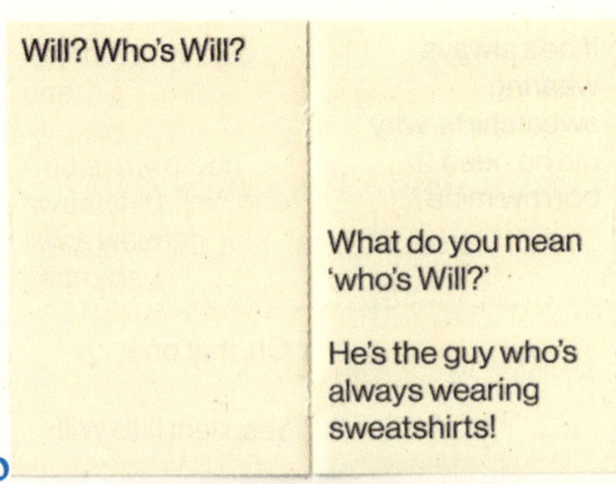

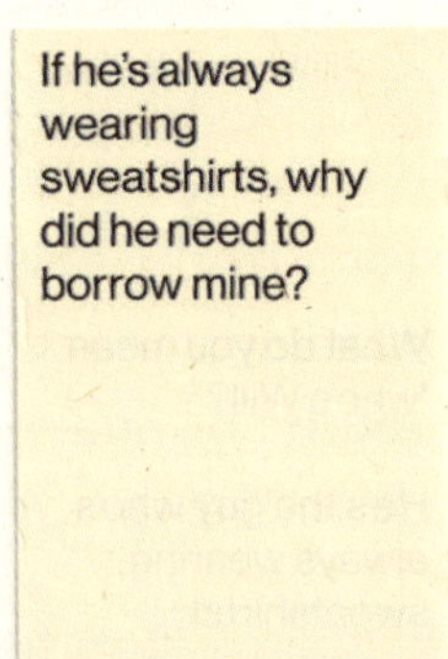

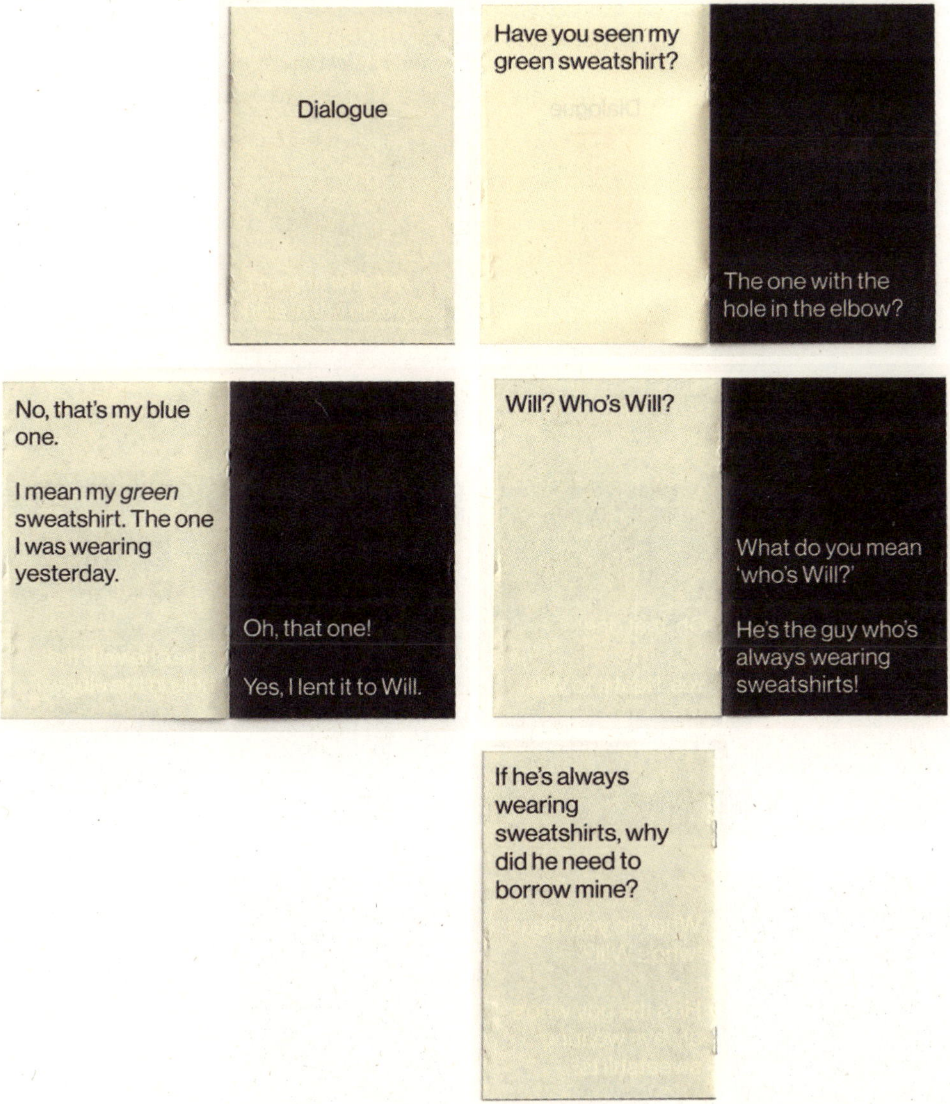

Sample 1b: Two voices on opposing pages, using black and white backgrounds to further denote speaker

Sample 2a: Collection of images, distinguished from one another through colored pages

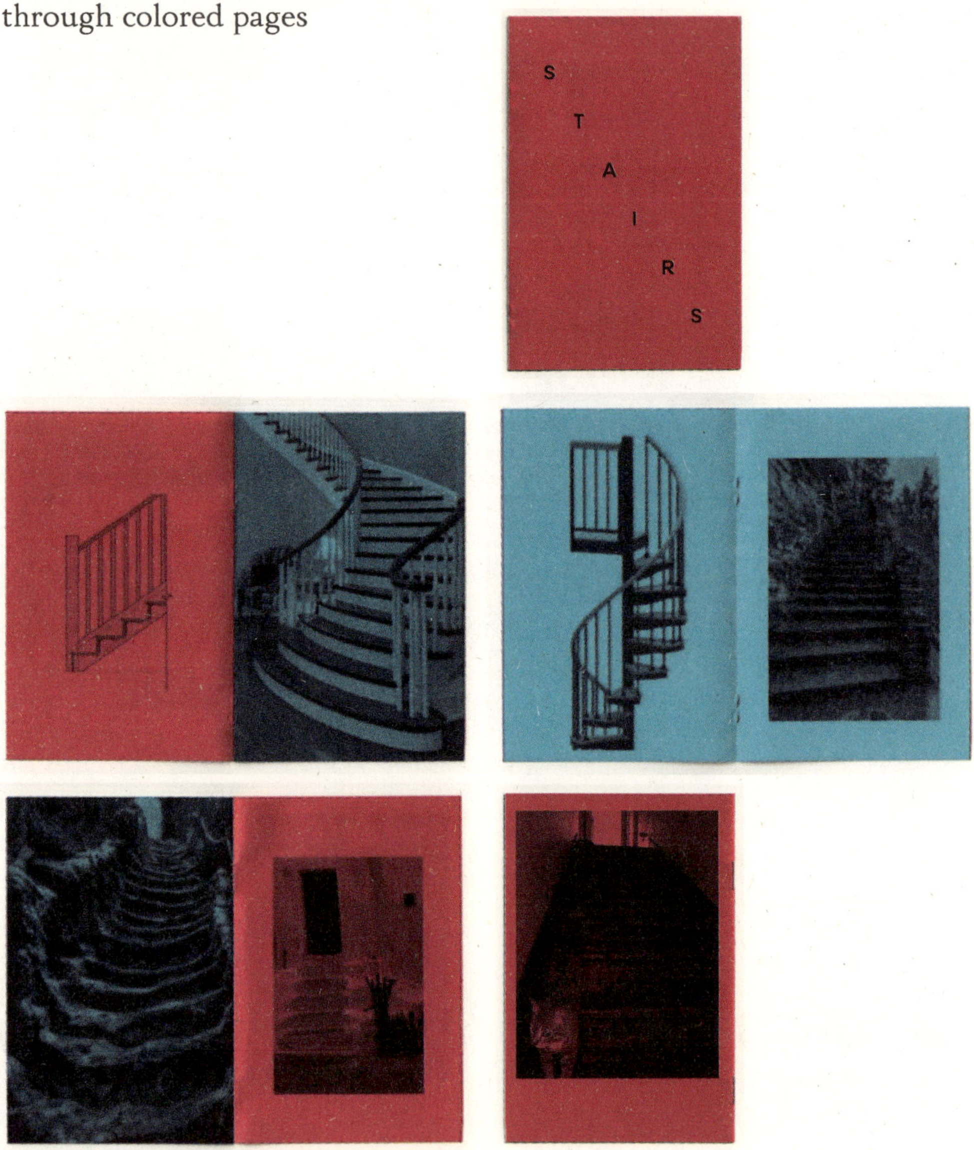

Photo credit: Brian Hitselberger

Sample 2b: Collection of images, distinguished from one another by descending sizes of page

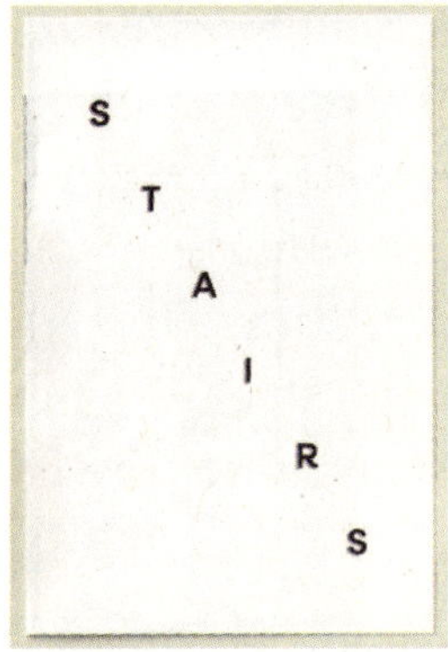

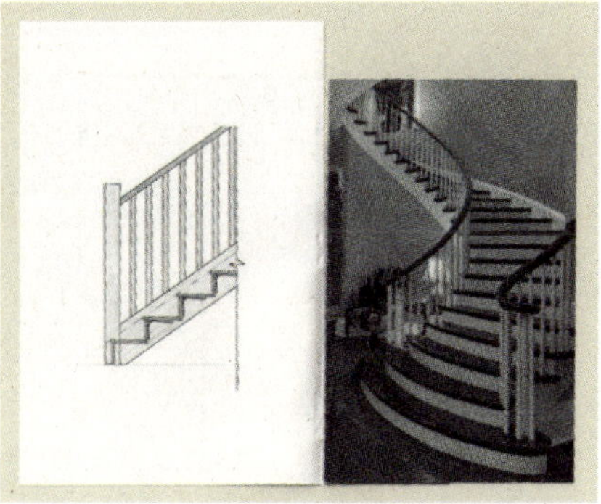

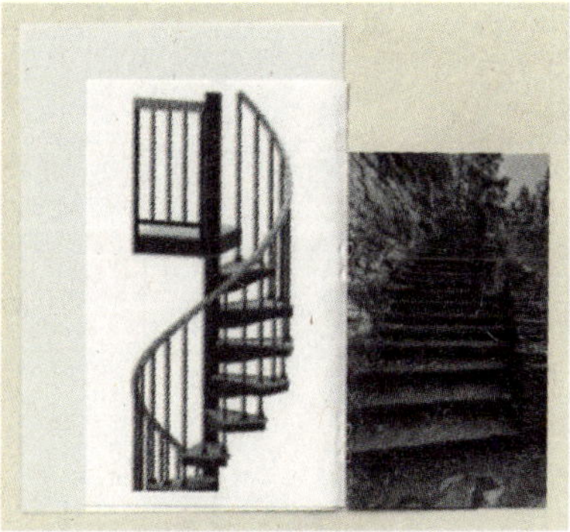

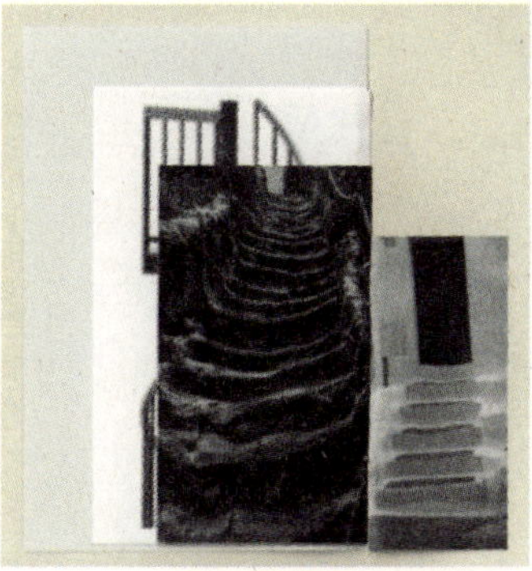

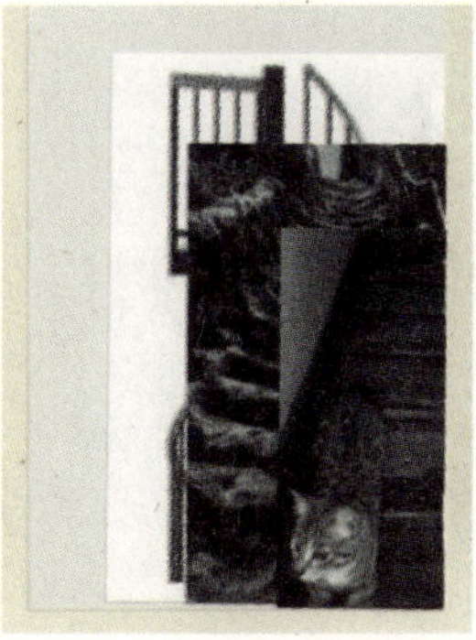

Instructor Try-It Activity

1. Make an eight-page book from two folded-and-stapled folios, illustrating several moments from your day. Use only the following:

> Cut paper shapes collaged onto your book's pages

> Three colors (maximum)

2. Questions to ask yourself:

> How did the book structure limit you?

> What did the book structure convey that language or other forms did not?

> Is there a topic in your course where structure would benefit student learning? If so, what and how?

RESEARCH BEYOND THE PAPER: EXPLORING KNOWLEDGE CREATION THROUGH ZINES (PART 1)

By: Sarah Huber

Discipline: Library and Information Science

Subject: Alternative Forms of Knowledge Creation and Dissemination

Information Qualities of the Format

Zines—small, affordable, self-published booklets—have the potential to both conduct research and communicate findings. Natalie Loveless's concept of research-creation (2019) presents "making knowledge" as a valid method of inquiry, positioning this approach within art and design. This lesson plan bridges to other disciplines, recognizing the role of creativity across fields. When students cut, fold, collage, and sequence information, they're not just illustrating knowledge but actively generating it. For example, arranging interview quotes alongside textures or symbols, and intentional use of color, can generate new insights, revealing connections a written outline might miss. Zines can also reimagine how research reaches audiences beyond academia—peers, local communities, or non-academic groups. As Rasch, Gijsen, and Staal explain:

> *The activity of making activates the implicit or tacit knowledge of the hands and body—something that can not be read in a book or learned from an expert. It is an embodied way of doing research that invites you to step out of your head and into the world*
> (Rasch, Gijsen, and Staal 2025, 7).

Zines as a Method for Research

> **Fieldwork Journal:** Use the pages of a zine to collect

sketches, words that stand out, and sensory impressions during data gathering. Does a narrative thread emerge? Or is there an underdeveloped idea that stands out? What are the future potential pages that could unfold?

> **Idea Mapping**: Fold and sequence, even cut and rearrange pages, of early findings to test narrative flows or relationships between conepts. These acts can reveal gaps or unexpected links.

> **Processing Through Design**: Use textures, colors, even page sizes, to represent relationships at play (e.g., overlapping shapes, vivid or faint colors, small compared to large pages) to explore power dynamics in a community study.

> **Iterative Reflection**: Draft multiple quick zines across the research process to document and highlight evolving questions, interpretations, and insights.

Zines to Communicate Research Results

> **Audience-Focused Design**: Identify a specific audience (e.g., family, politicians, or community members) and tailor the zine to their experience. This includes how the zine unfolds (e.g., the lotus fold may work well when teaching something about botany or horticulture) as well as the tone created through colors, choice in images, textures, and language. The section with resources has links to variations on folds.

> **Zine Summaries**: Use drawings, collage, diagrams (which could be created in software like Excel and printed), or found images to highlight key findings with minimal text that support visuals.

> **Narrative Navigation**: Arrange findings so readers feel like they are "traveling" through the argument or story. Use visuals, text, and the folding of the zine to create a map-like experience, rather than requiring the viewer make sense of lists of information from only one perspective. Comic-style zines allow for characters or

points of view to travel throughout the zine through a narrative thread.

> **Access and Reach**: Print multiple copies to give peers and leave in different physical spaces in academia or the community, or scan and distribute digitally to broaden access. One of the strengths of zines is their ease of reproduction. Using a simple photocopier, they can be scaled up cheaply and widely.

Who This Is For

Students across undergraduate and graduate courses can experiment with this approach, but especially those in courses introducing research methods, information literacy, or alternative forms to scholarship.

Instructional Context

> 1–2 sessions to either introduce students to the idea or to prepare them for a longer research project.

> Workspace is needed for materials to be spread out.

> Present early in the semester to help students think about possibilities.

Learning Outcomes

> **Explain** different ways research methods and outputs can take diverse forms.

> **Create** a visual or mixed-media representation of a research method or output.

> **Analyze and evaluate** how format shapes meaning, audience engagement, and accessibility.

Materials and Equipment

> 8.5 × 11 paper, scissors, glue sticks, markers or pens, printed copies

of students' words or words cut out of magazines, images cut from magazines or photocopies
> Optional: Shape cutters for paper, washi tape, stencils, stapler
> Access to a photocopier (consider how black and white will look compared to color)
> Examples of zines or non-traditional scholarly outputs for inspiration
> Alternative: Students may choose to make a digital version using programs like Canva or Issuu

Resources Students Should Review for the Assignment

> An example of a research project relevant to the field for students to read, such as an aspect of Madame Curie's process in isolating radium. Below is an example of visual storytelling on the topic:
o Redniss, Lauren. 2010. *Radioactive: Marie & Pierre Curie: A Tale of Love and Fallout.* HarperCollins.
> A brief history of zines:
o Van Leuven, Laura. October 25, 2017. "A Brief History of Zines " *The Chapel Hill Rare Book Blog.* https://bit.ly/49hXP4W.
> Examples of scholarly zines:
o University of San Diego Ethnic Studies Student Zines: https://bit.ly/4hMMfBn
> How to fold paper to make a zine:
o How to Fold a Zine from Cambridge University Museums: https://bit.ly/47sRYIZ
o The Lotus Fold and Other Unique Folds from Columbus College of Art & Design: https://bit.ly/49Dcolo
o Canva: Brochure Design ideas: 25 Tips to Create Marketing Materials That Sell: https://bit.ly/3JmSSO9

Assignment

This assignment may be done individually or in pairs. Some students may be intimidated by drawing, or they may second guess their creative decisions. Collage work or photography is an excellent approach to creating zines, especially for those intimidated by drawing. If working in pairs, students can brainstorm together how they will visually approach the assignment.

Process and Steps

1. **Presentation**: The instructor shares the above information on how to use zines during research or to communicate research findings.
2. **Prepare**: Students should either complete the "Hands-on Hierarchy: Designing a Concert Poster" lesson or review the "Design Basics" resources on using font, color, alignment, and spacing to create effective page layouts.
3. **Choose a path**: Students choose whether they want to explore zines for use in research or to communicate findings.
4. **Make**: Students choose a type of fold to represent their chosen idea through visuals, essential words, and sketches. This is a time to experiment. Use the Curie example above.
   - o **Method**: Use the accordion fold for lab notes documenting tools used, steps taken, and observations. (Curie's writings can be found online.)
   - o **Results**: Use the lotus fold to reveal layers of revelation or discovery.
5. **Sharing and Reflection**: Students exchange zines in small groups. Each student takes time to discuss how both the format of the zine (including the chosen fold) affected their thoughts on how research can be conducted, as well as an approach to sharing results.

Research Beyond the Paper: Exploring Knowledge Creation through Zines (Part 1)

Assessment

> **Formative**: Participation in creating and sharing the zine.
> **Summative**: Students write a reflective memo (as can be found in the lesson plan "Writing: Leveraging an Old Medium to Reflect on Learning") about their process and how they may or may not use zines in their research process going forward.

Cross-Disciplinary Adaptation

> **Anthropology**: Gather stories from peers (or any community of interest) on a shared theme (e.g., favorite restaurant or teacher). Present the qualitative data gathered by using photos, sketches, quotes, and a timeline of when the data was collected. Use this to generate ideas about a larger study.
> **Engineering**: Choose an object of interest. Gather details such as materials, cost, data on the demographics the item is most used by, and locate stories of cultural significance. Try the accordion-fold zine to represent the Lean Manufacturing decision-making process. Use this to walk through the different types of information needed when developing a product going to market. Identifying gaps or excess in the required information.
> **Data Science**: Gather personal data, such as steps walked or cell phone screen time. Try the different gate folds (closed, double, or open) to see which would best display the data. Use hand-drawn or printed digital visualizations of the data and include the methods used on the back page. Reflect on how this engaged the audience.

Examples

This example of sharing research was done by Purdue Archivist Jo Otremba:

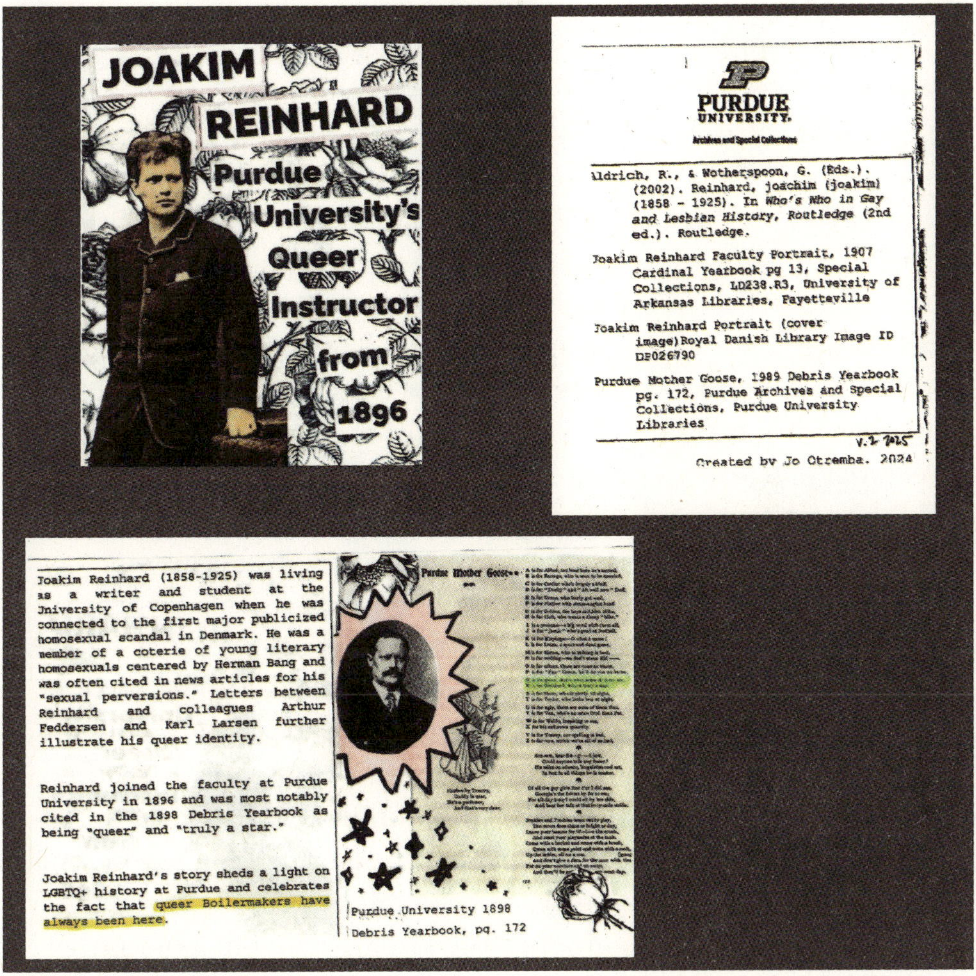

Images 1-3: Joakim Reinhard zine

Below is an example of UW-La Crosse, WI, Assistant Professor & Cataloging Librarian, Mike Olson, sharing the process of transforming one of his articles into a zine. Olson draws on his work in critical visual activism to create scholarly zines that empower communities and challenge information privilege.

o **Article:** "Critical Visual Literacy in Activism: Artist Violet Ray's Counterimages" https://bit.ly/4aq9Vtq

The original article analyzed Ray's appropriation techniques through frameworks of critical visual literacy, counterimages, and the intersection of advertising and warfare. The zine transformation eliminated theoretical scaffolding and academic framing entirely. Formal citations were removed, but references remain to acknowledge context and origin. Rather than discussing "critical visual literacy as research practice" or citing Kim & Serrano's definitions, the zine simply shows Ray's work and explains his method in plain language. Complex discussions about power dynamics and visual rhetoric became straightforward narratives: LIFE magazine published both war photography and consumer advertising; Ray cut out war photos and pasted them into the ads. The academic article's careful analysis of visual syntax and political encoding was replaced with direct presentation of the collages themselves—full-page spreads that let viewers experience the jarring juxtaposition firsthand. Theoretical concepts about appropriation ethics and image manipulation became concrete examples: the Fresh Spray deodorant paired with napalm, for example. The zine foregrounds the visual argument itself rather than explaining it through academic frameworks, trusting readers to grasp the critique through direct exposure to Ray's subversive counter-advertisements and brief contextual explanations of his activist intentions.

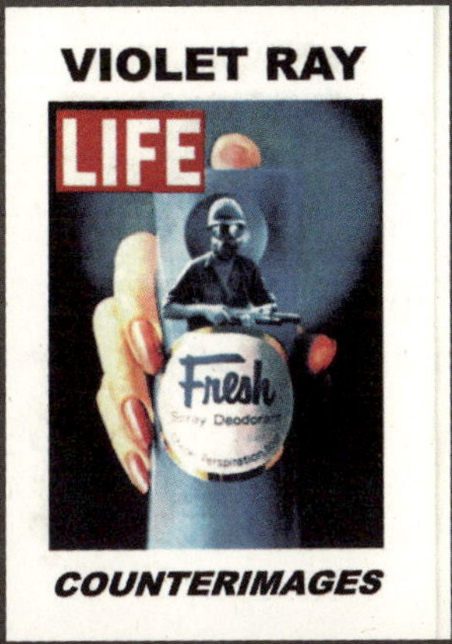

VIOLET RAY

LIFE

Fresh Spray Deodorant

COUNTERIMAGES

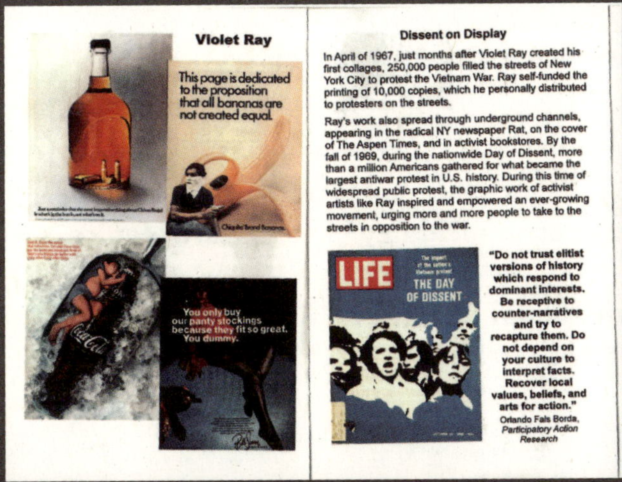

Violet Ray

This page is dedicated to the proposition that all bananas are not created equal.

Chiquita Brand Bananas

Coca-Cola

You only buy our panty stockings because they fit so great. You dummy.

Dissent on Display

In April of 1967, just months after Violet Ray created his first collages, 250,000 people filled the streets of New York City to protest the Vietnam War. Ray self-funded the printing of 10,000 copies, which he personally distributed to protesters on the streets.

Ray's work also spread through underground channels, appearing in the radical NY newspaper Rat, on the cover of The Aspen Times, and in activist bookstores. By the fall of 1969, during the nationwide Day of Dissent, more than a million Americans gathered for what became the largest antiwar protest in U.S. history. During this time of widespread public protest, the graphic work of activist artists like Ray inspired and empowered an ever-growing movement, urging more and more people to take to the streets in opposition to the war.

LIFE

THE DAY OF DISSENT

"Do not trust elitist versions of history which respond to dominant interests. Be receptive to counter-narratives and try to recapture them. Do not depend on your culture to interpret facts. Recover local values, beliefs, and arts for action."

Orlando Fals Borda, *Participatory Action Research*

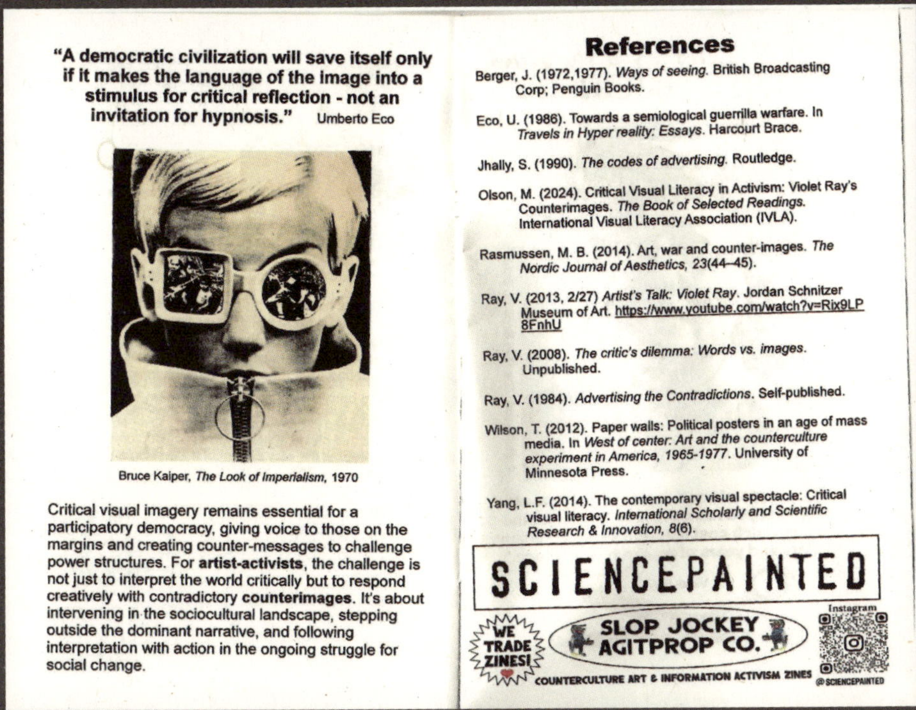

"A democratic civilization will save itself only if it makes the language of the image into a stimulus for critical reflection - not an invitation for hypnosis." Umberto Eco

Bruce Kaiper, *The Look of Imperialism*, 1970

Critical visual imagery remains essential for a participatory democracy, giving voice to those on the margins and creating counter-messages to challenge power structures. For **artist-activists**, the challenge is not just to interpret the world critically but to respond creatively with contradictory **counterimages**. It's about intervening in the sociocultural landscape, stepping outside the dominant narrative, and following interpretation with action in the ongoing struggle for social change.

References

Berger, J. (1972,1977). *Ways of seeing*. British Broadcasting Corp; Penguin Books.

Eco, U. (1986). Towards a semiological guerrilla warfare. In *Travels in Hyper reality: Essays*. Harcourt Brace.

Jhally, S. (1990). *The codes of advertising*. Routledge.

Olson, M. (2024). Critical Visual Literacy in Activism: Violet Ray's Counterimages. *The Book of Selected Readings*. International Visual Literacy Association (IVLA).

Rasmussen, M. B. (2014). Art, war and counter-images. *The Nordic Journal of Aesthetics*, 23(44–45).

Ray, V. (2013, 2/27) *Artist's Talk: Violet Ray*. Jordan Schnitzer Museum of Art. https://www.youtube.com/watch?v=Rix9LP8FnhU

Ray, V. (2008). *The critic's dilemma: Words vs. images*. Unpublished.

Ray, V. (1984). *Advertising the Contradictions*. Self-published.

Wilson, T. (2012). Paper walls: Political posters in an age of mass media. In *West of center: Art and the counterculture experiment in America, 1965-1977*. University of Minnesota Press.

Yang, L.F. (2014). The contemporary visual spectacle: Critical visual literacy. *International Scholarly and Scientific Research & Innovation*, 8(6).

SCIENCEPAINTED

WE TRADE ZINES!

SLOP JOCKEY AGITPROP CO.

COUNTERCULTURE ART & INFORMATION ACTIVISM ZINES

Instagram

@SCIENCEPAINTED

Images 1-3: Violet Ray zine

Instructor Try-It Activity

Fold a zine to reflect on a small piece of your own research. Ask yourself what shifts when your ideas move from text to image and sequencing. Take notes on what your students may encounter (including challenges) when doing this themselves.

Additional Resources/References

Loveless, Natalie. 2019. *How to Make Art at the End of the World: A Manifesto for Research-Creation*. Duke University Press.

Rasch, Miriam, Jojanneke Gijsen, and Harma Staal, eds. 2025. *Hands On Research for Artists, Designers & Educators*. Eindhoven: Set Margins' publications.

HOW MEDIA CHOICE IMPACTS READERS' ZINE EXPERIENCE (PART 2)

By: Sarah Huber

Discipline: Library Science

Subject: Alternative Forms of Knowledge Creation and Dissemination

Information Qualities of the Format

When people think of zines, they often picture black-and-white photocopied booklets with cut-out strips of typewriter font/text (which is fantastic!). However, experimenting with different folding styles and media can change how the viewer experiences and understands the material. In this lesson plan, students explore various media to see how their work is perceived differently depending on the medium used.

A similar decision in writing an academic journal article is choosing whether to use discipline-specific jargon or everyday language and considering how that choice affects the reader. For example, by choosing watercolor to communicate an oral history, the use of soft, blurred lines may evoke the interpretation that not all the details of memory are perfect. We rarely see people's handwriting anymore, but when we do, it creates a sense of intimacy—handwritten notes and hand-drawn sketches are powerful ways to grab the reader's attention. RISO printing adds vibrant, unpredictable color overlays that can reflect experimentation and alternative ideas. A digital zine might give an impression of precision and professionalism, while black-and-white zines aim for an underground, alternative feel.

By experimenting with different media, students learn that the medium is not just decorative but actively influences how research or stories are received and read. This lesson builds on Natalie Loveless's (2019) concept of research-creation, where knowledge develops through material practice as much as through textual analysis.

Who This Is For

This builds on the previous lesson plan on zine making, "Research Beyond the Paper: Exploring Knowledge Creation through Zines (Part 1),"but is suitable for students with a basic familiarity with zine creation who are ready to explore a variety of aesthetics. It is ideal for courses on information design and creative scholarship.

Learning Outcomes

> **Analyze** how different media (e.g., watercolor, hand-drawing, RISO) affect tone, accessibility, and audience engagement.
> **Create** a zine using different media to communicate research or storytelling content.
> **Evaluate** the relationship between media choice and information interpretation.

Instructional Context

> One or two 50-minute sessions, or an extended workshop
> Works best in a makerspace, art studio, or classroom with access to various making tools. The experiments students conduct will depend on what is available through a university makerspace or a collaboration with an art or design program. Students may only have basic zine-making materials, or they may access old letter presses, paints, or materials for creating wood blocks. It might be helpful to ask students what media they would like to work with and then seek out resource collaborations.

> Can connect to an ongoing research project or serve as stand-alone exploration

Materials and Equipment

> Basic: 8.5 × 11 paper, scissors, glue, markers
> Media options:
o Watercolor sets and brushes (thick paper or cardstock is suggested)
o Woodblock printing tools and ink
o Hand-drawing tools
o RISO printer or other specialty printers (coordinate with maker-space staff)
o Magazines, stencils, or digital tools for hybrid approaches
> Drying racks or protective sheets for wet media
> Access to Photoshop, Canva, Issuu, or Photopea. Students may work in any medium and either scan or photograph their work to include in a digital zine or assemble it as an analog (hard copy) zine.
o Alternatively, they can create the entire work in digital format.
> Have images to pass around in a book or photocopies so students can view different examples. Below is an example of a zine by Rachel Hendel.

Assignment

Students can work individually or in pairs to support each other making visual decisions.

Process and Steps

1. **Discussion**
> Review the previous zine exercise and discuss how students' media choices may have influenced the reader's experience.
> Review Hendel's zine, created with 14 traditional media (water-

color, pen, linocut, cut paper, etc.) for a class by Il Sung Na at the Kansas City Art Institute. Hendel chose a snail for its varied textures and colors, which was ideal for exploring different media.

o Use this as a model. Projects in fields like agriculture or science can focus on experimenting with media to highlight aspects of the subject rather than the story itself.

> Discuss the media used in the zine. What are the different tones created, and what are the various contexts the media might be used in?

> Discuss how the different media might affect who feels invited to engage with the content (audience)?

2. **Media Selection and Planning**

> Students choose a medium or a couple of media they're less familiar with or excited to explore. Time is given to search online for examples, and if a printer is available, to print them off.

> Students identify a research idea or story they can re-express through a new medium or media.

> Students fold a piece of paper into a zine (fold of choice) and sketch a quick layout.

3. **Experimentation to Create**

> Create zine (single-sheet or small booklet).

o Note: When using different media, consider the type of paper. For example, it might need to be cardstock, or the paper may need to be cut into small rectangles to allow more flexibility when working with media like watercolor.

> Assembling: Images or scans of work can be dropped into a digital zine or taped to a piece of paper and scanned.

o *Note*: It's good to give a little room at the edges of each image as some paper real estate is lost when folded.

> Encourage experimentation: Overlap watercolor textures with text, layer RISO colors for misregistration effects, or use woodblock

shapes as metaphors to represent data or something non-yet discovered in science.

4. **Sharing and Reflection**

> Display zines on a table.
> Students circulate, flipping through and taking notes on what they believe worked and what could have been further developed.
> Students share out their notes/thoughts.
> Students write a brief reflection to be turned in with their zine:

o What did your medium emphasize or obscure? How might this choice influence a reader's understanding of your research, story, or subject?

Assessment

> **Process**: Participation and risk-taking in trying a new medium
> **Product**: A finished experimental zine
> **Reflection**: A reflective paragraph connecting material choice to meaning and audience engagement

Cross-Disciplinary Adaptation

> **STEM**: Use woodblock shapes to depict molecules or processes abstractly or utilize an available specialty printer for data visualizations.
> **Social Sciences**: Layer ethnographic quotes with expressive media to explore participant voices.
> **Humanities/Arts**: Reinterpret a poem or historical artifact using a medium associated with its era or theme, such as dip or fountain pens to mimic a quill used in medieval manuscripts.

Instructor Try-It Activity

Create two mini-zines on the same topic using different media (e.g., hand-drawn sketches and collage). Compare your reactions and the perceived audience for each. Ask yourself how the media supported or did not support the topic and what you might do differently if you were to repeat it. Share your observations with students to model critical reflection.

Additional Resources

Loveless, Natalie. 2019. *How to Make Art at the End of the World: A Manifesto for Research-Creation*. Duke University Press.

For more information on Rachel Hendel's work: https://bit.ly/4poCSR1

Examples

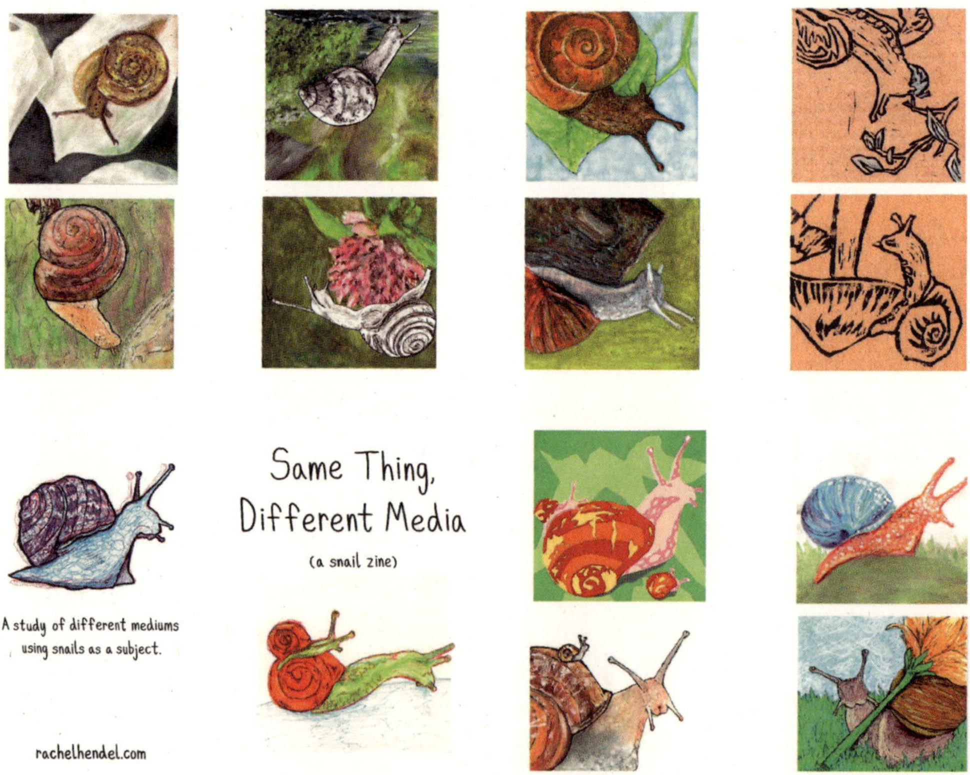

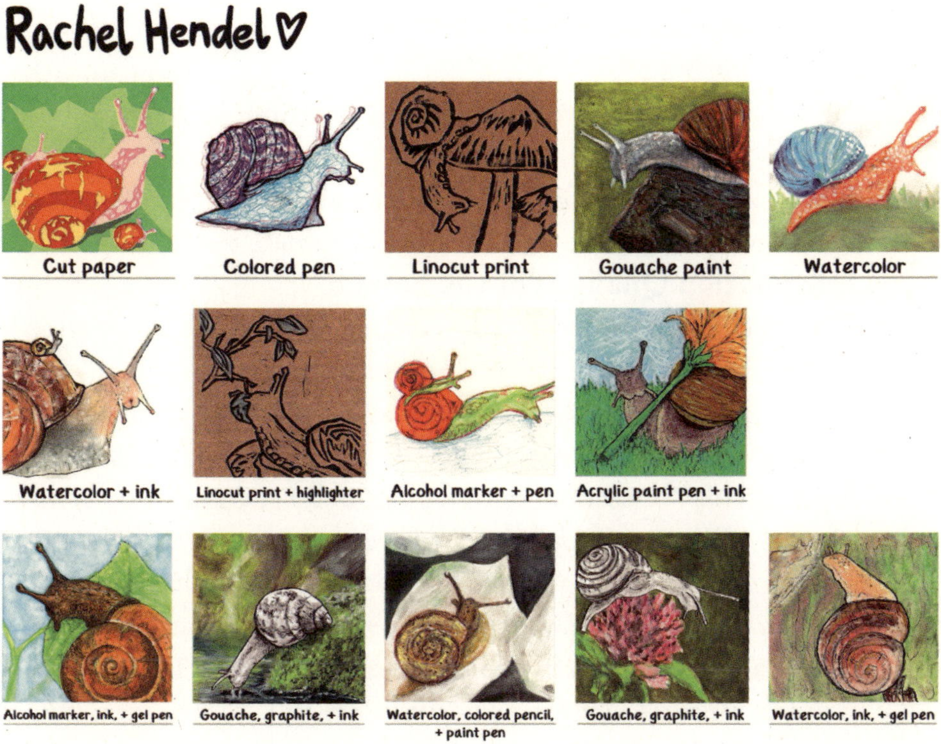

Images 1–2: Same Thing Different Media Photo credit: Rachel Hendel

REMEMBERING AIR

By: Matt Olson

Discipline: Design, art, architecture, landscape, writing, breathing

Subject: Play, Experimentation, and Expansiveness

Information Qualities of the Format

Design is often unnecessarily constrained by professionalized definitions that are outdated and based in business thinking rather than creative thinking. I teach with open experiences, using disruptive group activities followed by joyful dialogues. This "lesson" or activity has been successful both as a playful, silly "art happening" and/or with more seriousness when paired with teachings by Luce Irigaray, who wrote *The Forgetting of Air in Martin Heidegger*, and other texts committed to a deep poetics in ecological emergences. This assignment is meant to create curiosity, not skills or answers. It's meant to use collective experience as a space of freedom. Generative and uncertain, filled with aliveness. Funny. Humble. Gentle.

In her book *Ordinary Affects*, Kathleen Stewart starts by saying what the book is and isn't:

> . . .[it] is an experiment, not a judgment. Committed not to the demystification and uncovered truths that support a well-known picture of the world, but rather to speculation, curiosity, and the concrete, it tries to provoke attention to the forces that come into view as habit or shock, resonance or impact. Something throws itself together in a moment as an event and a sensation; a something both animated and inhabitable (Stewart 2007, 1).

This lesson travels in a similar direction. The intended outcomes are alive and continue to develop in our memories. It may even have a structurally unsolvable quality, so I encourage students not to seek an answer or fixed result. It draws on what Peter Sloterdijk calls "Atmospheric Knowledge"—knowledge in the air that is ephemeral rather than fixed, shifting shape as we interact, play, and experiment with our surroundings. It reminds us that information can change and move, remaining impermanent, yet still taking form, alive in the spaces between us.

Who This Is For

Everyone, anyone . . . Joining the air with a group is poetic, philosophical, scientific, mathematical, social, factual, functional, fictional, innocent, open and neutral, elusive and charged. Open.

Learning Outcomes

> **Making as thinking**: Students make as a form of speculative inquiry.
> **Attention as place**: Students observe how focused attention shapes and reveals atmospheric structures.
> **Participation as performance**: Students evaluate how participatory acts construct shared experience.
> **Moving as seeing**: Students experiment with movement as a way of perceiving what the air is communicating.

Instructional Context

> Open, outdoor space
> Small to large groups (15-30)

Materials and Equipment

> Biodegradable bags that, when filled with air, are no larger than a single person can carry in their arms

> Cameras for documentation
> Air and breath

Resources Students Should Review for the Assignment
Pre-Activity Discussion Questions

> Do you remember the air?
> Is everything made of air?
> Who, what, where, why, when . . . and forget while moving as a group.
> Did you laugh?
> Is air happy?
> Are we separate?
> What does it mean when we say something is "in the air"?

Pre-Activity Group Work (optional)

Make a Mixtape of Songs About the Air.

> Bush, Kate. 1980. "Breathing." Track 3 on Never for Ever. EMI Records.
> Radiohead. 1997. "Airbag." Track 1 on OK Computer. EMI Records.
> Talking Heads. 1979. "Air." Track 7 on Fear of Music. Sire Records.

Readings

Coccia, Emanuel. 2016. "Like an Atmosphere: Philosophy as a Climate of Knowledge." *The Brooklyn Rai*l. https://bit.ly/4hIBTCi.

Irigaray, Luce. 2021. "Luce Irigaray." Interviewed by Octave Larmagnac-Matheron. Translated by Mélani Salvi. *Philosophy Now 162*. https://bit.ly/4p21RDv.

Sloterdijk, Peter. 2009. "Something in the Air." Interviewed by Eric Morse. *Frieze 127*. https://bit.ly/47Gri6q.

Assignment
Part 1: Experience and Actions

In one large group or in small groups, form a line. The first person in the line takes a deep, contemplative breath, exhaling into the plastic bag. Handing the bag to the next person, they move to the end of the line and wait for the bag to reach them again. This circular pattern is presented as a widening circle. When the group has filled a bag with exhales, it's tied closed tightly and a new bag begins. When the group has five filled bags, proceed to part 2.

An alternative option has people breathe into an individual bag and add it to the group bag.

Part 2: Open Dialogues and Playful Explorations

Use the bag(s) full of exhales as objects and try to use them for anything from sculptures, a seat, a table, a ball, or however the air itself suggests.

Discussion

> Do you remember the air? How often? Why? And how deeply?
> Is everything made of air?
> Who, what, where, why, when . . . and forget while moving as a group.
> Did you laugh?
> Is air happy? Is it alive? Or just life giving?
> Are we separate?
> What does it mean when we say something's "in the air"?

Deliverables

Take two 15-minute walks and observe breathing and air. Write a reflection that honestly speaks to how you've changed from this activity. No word count requirement.

Cross Disciplinary Application

> **Media or Theater**: Record the sounds of breath, wind, or air in varied environments and write a short reflection on how air changes meaning across these spaces.

> **Anthropology / Sociology**: Investigate communal rituals of breath, air, or atmosphere across cultures and write a reflection that compares these findings to personal experience.
> **Philosophy/Ethics**: Read Sloterdijk, Irigaray, or Coccia to discuss how air complicates boundaries between self and world.

Instructor Try-It Activity

Think of air as a source of information in your discipline. Ask:
> What does air communicate in my field? (HVAC, pneumatics, particle accelerators)
> How is it measured, represented, or felt?
> What happens when we treat it as a carrier of meaning, not just matter?
> How could looking at air as "Atmospheric Knowledge" help my students view the way they interact with air from a new perspective?

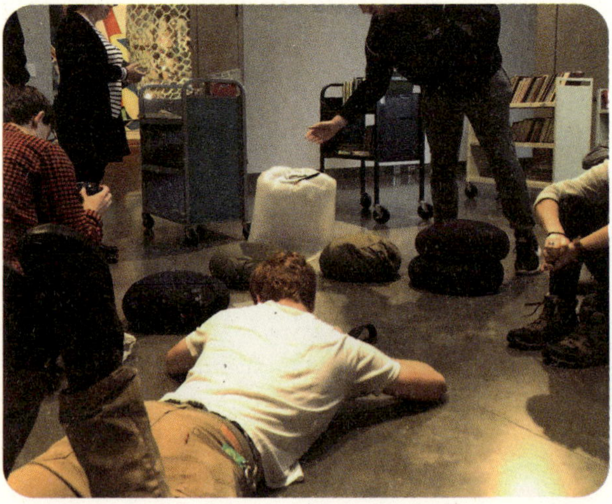

Additional Resources/ References

Irigaray, Luce. 1999. *The Forgetting of Air in Martin Heidegger*. Translated by Mary Beth Mader. University of Texas Press.

Stewart, Kathleen. 2007. *Ordinary Affects*. Duke University Press

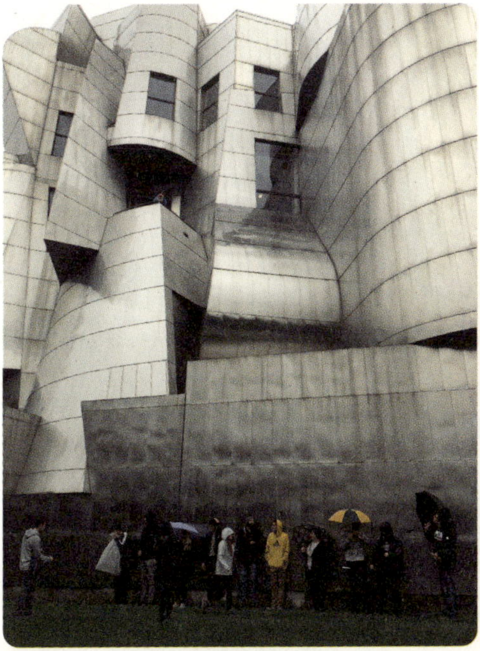
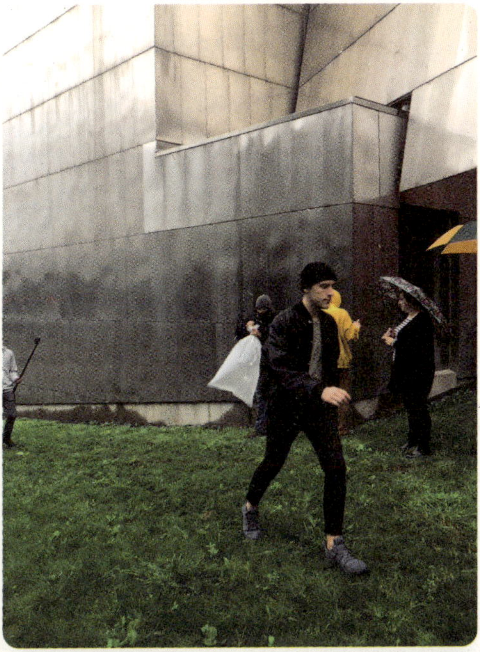
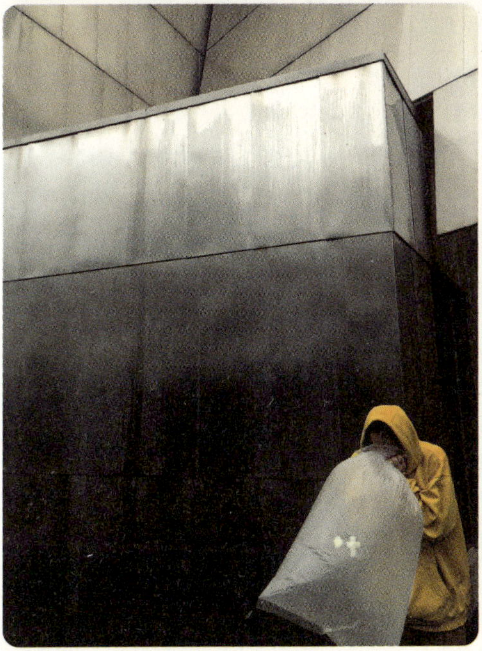
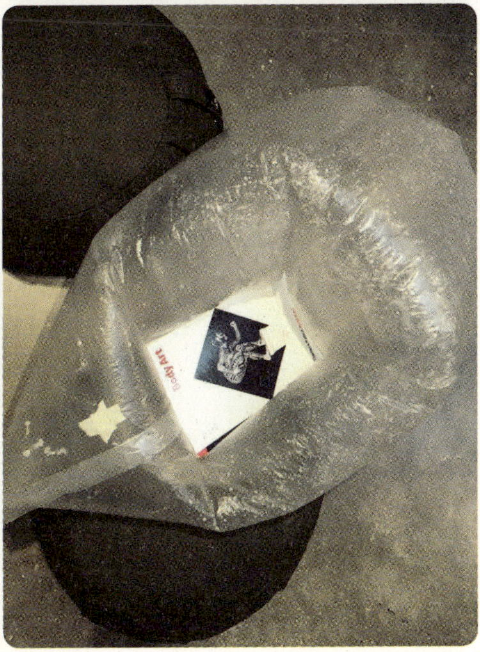

Images 1–5: Remembering Air
Photo credit: Matt Olson

MEANING IN MUSIC: EVERYONE CAN BE CREATIVE

By: Dan Guberman

Discipline: Music

Subject: Write Your Own Song

Information Qualities of the Format

Debates about whether music has intrinsic meaning or only meanings constructed by listeners have been active for centuries (Hanslick 1986; Abbate 2004). At a minimum, we can say with confidence that elements of music combined—including lyrics, tone, timbre, structure, and musical tropes—communicate meaning to listeners, both individually and culturally. This shapes not only our experience of music itself, but film, television, video games, and even novels, where music is often described to evoke mood and/or meaning. It influences our sense of identity and belonging, how we express ourselves (through choice in clothing and hairstyle, for example) and how we remember the past. Yet, there is a perception that music making is limited to those with significant formal training and "natural talent." This assignment is available to students with no formal training. It explores music as an information format through which ideas, emotions, cultural values, or discipline-specific topics communicate meaning and understanding.

Who This Is For

Faculty who want their students to share their experiences, narratives, perspectives, or understanding of a concept or process through more abstract means. Songwriting and reflection are used to creatively engage students in their learning and personal meaning-making.

Originally designed for non-music majors in a music class, the assignment is adaptable across disciplines.

Learning Outcomes

> **Communicate** experiences and ideas through alternative formats.
> **Consider** music's ability to convey meaning in various forms.
> **Explore** how AI tools can help navigate creative challenges.
> **Find** connections between music and meaning.
> **Identify** basic components of a song (verse and chorus) and reflect on how they work together to create narrative or meaning.

Instructional Context

> Can apply to large or small classes.
> Ideally designed for a peer sharing/discussion or showcase environment.
> It is recommended that grading focus more on completion and the student's reflection process than on the quality of the song itself.

Resources Students Should Review for the Assignment

> Listen to some songs that have meaning to you and reflect on how the music and lyrics synthesize with each other. Listen for distinct sections (particularly verses and choruses) to understand the structure.
> Use Genius (https://genius.com/) to follow the lyrics and form of songs you know, but don't feel constrained by the meaning described therein.
> Use Music Map (https://music-map.com) or Every Noise at Once (https://everynoise.com) to explore genres.
> Find examples of educational or narrative songs—"The Elements" from the musical *Hamilton* or Bill Nye the Science Guy songs.

If you want students to delve more deeply into thinking about analyzing the meaning in songs:

> **12tone** (https://www.youtube.com/@12tone) creates deep dive videos that explore song creation from multiple angles with an engaging drawing approach to visuals. For example, his video about The Eurythmics' "Sweet Dreams" (https://bit.ly/4nDx1Ql) provides context about the performers background and breaks down individual instruments and how they contribute to narrative and meaning. This uses a lot of terminology.

> **Middle 8** (www.youtube.com/@Middle8) also creates deep dives into individual songs, although does it with less emphasis on music theory. As demonstrated in his video about OutKast's "Hey Ya" (https://bit.ly/4hKoqdf), he provides background about the album and song, and then a deeper dive around the lyrics and how those lyrics in this case contrast with the overall sound of the song.

Assignment

This assignment was drawn from the work of Stimeling and Katz (2012).

Process and Steps

1. **Decide What You Want to Communicate**
   Choose a topic, idea, or theme that has personal meaning or interests you. Some examples include:
   - o A scientific principle
   - o A social justice issue
   - o A personal experience
   - o An historical moment
2. **Write Lyrics**
   Write at least:
   - o One verse: Part of a song where the lyrics change with each repetition, evolve

o One chorus: Part of the song where music and lyrics repeat for reinforcement

If the idea of writing lyrics is intimidating, consider using a language generation AI tool such as ChatGPT or Gemini.

Note: If you use one of these AI tools make sure to edit and adjust the lyrics as you see fit for the meaning you want to convey.

3. **Describe the Music**

o Describe what the music *sounds* like.
o Describe how much the music differs between the verse and the chorus and whether the transition is smooth or abrupt.
o Describe an intro and outro (which can include additional lyrics if you choose) and or a bridge that may be a musical section connecting parts of a song (often going back from a chorus to a verse).

As you're writing, think about how the music can help convey what you want in the lyrics (the music may imply a second hidden meaning that is not on the surface of the lyrics as well). Things you might consider are what instruments may be playing and with what qualities and speed. Drums for example may quietly maintain the speed of the song in the background or they may overwhelm our senses and make us feel like we are constantly speeding ahead with no control. A violin may provide short, pointed accents, as often in horror scenes, or may play a slow, enchanting melody. The singer of the lyrics may scream in largely incomprehensible ways or may whisper gently into the microphone.

Consider:

> Instrumentation: E.g., violin, acoustic or electric guitar, piano
> Tone and tempo: E.g., upbeat, eerie, slow, fast, chaotic

4. **Write a Reflection**
Address:
> How did you generate the lyrics?
> If you used AI, explain how it shaped your process?
> What meaning are you trying to communicate – emotionally, intellectually, socially?
> How does the musical structure support your message?
> Who is your intended audience? Why would this information format be effective for them?
> What was most challenging and/or most rewarding?
> What advice would you give future students?

5. **Peer Engagement**
Upon reading a peer's work:
> What meaning do you take from this?
> How did the lyrics and described sound support the message?
> Who would benefit from this song?
> If you have one, what is a suggestion you would give to enhance the lyrics, music, or both?

Example

This example song was inspired by an example from a student nearly a decade ago. I generated the lyrics by first asking ChatGPT to:

"Write lyrics including 3 verses and a chorus for a song that explores a college student's experience with coffee. Consider how it helps when there is not enough sleep and when assignments are due as well as the health benefits and drawbacks as might be discussed in a class about well-being."

I found the first iteration alright, but it was too positive in its perspective on coffee and for my taste in music, I really enjoy songs that have a darker undertone, and I think it makes for a better palette to explore musical sounds. So, I made a second request:

> "Revise the lyrics to emphasize the physiological effects of coffee (as one might learn them in a class) and create more of a narrative that slowly reveals the coffee to be an addiction that might be harmful. The chorus should be primarily positive, but have subtle hints of this negative element."

I was much happier with the second iteration, and I asked it to create a bridge after the second chorus that would support the transition to the mood of the third verse (this was a suggestion ChatGPT made that I asked it to follow up with). But then, as I thought through the music, I decided to take that bridge out and replace it with a short instrumental transition.

I was mostly happy with the lyrics, envisioning a folk-rock style suited for a coffee shop—guitar and vocals up front, with subtle bass and drums. I initially considered a dramatic shift at the end but opted for a subtler darkening to preserve the coffee-shop vibe. The table below outlines my musical ideas for each section, with half-verses separated and key words that I thought about informing the music in blue.

Lyrics	**Musical Commentary**
[Verse 1] 7 a.m., alarm like a bell I stumble through dreams I don't quite quell Eyes like sand, brain still stuck in sleep	I like the idea of a brief musical intro that approximates in some way one of the common phone alarm melodies. While the instruments would be fairly static and subdued in the

But dopamine's a promise I plan to keep	background, I think the voice of the singer here can do a lot to convey a sense of waking up through poor diction, maybe eliding some of the words. Gradually I think by the word "promise" it would reach a point of clarity in the singing I want for the rest of the song.
One pour, then two—my ritual starts Caffeine kicks in, quickens my heart Blood pressure climbs, I feel alive The lecture starts—I just might survive	This second half of the verse I imagine being a little more upbeat by having the guitar and drums be more active (not overpowering). For the last two lines I imagine the voice of the singer entering a higher range to convey more excitement and that continues straight to the end of the verse.
[Chorus] Cup by cup, I chase the light Turn the fog into clear daylight You help me focus, help me try With every breath, I'm flying high You lift me up when I fall flat But sometimes I wonder where I'm at Oh coffee, you keep me near	The chorus, overall, I imagine being more anthemic than the verses continuing from the type of energy built up at the end of the first verse. This means that the instruments continue to become more present and energetic as well. The rhyme of light and daylight is poor on the part

To the edge I didn't know was here	of ChatGPT but I don't have a replacement, and I really want to emphasize those words in the sound throughout. Even with the more negative ideas at the end the energy doesn't change, it implies a sort of blissful ignorance.
[Verse 2] Afternoon crash, I feel it descend So I brew again—my faithful friend A jolt of joy, a sharpened mind But cortisol whispers from behind	The music in this verse follows the same pattern as the first. And the transition from chorus to verse captures the idea of a crash. Even though in the second verse the transition to more positive words happens earlier, I like that the music is actually slower to respond signifying that coffee can deceive us.
My hands now shake in quiet revolt My stomach turns like a lightning bolt I tell myself it's just the grind But sleep won't come, though I've reclined	This second half of the verse again follows the same pattern again with more upbeat and active and the ending now with more excitement contrasts with the desire for sleep.
[Chorus] Cup by cup, I chase the light Turn the fog into clear daylight You help me focus, help me try With every breath, I'm flying high	Repeat of the same music in the first chorus.

You lift me up when I fall flat But sometimes I wonder where I'm at Oh coffee, you keep me near To the edge I didn't know was here	
[Instrumental]	I generally like instrumental sections at this part of a song and as I went back I thought this would be better than the lyrics in the bridge ChatGPT generated so I took them out. I imagine this being only half of the length of a regular verse and following the same pattern of starting fairly subdued but growing in intensity.
[Verse 3] 3 a.m., screen's burning bright I've lost my calm, I've lost the night One more shot to push me through Though half my thoughts no longer feel true	Unlike the other verses this one already starts with the intensity we normally find at the end of a typical verse.

We talked in class of healthy bounds How sleep repairs and slows us down But here I am, pulse on repeat Trading health for half-complete	This follows the inversion of the previous verses and ends by getting less excited. The idea is that it almost seems like fading out to go to sleep, but it still gets interrupted by the return of the chorus.
[Chorus] Cup by cup, I chase the light Turn the fog into clear daylight You help me focus, help me try But something's hollow in this high You lift me up, I don't regret But I forget what rest feels like yet Oh coffee, you keep me near To the edge I didn't know was here	Repeats the same music, but the beginning has a more abrupt transitional sound to start. Ends with repetition of the last two lines while it fades out.

Cross-Disciplinary Adaptation

> **Education**: Create songs to support memory and learning in children's education.
> **Health**: Write songs for public messaging and mental health.
> **History:** Reinterpret historical events or voices through lyrical storytelling.
> **Humanities/Social Sciences**: Explore identity, culture, social movements, and lived experiences.
> **STEM**: Translate a scientific process into song for memory or outreach.

Instructor Try-It Activity

Is there a concept, theme, or process in your course that has been difficult for students to understand in the past through reading alone? This could be a commonly misunderstood process, a moment of ethical tension, or a central idea.

Example ideas:

> **Biology**: Cellular respiration (or photosynthesis)

> **Philosophy**: The Trolley Problem (utilitarianism vs. deontology)

Process and Steps

1. **Write** a short chorus (2–4 lines) that captures the essence of that idea, repeated like a chorus. Then describe what the accompanying music might sound like (consider mood, instruments, tempo, and transitions). Consider how your tone aligns with the message (urgent? ironic? hopeful? reflective?).
2. **Reflect** briefly on how thinking through music changed your understanding or teaching of the concept. What were the limitations? How can you see your students utilizing music as an alternative learning and communication format?

Additional Resources/ References

Abbate, Carolyn. 2004. "Music—Drastic or Gnostic?" *Critical Inquiry* 30 (3): 505–536. https://doi.org/10.1086/421160.

Hanslick, Eduard. 1986 [1854]. *On the Musically Beautiful: A Contribution Towards the Revision of the Aesthetics of Music*. Translated by Geoffrey Payzant. Hackett Publishing Company.

Stimeling, Travis D. and Mark Katz. 2012. "Songwriting as Musicological Inquiry: Examples from the Popular Music Classroom." *Journal of Music History Pedagogy* 2 (2): 133–52.

DANCE: COMMUNICATE MEANING FROM THE KINESPHERE

By: Renee Murray

Discipline: Dance

Subject: Creating Dance from Personal Experience

Information Qualities of the Format

Dance is composed of time, space, and effort. Each gesture or action carries meaning, just like words in writing or visuals in an infographic.

> **Time** is expressed through the length of the dance, the changing speed of the movements, and the duration of time it takes to perform movements or sections.

> **Space** is expressed through the dancer's kinesphere, through the performance space, and through changing proximity of performers to each other, to the audience, and to the boundaries of the performance space. Associated with the theories of Rudolf Laban, the kinesphere is the three-dimensional space around a dancer that they can reach/dance through with all the parts of their body. While exploring the kinesphere, a dancer can utilize different levels of dancing (low, mid, and high) and reach (near, mid, and far) in relation to their center.

> **Effort** is expressed through how the dancers perform the movements with shifting qualities and tone of muscles.

Dance composition can range from purely abstract, focused on bodies moving through space creating shapes, textures, and patterns, to thematic, focused on expressing additional meaning and symbolism through choreography.

Who This Is For

Originally designed for a university choreography course, this activity is applicable to students in disciplines exploring nonverbal storytelling as well as embodied learning such as psychology (body language and emotion), environmental studies (movement in nature), or STEM (communicating systems or processes through gesture and flow).

Learning Outcomes

> **Identify and describe** the key elements of dance composition: space, time, and effort.
> **Recognize** how movement can serve as a medium for expressing information, emotions, and experiences.
> **Analyze** how choices in movement, space, time, and effort affect audience interpretation and information clarity.
> **Build confidence** in nonverbal expression and embodied communication.

Instructional Context

This assignment can be completed in duets, trios, small groups and large groups. Each group size offers different ways to collaborate and will affect how the final dance looks and feels.

Materials and Equipment

> An open space for movement
> Journals or paper for reflection
> Music is optional in this assignment (see note regarding music under "Tips for Teaching")

Assignment

Using prompt given by the instructor (see example below), students will create an original dance composition utilizing space, time, and effort inspired by a personal experience.

Prompt

Think of a time this season (winter, spring, summer, or fall) when you participated in an outdoor activity. What made that moment meaningful? Did you try something new, face a challenge, connect with someone, or learn something about yourself or nature?

Alternative STEM (Agriculture) Prompt Example

Think of a time you were involved in growing, harvesting, or working with plants. What stood out to you about that experience? Did you notice how people, weather, tools, or timing affected the outcome? Did it teach you anything about nature, or food systems?

Process and Steps

1. **Discovering Choreographic Intent/Inspiration**

> Discuss personal connection/experience to the given prompt.
> One student documents a group's conversation writing down key words, phrases, and ideas.
> Two to four ideas are selected to be the key inspiration for their dance and generating movement. Select words, phrases, ideas that jump out to the group. (The ideas should be specific so that they offer clear imagery or information.)

2. **Creating Movement**

> Explore each of the two to four ideas physically, moving freely, for one minute.
> Choose two strong/impressionable movements per idea (four to eight total).
> Practice each with clarity and conviction to retain choreography.

3. **Creating a Phrase**

> Each student assembles their unique movements into one repeatable sequence, called a phrase.

> Create movement to connect the end of one movement to the beginning of the next. Sometimes a simple connection is the most satisfying and the most enjoyable.
> Experiment with changing space (levels and direction), time (fast, slow, still), and effort, (tension, ease). (Instructor can include additional objectives based on prompt.)

4. **Creating a Structure: Group Dance Composition Entrance**

> Dancers start offstage.
> Travel one to two movements from each student's phrase to enter the stage.
> Manipulate these movements to travel—change direction, change sides (right/left), and incorporate repetition.

Choreographic Decisions

> Timing: Do students want to enter together, staggered, or own their own timing?
> Pathways: Do students travel directly or indirectly? Curved or linear?
> Formations: Select an ending position (e.g., scattered, organized, linear, circular, symmetrical, asymmetrical).

Duet (Call and Response)

> Each student selects a partner in close proximity to them.
> Perform phrases in a call-and-response style:
o Student A performs one movement while B holds stillness.
o Then B performs their first movement while A holds stillness.
o Alternate until both phrases are complete.
> Stillness can reflect a shape from the phrase or a neutral pose.

5. **Shared Group Phrase with Kinesphere Exploration**

> Each student teaches one movement from their phrase to the group.

> Together, create a new phrase that all group members have in common.
> Manipulate each movement using individual's own kinesphere:
o First movement: Small and subtle/near space
o Second movement: Medium/mid-space
o Third movement: Large/far reach
o Fourth movement: Movement that explodes past their kinesphere.
> Repeat this process of manipulating with the kinesphere until all movements in the phrase have been adapted.

6. **Exit**
> Students travel offstage using one to two movements from their choreography.
> Consider direction changes, repetition, side shifts, timing, and pathways.

7. **Performance as Assessment**
Dance is a communal experience, therefore performing for an audience helps complete the process and brings a level of gravitas to the experience.
> Pieces are presented to the audience (classmates, other faculty, or visitors)
> Discuss what the dance is communicating – possibly information, emotions, or a theme with the audience.

8. **Reflection**
Reflecting on a creative process helps students digest the experience and learn about the collaborative process and the artform.

Prompt:
> Share one moment that you enjoyed about your creative process.

> Share one moment that challenged you during the creative process.
> How did you work with or through this challenge?
> How did the ideas from your discussion inform your movement explorations and choreographic structure?

Teaching Tips

Repetition is key while creating choreography. It supports retention and clarity.

At every step of the process, you can layer space, time, and/or effort into the assignment. Add prompts like:

> Change level (high/medium/low)
> Reverse the movement
> Change the movement from one body part to another or restrict a body part
> Add stillness or speed
> Add a quality: make it bouncy, make it jerky, make it punchy
> Change muscle tone: if a movement is tense, relax muscle tension
> Repetition

Music: To use or not to use

> No music: Encourages own unique timing and accents.
> Music: May help reluctant students enter into movement. If using, students can choose a piece that supports their choreographic intention.

Cross-Disciplinary Adaptation

> **Psychology**: Express the intersections of social dynamics through dance
> **Environmental science**: Use movement to embody the dynamics of ecosystems
> **History**: Choreograph a dance as a form of cultural storytelling
> **Engineering**: Use movement to explain mechanical processes

Instructor Try-It Activity

Take a concept or process in your course design you believe dance could support learning. For example, in Computer Science, code execution.

Process and Steps

1. Write two to four core elements of code execution
> Lexical analysis
> Parsing
> Compilation or interpretation
> Execution

Walk through the above steps of moving freely, creating a movement phrase, manipulating with the space, time and effort (levels, proximity, stillness vs. speed, and dynamics).
Then reflect on what you experienced, asking how you see students working on this individually or with peers to learn or generate a process.

Additional Resources/ References

Newlove, Jean and John Dalby. 2003. Laban for All. Nick Hern Books.

Newlove, Jean. 1993. Laban for Actors and Dancers: Putting Laban's Movement Theory Into Practice: A Step-by-Step Guide. Routledge.

Smith-Autard, Jacqueline M. 2010. Dance Composition. 6th ed. Methuen Drama.

TRY ON AN ARTIST'S FORMAT: REIMAGINE THE FIT FOR YOUR OWN PRACTICE

By: Kathleen Hickey

Discipline: Dance, Visual Arts, and Performance Art

Subject: Theatre and Dance

Information Qualities of the Format

This assignment lives in a variety of formats. The direction it takes depends on which format the student wants to explore. Students investigate another artist's process—including format choice —to relate it to their developing practice. Through this work, students examine how artists' choices reflect social, behavioral, and historical influences, and analyze how artistic work shapes cultural understanding. By connecting their own creative decisions to broader personal, civic, ethical, or global perspectives, students begin to articulate how art functions as a form of social inquiry and expression.

Format Focus Areas

- **Visual arts exploration**: Communicates ideas through embodied engagement with visual principles such as line, shape, color, texture, and space.
- **Choreographic/dance exploration**: Communicates through movement as the primary medium, emphasizing technique, rhythm, and musicality.
- **Performance art**: Communicates concepts, ideas, or critiques through the body, which may include movement, gesture, or action.

Try on an Artist's Format: Reimagine the Fit for Your Own Practice

Who This Is For

This is for instructors interested in giving students a multidirectional approach to art making, encouraging student autonomy and self-directed decision-making in the creation of expressive artworks. This assignment is typically the first in a series of exploring one's creative voice and parallels in-class explorations.

Learning Outcomes

> **Explain** how major concepts, theoretical perspectives, and historical contexts influencing artists' creative choices relate to key ideas in the social and behavioral domains.

> **Analyze** how social, behavioral, and historical knowledge informs artistic practice and shapes cultural perspectives.

> **Evaluate** how the choice of artistic format influences the communication of personal, civic, ethical, or global responsibilities within groups, institutions, or communities.

Instructional Context

> One to three sessions (depending on depth), with time for research, creative experimentation, and reflective discussion.

> 10–25 students, allowing for individual exploration, small-group collaboration, and shared feedback sessions.

> Ideally, a hybrid space that supports both movement and visual art-making (paper, markers, scissors, glue); otherwise, ensure access to separate spaces for each activity.

Materials and Equipment

This is variable, but depending on what students choose, access to the following:

> Art making materials (paper, markers, scissors, glue)

> Tables to work at

> Research resources: Locating authoritative sources on artists' and their processes
> Audio/video/photography equipment for recording (or students' phones)
> Editing software (Audacity)

Assignment

This assignment invites students to research an historical work, analyze the artist's process, and then reimagine the piece through their own creative lens. Students will explore how format—visual art, dance, or performance—shapes meaning and communication.

Examples

Show these works at the beginning of the project and discuss how the artists' creative choices reflect their social or historical context, and how the format they use shape what they communicate about responsibility or community.

> Visual Arts Exploration: Lygia Clark
o MoMA: *Part 1: Lygia Clark: At the Border of Art* https://bit.ly/4nLvDLr
o MoMA: *Part 2: Lygia Clark: At the Border of Art* https://bit.ly/3LvAlj6
> Dance/Choreography: Yvonne Rainer, *Trio A* (1966)
o MoMA Yvonne Rainer, *Trio A*, 1978 https://bit.ly/47ItsCn
> Performance Art: Yoko Ono, *Cut Piece* (1964)
o MoMA: Yoko Ono: *One Woman Show*, 1960-1971 https://bit.ly/47OFMkQ

Research Historical Work

1. Choose a historical piece within your selected format (visual arts, dance, or performance art).

Try on an Artist's Format: Reimagine the Fit for Your Own Practice

2. Study the artist's creative process and how the work was implemented.
3. Investigate the *why* behind each creative decision:

> What inspired the artist to make this piece?

> How did the work evolve throughout the creative journey?

> What were the critical responses or interpretations?

Analyze and Reflect

1. Identify how the artist's choices relate to broader social, cultural, or personal contexts.
2. Consider how the chosen format shaped the communication of the idea.
3. Respond to these guiding questions:

> Why did the artist make the work?

> Why is this format more effective than other options?

o *Visual Arts*: How are line, shape, color, texture, and space used to communicate?

o *Dance*: How are technique, rhythm, and musicality used to communicate?

o *Performance Art*: How do movement, gesture, or action communicate an idea or concept?

> Why am I restaging or redoing this work?

> What elements am I staying true to in the original?

> What elements am I changing or making my own?

Recreate or Reimagine

1. Recreate or restage the chosen work in the format of your choice, bringing your own commentary and interpretation.
2. You may reinterpret a piece from another discipline—for example, translating a poem into movement or a historical event into a performance piece.

3. The final piece must demonstrate intentional creative decisions, precision, and high-quality execution.

Work Process and Feedback

1. Create a Work Plan: Develop a timeline for how you will use your in-class and independent work time
2. In-Process Showings: Present your work at three checkpoints to share progress and receive feedback.
3. AOQS Feedback Framework:

> A – Affirmations: What is impactful, and why?
> O – Observations: What was noticed beyond the affirmations?
> Q – Questions: What are you curious or uncertain about?
> S – Suggestions: How might the artist push or expand the work?

4. Revise and Refine: Use feedback to iterate between showings.

Final Presentation

1. Present your completed project in an open-house showing.
2. Demonstrate how your creative decisions connect to your research, chosen format, and personal interpretation.
3. Discuss the work's historical context, its past cultural impact, and how your version speaks to the present moment.

Deliverables

> Completed responses to the guiding questions
> A detailed work plan and project timeline
> Active participation in three in-process showings
> Engagement in AOQS feedback for peers
> Revised final version of your project
> Presentation in the final open-house showing

Assessment

Points are given for the submitted questions, three in-class showings, and final showing. Criteria are based on the level of detail that goes into the research, the time taken to understand the strengths and purpose of the format, the level of reimagining, feedback given, and feedback taken and applied to iterations of the project.

Cross-Disciplinary Adaptation

Students reimagine a scientific idea or concept performed. Through the process of format change, students should consider where they see room for additional details due to qualities of the format, or details omitted, or changed, and the effects of those changes.

For example:

> Turn a physics equation into a dance illustrating forces in motion. Does the student see other dance elements that could be added, causing new forces to emerge and affect the world we live in?

> Reimagine a chemical reaction as a visual installation. What would happen if a chemical never tested with another was added? What does the student hope could happen to better our lives and what would it look like?

> Represent climate data as sound or movement. If new policies to protect the climate were passed, how does the student imagine the sounds and movements changing?

Instructor Try-It-Activity
Process and Steps

1. Select a familiar disciplinary artifact:

> A historical photograph, monument, or document

> A scientific model, diagram, or visualization

2. Briefly consider:
> What format was chosen to communicate this idea?
> What assumptions about audience, values, or norms seem embedded in that choice?
> How did this artifact help shape or reinforce cultural understanding at the time it was produced?
3. Imagine the work in another format:
> If communicated primarily through visual art principles, what cultural messages would become more visible?
> If communicated through choreographic/dance exploration or performance where might the audience notice different information or ideas being communicated?
> What aspects of meaning might be amplified or lost? Prompt:
o How would the cultural meaning change if the format changed?
4. Reflect:
> How could this kind of format-based analysis help students see how knowledge in your field both reflects and shapes its cultural values?

Additional Resources/ References

Goldberg, RoseLee. 2011. *Performance Art: From Futurism to the Present*. 3rd ed. New York: Thames & Hudson.

Lerman, Liz, and John Borstel. 2003. *Liz Lerman's Critical Response Process: A Method for Getting Useful Feedback on Anything You Make, from Dance to Dessert*. Takoma Park, MD: Dance Exchange.

STUDENT LIFE EXHIBITION USING UNIVERSITY ARCHIVES

By: Sammie L. Morris

Discipline: Special Collections and University Archives

Subject: Three-Part Archives Workshop

Information Qualities of the Format

Exhibits are curated presentations of information—visual, textual, audio-visual, or artifactual—that communicate interpretation to a public audience. They require selecting, contextualizing, and arranging items to tell a coherent story. Archives and special collections, once primarily used for humanities research, now support disciplines from STEM to social sciences and art.

Exhibits promote primary source literacy, historical empathy, and institutional belonging by connecting students with the history of their own university or community. In this lesson plan, students collaboratively use university archives to create a narrative exhibit. This experience helps students find meaning in their place at the university. In the following example, students highlighted voices from Purdue's past that are often unheard

As stated in the example exhibit for this lesson plan, "By opening up and looking into the stories and artifacts that were left aside in order to create the dominant narrative, researchers can help to transform that narrative into something that more accurately reflects the world that formed that prior moment in time and space."

Who This Is For

> Faculty: Those interested in developing students' primary source analysis, communication, and curation skills.
> Students: Learners who benefit from hands-on exploration of archives or personal artifacts to understand information creation, preservation, and presentation.
> Additional Benefits: Strengthens institutional connection and helps students situate their own experiences within broader histories.

Learning Outcomes

> **Analyze** archival collections, considering their context, provenance, and limits.
> **Select, evaluate, and synthesize** sources to build a clear research narrative.
> **Interpret** archival materials and **communicate** their significance for a public audience.
> **Create** a physical exhibition with a clear theme and logical flow.

Instructional Context

> Structure: Three workshops (plus optional installation session)
> Class Size: Best for ≤12 students for collaborative curation
> Preparation:
o Conduct an introductory session on archives: locating, handling, and citing materials.
o View physical or digital exhibits for inspiration (study label tone, layout, flow).
o Arrange with archives staff regarding access, handling, and materials.

Materials and Equipment

> Smartphones for photographing non-digitized items

- Exhibit cases or display boards; labels or cardstock
- Preservation-quality mounts or cradles (provided by archives or museum partners if needed)
- Optional: digital tools for virtual exhibits (e.g., Padlet)

Resources Students Should Review for the Assignment

If your university has online finding aids for archival collections or an online catalog of the collection(s) students will be working with, have them review before the first workshop. This will help them prepare for new terminology and get a better understanding of all that goes into preserving and making a collection accessible. Below is a list of terms, adapted from the Society of American Archivists' Dictionary of Archives Terminology, to help students prepare for their visit. Students can reference this resource throughout the workshops. https://dictionary.archivists.org/

Archival Basics

- **Archives / Special Collections**: A repository managing and preserving unique, primary source materials that fall outside the general library collection, such as archives, manuscripts, rare books, etc.
- **Primary Source**: Original, firsthand evidence (letters, photos, artifacts) created during the time under study.
- **Finding Aid**: A guide or descriptive record describing the contents, structure, and context of an archival collection.
- **Collection Identifier**: A unique code or name used to cite and locate materials.
- **Provenance**: The origin and ownership history of an item or collection.
- **Series / Box / Folder**: Hierarchical levels used to organize archival materials.
- **Handling Guidelines**: Rules for safely using materials (clean hands, no pens, proper supports).

Exhibition and Interpretation

> **Curation**: Selecting, interpreting, and organizing materials to convey a theme or narrative.
> **Exhibition Label**: Concise, audience-friendly text accompanying an object.
> **Contextualization**: Providing background or connections that explain an item's significance.
> **Interpretation**: Explaining the meaning or story behind a source, not just describing it.
> **Theme / Narrative Flow**: The unifying idea and logical arrangement guiding an exhibit.
> **Audience**: The intended viewers or readers and their information needs.

Rights and Ethics

> **Copyright / Permissions**: Legal considerations for reproducing or displaying materials.
> **Citation Practices**: Accurate attribution using collection name, box, folder, and date.
> **Cultural Sensitivity**: Respecting communities or identities represented in the materials.

Teaching Tips

> **Normalize Uncertainty**: Reassure students there are no "wrong" choices in what they select—choose what intrigues them. Having autonomy in the selection process will keep them engaged and help build confidence in their primary source research skills.
> **Focus the Search**: Provide parameters to prevent overwhelm (e.g., specific decades or themes that students can narrow their research within).
> **Model Analysis**: Show an example label and walk through its

components. Ask students to provide feedback on the effectiveness of the label, its visibility/readability and clarity. Discuss accessibility in planning for the class's selection of a uniform font size and color for all labels that will accommodate a range of visitors' needs.

> **Encourage Personal Connection**: If archives are limited, students can substitute meaningful items from their own lives (e.g., family photos, club memorabilia) and follow the same steps to curate a "personal archive" exhibit.

Assignment

As part of a semester-long Libraries and School of Information Science course on print and digital archives, graduate students from English, History, and Political Science programs collaborated to create a digital exhibition focused on diverse aspects of student life at Purdue University. This exhibition, titled by student curators, *Voices, Identities, and Silences: Investigating 150 Years of Diversity in the Purdue Archives* was created using Omeka. Each student selected a decade in Purdue's history and located an item relating to a diverse person or group in that decade. The lesson plan has been adapted for this work in recognition that creating an online exhibition requires more time to become familiar with digital exhibition tools than can be accommodated in a few workshops. In addition, digital exhibitions have a short life span as technologies evolve. The Purdue digital exhibit was captured by the Wayback Machine when it was not feasible to continue to maintain the original look and feel of it over time.

Voices, Identities, and Silences: Investigating 150 Years of Diversity in the Purdue Archives
(Please allow a few moments for the page to load as it is archived.)
https://bit.ly/47wtpuU

Session 1: Explore and Register
Process and Steps

1. Visit the university archives or browse online finding aids.
2. Choose a theme or parameter (e.g., student life in a specific decade, discipline-related clubs). Register as an archive's user on the university archives website and request one box from a relevant collection.
3. Read the finding aid, list initial questions, and gather contextual background (articles, department histories, websites).

Session 2: Analyze and Select
Process and Steps

1. Review your requested materials in the reading room.
2. Select one item that sparks your interest for inclusion in the class exhibit.
3. Record full citation details: collection identifier, title, box, and folder numbers.
4. Photograph your item and answer guiding analysis questions (e.g., What story does this tell? Who created it? What's missing or surprising?).

Session 3: Share and Curate
Process and Steps

1. Submit a photo of your item before class for a compiled slideshow.
2. Present your item: Why you chose it, key context, and one lingering question.
3. Collaboratively discuss how the items fit together into a narrative.
4. Draft an exhibition label for your item: concise, engaging, accessible, audience-friendly.
5. Reflect briefly on what you learned about archival research and storytelling and share with class.

Artifact

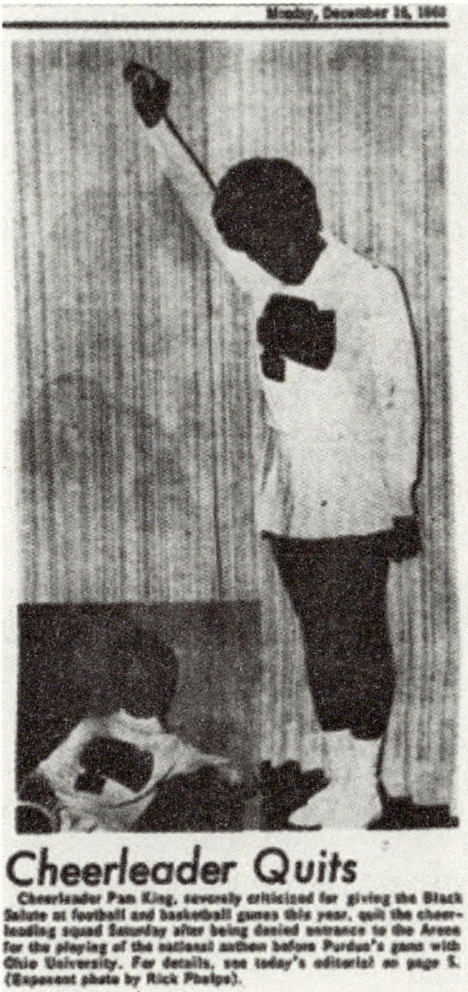
Monday, December 16, 1968

Cheerleader Quits

Cheerleader Pam King, severely criticized for giving the Black Salute at football and basketball games this year, quit the cheerleading squad Saturday after being denied entrance to the Arena for the playing of the national anthem before Purdue's game with Ohio University. For details, see today's editorial on page 5. (Exponent photo by Rick Phelps).

Example Artifact Label

Pam King Takes A Stand

Purdue University, 1968

In December 1968, cheerleader **Pam King**, the first African American woman on Purdue's squad, **resigned after being barred from entering the basketball arena during the national anthem**. She had earlier faced criticism for raising the **Black Power salute** at games. Her actions reflected student activism and the fight for racial justice during the civil rights era.

Newspaper clipping, December 18, 1968

Image 1: "Cheerleader Quits."
Photo credit: Purdue Exponent, December 18, 1968.
Reproduced with permission.

Optional: Session 4: Install or Publish

> **Physical Exhibit**: Work with archives staff to install items or submit label text and images for them to mount. Discuss with the archives staff whether there are opportunities for the students to share and discuss their work by giving talks at an exhibit opening or event, for example.

> **Digital Exhibit**: Upload curated images and labels to an online platform (if available). If the archives has a blog or easy-to-use tool for sharing the exhibit online this can be an easier entry point than taking the time to learn digital exhibits software.

Cross-Disciplinary Adaptation

> STEM: Prototype Evolution Exhibit—Students locate early lab notebooks, blueprints, or hardware from the department archives and pair them with their own prototypes. The exhibit traces the evolution of design thinking and shows how past innovations influence current projects.

> Computer Science: Code Histories—Computer science students uncover punch cards, legacy code, or software manuals in the archives, curating a display that connects historic programming practices to modern development.

> Fine Arts: Artistic Histories—Art students select archived student or faculty artworks and exhibit their own re-interpretations alongside, showing how style and themes evolve.

Instructor Try-It Activity
Process and Steps

1. Select an Object:

> Choose a personal or nearby item (e.g., a lab tool, photo on your phone, or book on your desk).

> Imagine it as an artifact for an exhibit in your discipline.

2. Create a Quick Label:
> Explain the item's relevance within an exhibit being held for your department.
> Include:
o Title (creative, audience-friendly)
o Discipline lens (e.g., environmental science, sociology, design)
o Key takeaway for a public audience
3. Share and Discuss:
> Pair with a colleague or small group of colleagues: read your labels aloud.
> Discuss:
o How the exhibit format reframed the object's meaning
o Ways this method could foster critical thinking, storytelling, or cross-connections in your courses
o Whether the format, font size and type, color selection, and wording support accessibility and diverse audience needs

Accessibility considerations: Use sans-serif fonts, and take into account the distance the label will be from the audience, ensuring it can be read easily. Avoid information overload. Using less text is often more impactful and memorable.

Additional Resources/ References

Lacher-Feldman, Jessica L. 2013. *Exhibits in Archives and Special Collections Libraries*. Society of American Archivists.

Bogle, Elizabeth. 2013. *Museum Exhibition Planning and Design*. 2nd ed. AltaMira Press.

Bedford, Leslie. 2014. *The Art of Museum Exhibitions: How Story and Imagination Create Aesthetic Experiences*. Routledge.

PART 4:

Student Stories

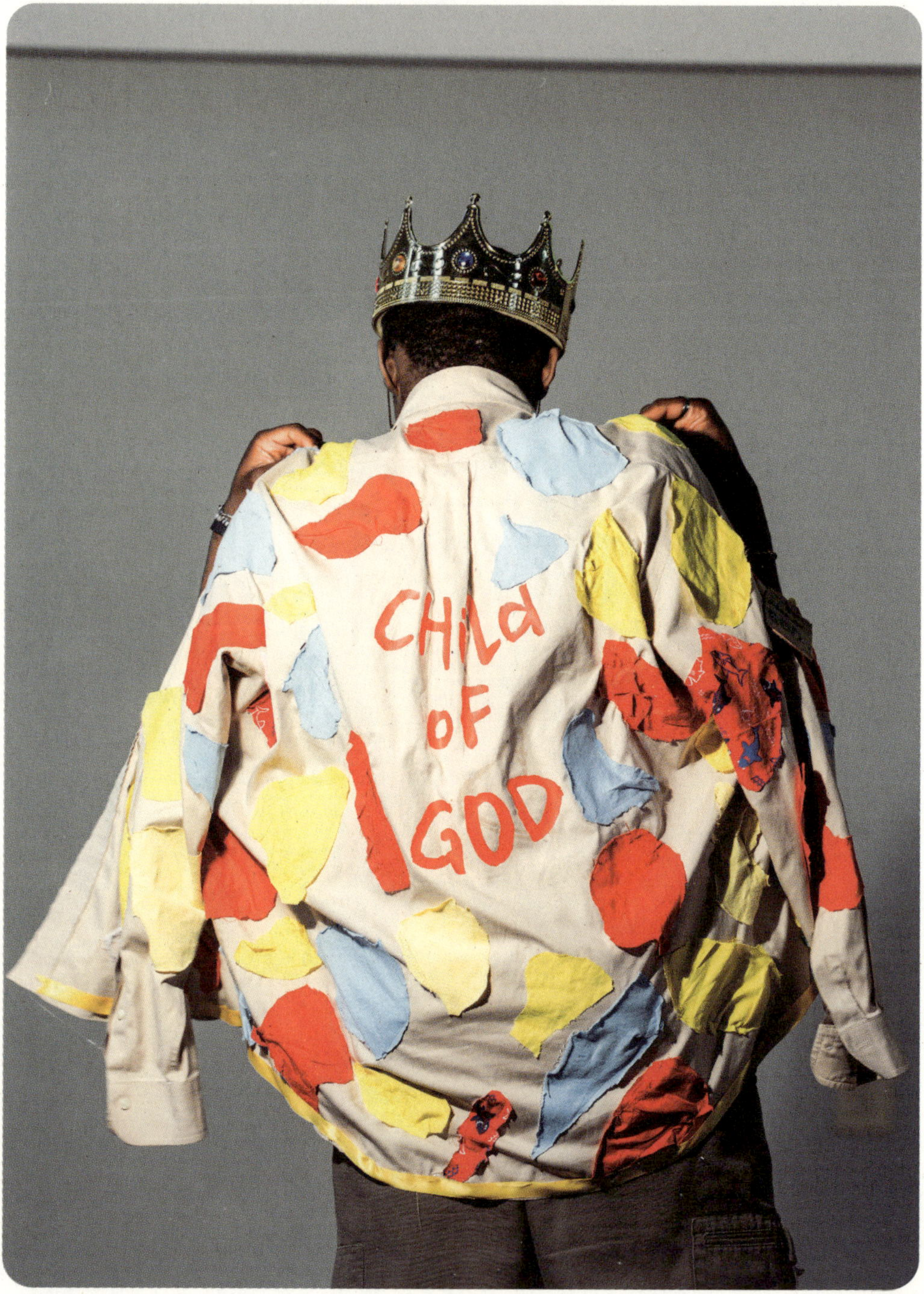

Image 1: Aurum fashion show 1 Photo credit: Jeremy Chen

Networks to Needles: Sewing to Communicate Belief, Identity, and Sustainability

I began exploring how academia might recognize textile formats as scholarship after meeting PhD candidate Kadari Taylor-Watson, who studied African print fabrics and created African American print fabrics as scholarly work. Her exhibit demonstrated how textile prints could tell stories of culture, community, and self-expression. Later, seeing another student, Osighe "Osi" Akpeokhai, communicate stories of faith through clothing design reinforced for me the power of making within textiles as a way for students to learn, process, and share knowledge.

A familiar presence in the libraries' makerspace, the Knowledge Lab, Osighe could regularly be spotted switching between Cricut machines and presses, his workflow on bags and t-shirts unfolding like a small production line. It was apparent that Osighe enjoyed developing technical expertise along with creative practices. At *Aurum*, a fashion show co-hosted by the Sewing and Design and Fashion and Retail Organization clubs, I learned that while he already ran a clothing business, his participation in the fashion show marked his first time sewing. The designs in his line combined religious iconography with sustainability themes. What follows is a narrative of how sewing became a tool for expressing his style and beliefs with others.

Osighe "Osi" Akpeokhai is a recent Purdue University graduate with a double major in cybersecurity and network engineering and a minor in art and design. Osi moves effortlessly between highly technical systems work and creative design, explaining, "I like to design either significantly asymmetrical or very symmetrical." He looks for a kind of "weight balance" in both networks and visual compositions. As a kid, he would draw and study characters, deciding where visual weight should be distributed—"one had to be heavier on top and one heavier on the bottom." That way of seeing carried into his teaching. As a teaching assistant, he often sketched systems and diagrams rather than relying on text-based explanations: "It's easier to draw it out than to write it . . . when you draw the certain segment that you need to look at, it's a lot easier." By visualizing systems, he identifies imbalances—gaps or failures—and fills them "with some kind of pattern that works," much like in his early drawings.

Osi's creative work began in 2017 with Osi Draws, an art and design business he started while moving from middle school to high school. Encouraged by peers, he created and sold commissioned artwork—logos, wallpaper, customized phone cases, and designs on sneakers. When asked what company produced the items from his designs, he replied, "You want to hear the spoiler? I just did it all myself." He used Angelus acrylic leather paint on shoes, Mod Podge to adhere drawings to cases, and experimented with apps like Procreate and MediBang Paint, as well as COPIC Markers. Entirely self-taught, Osi recalled his parents' concern: "What's he doing in the kitchen now?" they would ask. They weren't unsupportive, but worried his growing interest in art might lead to a career that wouldn't provide a living. Osi emphasized otherwise: "You can still make money as an artist." His experience has confirmed this, even amid the rise of AI art.

In 2021, Osi had an idea: "No Type," a concept rooted in individuality. "Every single piece was going to be different except it would have a little stripe to represent that it's the same brand," he explained. By 2023, the idea evolved into SUDL, a Christian streetwear label featuring understated faith-based symbolism. Once he had the idea, Osi said, "I immediately texted my brother." His brother supported the idea. "It's not extremely loud," Osi said, "but if you know, you know." Designs like Cornerstone ("the stone the builders rejected") and Joy 'n' Sun (Son) carry layered meaning—appealing broadly yet resonant for those versed in biblical references. SUDL prioritizes sustainability with 100% cotton or recycled fabrics. Osi turned to professional suppliers as demand increased.

The brand made notable achievements, including collaborations with campus organizations, a cultural festival hosted by Origin Black Creatives Collective Purdue, a pop-up event with Freemind Garments, a feature in *Aurum*, and upcoming events such as a Juneteenth pop-up with Future Black Leaders, Inc., an Indiana organization.

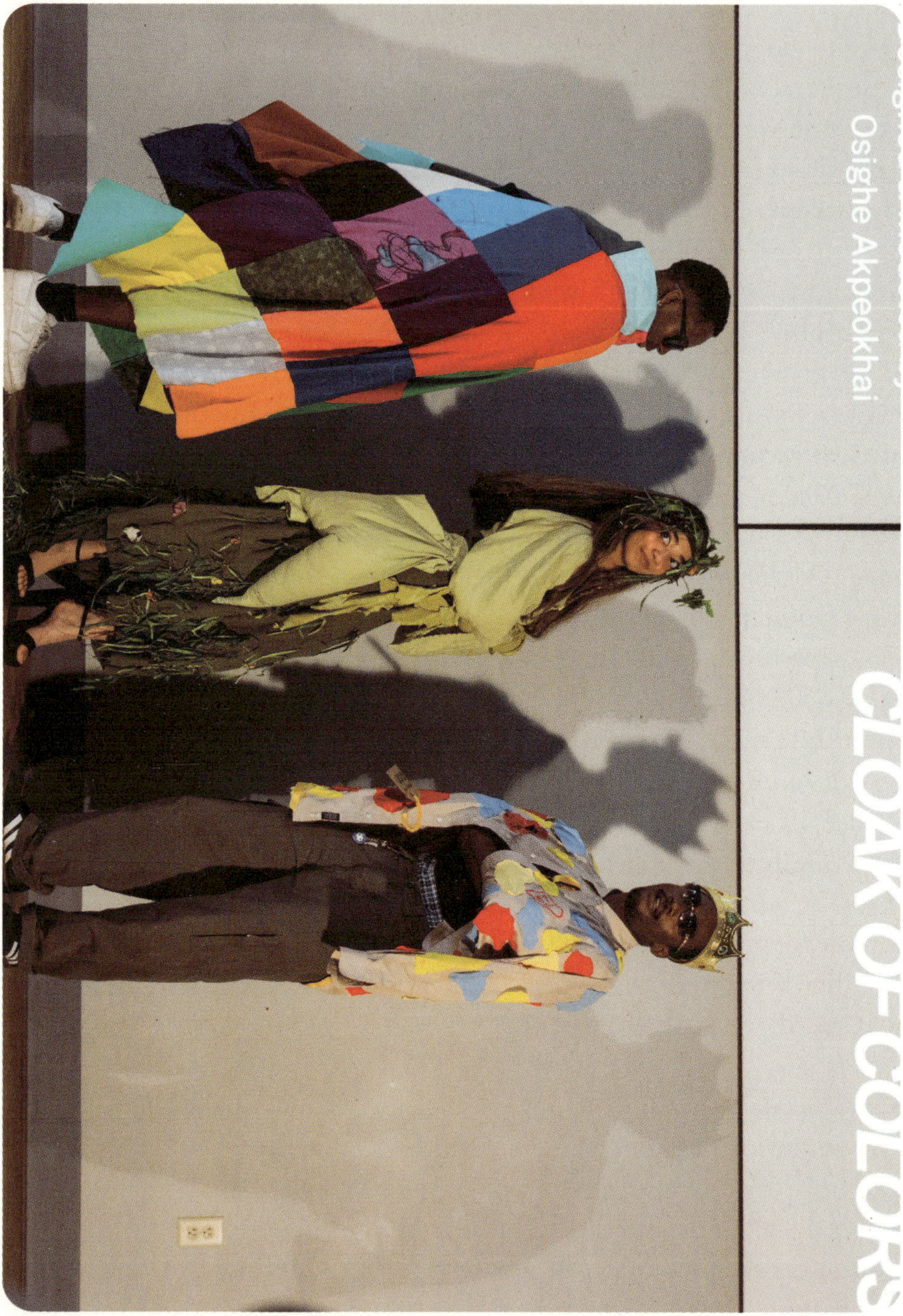

Image 2: Aurum fashion show 2 Photo credit: Sebastian Murariu

Osi's introduction to sewing began with a chance encounter that introduced him to Purdue's Sewing and Design and Fashion Retail Organization clubs. When he asked about participating in their fashion show, *Aurum*, he was welcomed immediately. "I felt like such a side piece that just got inserted into the Lego set that was already finished." *Aurum's* theme was sustainability, with participants upcycling or repurposing clothing and other items. He had just three weeks to learn sewing and create his entire collection. Patricia, the Knowledge Lab manager, taught him the basics on the Lab's very basic, non-automated machines. "Threading the needle was the hardest part!" OSI said. "Patricia showed me how to adjust thread, and if the thread bunched up, it could be because the sewing foot wasn't down." Laughing about his early attempts, he added, "Patricia showed me how to practice. I never really did practice pieces, though. That's the reason I sewed my first patch backwards." He decided to keep the backward sewn patch, both for lack of time and to signal that mistakes are acceptable.

Osi's collection, *Children of God*, featured three pieces shaped by quick sketches and refined in Procreate: a patchwork coat inspired by the Admirals in the anime series *One Piece*, and stitched from second-hand children's clothes and material; "Cloak of Colors," a reference to the coat the biblical Joseph wore, and made from thrifted and gifted fabric that evoked childhood joy through its vibrant primary colors; and "Garden of Genesis," a living gown of grass, leaves, and real flowers that symbolized play and new beginnings. As the model walked, "flowers were left behind," Osi recalls, transforming the runway into part of the installation. "It was a living piece, literally."

Working closely with the models was just as essential. Osi went back and forth between fittings to ensure comfort and confidence, incorporating feedback and adapting designs for wearability. "I almost didn't go to sleep, yeah, that Saturday night," he admitted. "I had to do a lot of work on the sizing for the model." Eyeballing fabric needs, responding to feedback, and making repeated restock runs, he embraced improvisation and creative reuse—turning sustainability, faith-driven storytelling, and childhood wonder into a vivid narrative aligned with the show's environmental theme.

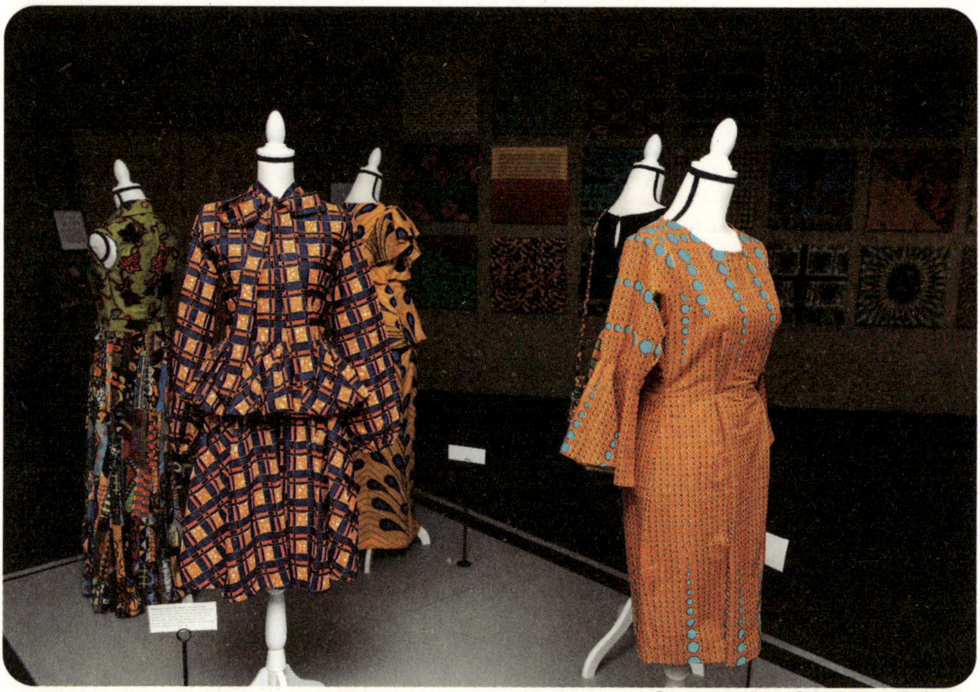

Image 3: African print fabrics exhibit
Photo credit: Kadari Taylor-Watson

Reflecting on his own wardrobe, he shared, "I find it so satisfying to wear something that I made." Newly graduated and moving to a new city for a security analyst position, Osi plans to outfit his apartment studio with sewing machines and screen-printing presses to continue fueling his ideas and scaling SUDL. Bright colors define both his personal style and design philosophy. "Bright and bold is not dead,"

Osi says, rejecting the trend toward neutral palettes. "I love color. I'd rather be, you know, dressed like a highlighter than fade into the background." With a smile, he added, "My friends say I dress like a highlighter." Gesturing to his outfit, he explained, "I try to wear analogous or complementary colors. For example, currently I'm wearing red and green." He stressed that he has spent time studying color, and that SUDL colors are meant to convey a certain feeling. "I'm not trying to spit out negativity," he added. His clothing communicates individuality, confidence, and energy—values he embeds across his visual creations.

Osi's education and professional path from networks to sewing needles is an example of someone who can work across technical expertise and creative practices to communicate meaning. Sewing, once quickly learned, became a language of belief, identity, and sustainability that resonated widely. Whether sketching network diagrams, balancing color palettes, or patching together fabrics, Osi treats each medium as a system to understand and reconfigure. In doing so, Osi builds community through designs that invite both recognition and dialogue.

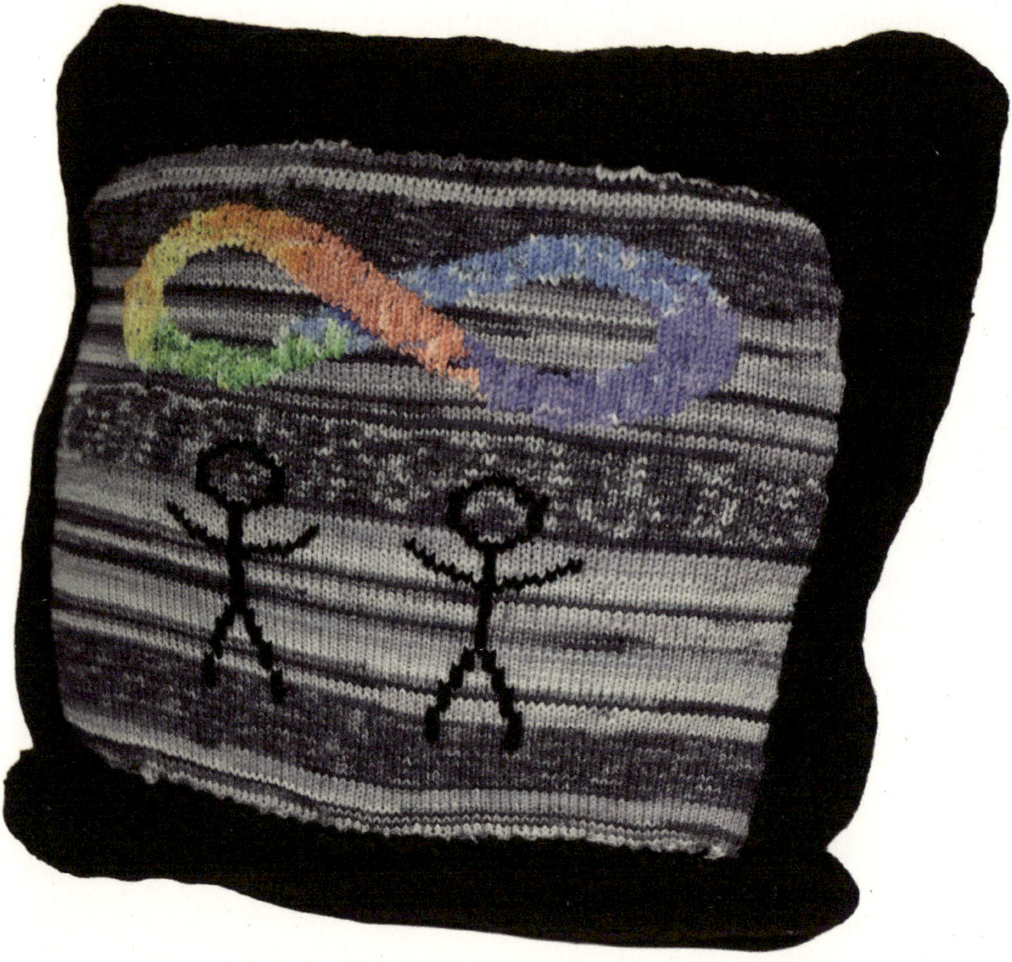

Image 1: TV Pillow
Photo Credit: Rebecca-Eli Long

Materialized Narratives: Knitting as Both a Method of Research and an Output

I met Dr. Long when they were seeking a venue for their PhD dissertation—an exhibit of knitted narratives. Drawn to the Knowledge Lab's focus on craft and textiles, they arranged a visit with their service dog, Tizzy, a bright-eyed terrier eager to earn treats. I had never encountered research "written" and "published" in knitted form. Unfortunately, the Lab lacked the exhibition space they needed. Instead, I eagerly awaited the opening of their exhibit in the Anthropology department, which had developed a lab dedicated to displaying made research.

On opening day, I stepped into the exhibit and felt a wave of emotion. Information and knowledge, and what I read as respect and care, radiated from the knitted works. I wasn't reading in the traditional sense, but instead was "reading" through color, texture, images, and placement. I was required to use a completely different set of senses to understand and interpret what was being presented than if I were reading a text-based dissertation. The experience affirmed that research and knowledge-sharing can take forms beyond those historically recognized in academia, creating space for broader participation. What follows is a narrative summary of a discussion I had with Long about their dissertation.

Long, who recently earned a PhD in anthropology and gerontology from Purdue, works across disciplines with a focus on critical disability studies. They approach their research through the research-creation framework developed by Natalie Loveless. "It sees research and creation as intertwined and recognizes research as something that is creative and is a creative process," Long explains.

They emphasized Loveless's argument in *How to Make Art at the End of the World* that creative practices are valid forms of inquiry and "knowledge-making." Long uses knitting as both method and medium to tell stories of autistic joy, critique diagnostic systems, and create accessible, multimodal scholarship. Their dissertation, "Crafting Autistic Futures," centered on three areas: life history interviews with autistic adults, a virtual fiber crafting circle, and critical reflexive knitting.

Life History Interviews with Autistic Adults

Long, experienced with interviews, but aware of their potential for fostering awkward conversations that lacked open dialogue, turned to knitting. They learned knitting from a roommate before entering their master's program and was surprised by how quickly they were moving from one level to the next—first making hats and then making sweaters. They experienced it as a calming, focus-enhancing practice. Incorporating it into their research, knitting served as an assistive technology, easing anxiety and softening interviews for both researcher and participants.

Long's interviews explored autistic people's special interests—passions often framed in the Diagnostic and Statistical Manual of Mental Disorders (DSM) as "intense" or "restrictive."

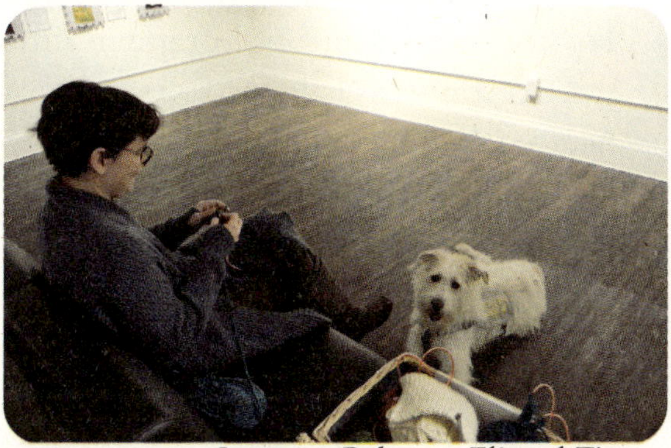
Image 2: Rebecca-Eli and Tizzy
Photo credit: Rebecca Eli-Long

Participants, however, described them as sources of joy, identity, and emotional regulation: "It's how I see the world," one shared. Interests ranged from 3D printing and gaming, to storytelling, music, and the US Postal Service. Long critiques the DSM's contradictory framing, noting that special interests inherently foster connection: "It's a damned-if-you-do, damned-if-you-don't framework," they said. Their project shifts the narrative from autism as a "tragic life" to be prevented to one rooted in meaning and community.

After each interview, Long collaborated with participants to design a knitted piece—a pillow, wall hanging, or wearable—that preserved their stories in material form. They invited participants to choose meaningful details; one requested a pillow shaped like an old box TV. Long responded to this by using yarn "speckled like static" to mimic analog screens. This practice of materializing narratives became central to their methodology: "Knitting almost documents time passing and conversations had," they explained, with dropped stitches and changing tension serving as traces of their shared experience—experiences that are often "erased, forgotten, or easily dismissed."

Virtual Fiber-Crafting Circle

For their dissertation, Long had interviewed autistic individuals who were not necessarily knitters. As a type of focus group, and to connect with other knitters, they developed an online fiber craft circle—including crocheters, spinners, and a nalbinder (a Scandinavian precursor to knitting)—to further explore how autistic people experience craft spaces and identity. Long was unable to perform the same analysis on the Zoom transcripts from this group as they did with the interviews; however, the Zoom conversations offered insights that influenced aspects of the dissertation.

Participants expressed mixed feelings about the term "special interests." Several found it pathologizing or infantilizing, insisting their interests were simply parts of their daily life. Still, many identified knitting as integral to their autistic identity and well-being. One participant described designing a dragon with glow-in-the-dark yarn and fairy lights, explaining that it felt alone until another was made, and that this project was a creative expression of autism acceptance and their own diagnostic journey. Long reflected that this knit piece offered a means to tell a story that felt manageable and less personal, allowing the creator to analyze the dragon and share it without feeling it was directly about themselves. This illustrated how fiber craft provided a safe, tangible mode of communication.

Image 3: Quotes pinned to knitted piece Photo credit: Rebecca-Eli Long

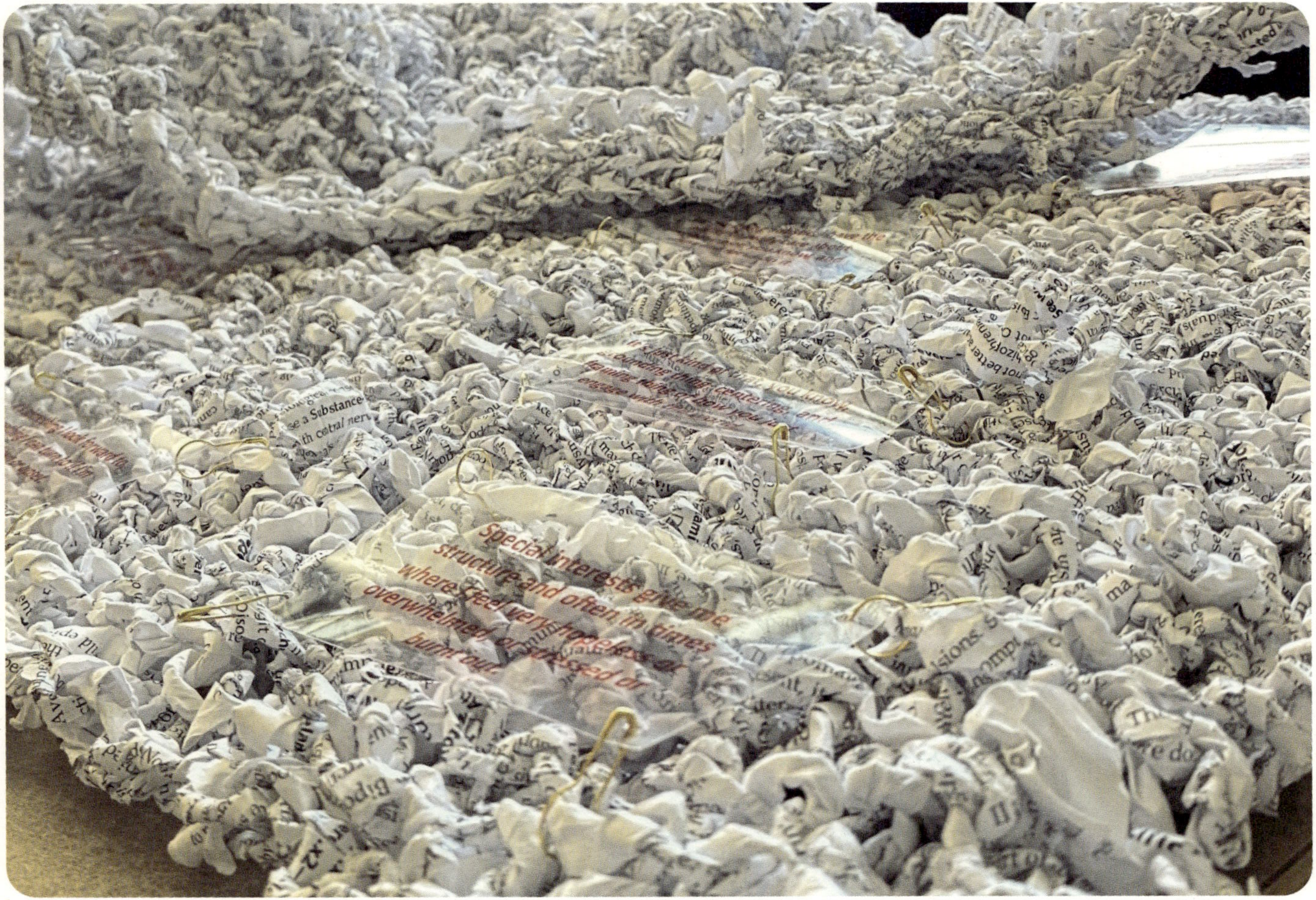

Critical Reflexive Knitting

The third element to Long's work was reflection. It included an art piece that deconstructed and reimagined scientific texts. As someone in academia who continuously interacts with papers, journal articles, and books, Long asked "is it possible to like, destroy or refigure or re-engage with texts?" Their largest work involved knitting a former edition of the DSM as a wall hanging, titled "Disordering the DSM." By tearing each page out of an old copy of the DSM, crumpling the pages to soften the paper fibers, cutting the pages into spirals, and twisting the strips on a basic wooden spindle, Long was able to create a kind of yarn. Using a basic wooden spindle, Long twisted the strips into yarn and skimmed the pages as they worked with them. They noted the category of mental disorders was broad—covering everything from Alzheimer's and dementia to childhood conditions, eating and body image disorders, autism, and even outdated entries on gender and sexuality.

Long knit two layers: a dense garter-stitch background symbolizing diagnostic categories as a framework for understanding experience, and a more open triangular piece displayed several inches in front to suggest how autistic identity and knowledge reshape that framework. Long then used calabash pins on the back layer to attach their favorite interview questions and special interest quotes on transparency film. Included were, "comfort food for your brain," "autistic joy that can't otherwise be explained," "emotionally rich," and miscellaneous "beautiful" quotes.

When asked how to begin capturing people's stories in a similar way, Long suggested approaching research-creation by rethinking your role in the research and emphasizing materialized narratives. Though not everyone knits, this craft-based perspective and method can inspire new approaches and outcomes. When asked how they submitted their dissertation, Long said they organized their dissertation as a collection of articles, along with a chapter sharing the exhibit of their work at The Arts Federation in Lafayette, Indiana. The piece "Disordering the DSM" was also displayed at the Pratt Institute in Brooklyn, New York.

Long's contribution to new knowledge lights a path toward creative ways of engaging with research, revealing new perspectives that can deepen our understanding of humanity for the world to "read."

To learn more about Dr. Long's work,
visit https://rebecca-eli.com/
and www.craftingautism.com.

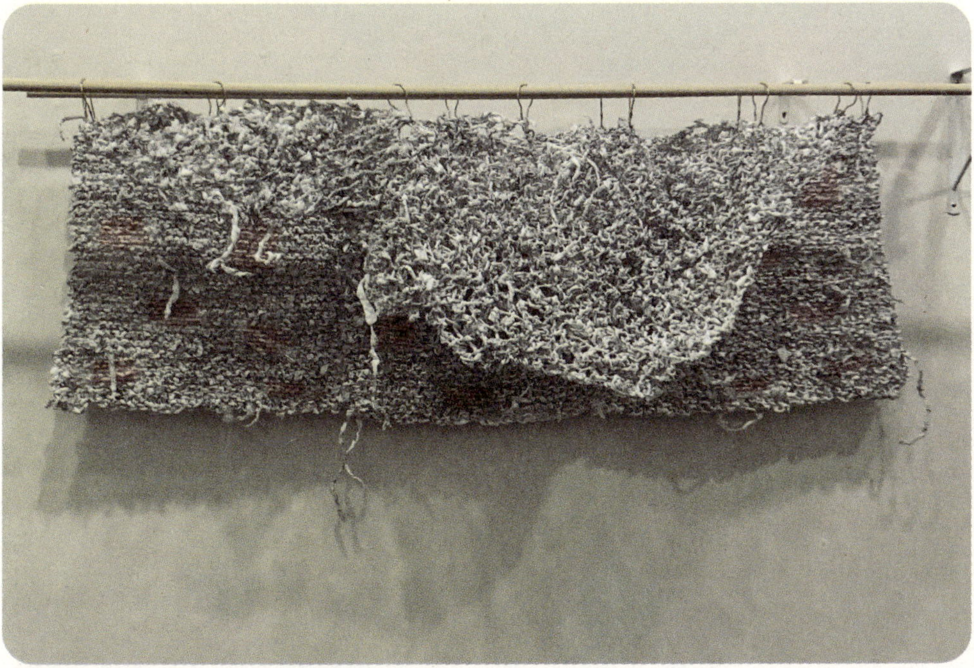

Image 4: Disordering the DSM
Photo Credit: Rebecca-Eli Long

PART 5:

Lesson Plans

Formats Across the Disciplines

PODCASTING AS PUBLIC SCHOLARSHIP IN AFRICANA STUDIES: A LABORATORY MODEL

By: Jasmine L. Harris

Discipline: Africana Studies

Subject: Podcast as Pedagogy

Information Qualities of the Format

The podcast as a pedagogical format transforms learning from a static, text-based experience into a dynamic, participatory one (Harris 2025). Whether focused on a specific idea or a wide-reaching theme, podcasts bridge academic inquiry with public discourse, positioning students as researchers, producers, and storytellers. In the context of Africana Studies, this approach embraces oral traditions, community dialogue, and intergenerational knowledge transmission—modes of knowing deeply rooted in African diasporic epistemologies. Unlike traditional essays or exams, the podcast requires students to synthesize scholarship, narrative, and sound. It values voice—both literally and figuratively—as a vehicle for critical thought.

Who This Is For

This pedagogy is designed as applied practice for undergraduate students in Africana Studies and related disciplines such as history, communication, sociology, and education. It is particularly well-suited for instructors seeking to integrate community-based learning, center Black voices and storytelling, and provide creative practical skill-building alternatives to traditional written assignments.

Learning Outcomes

> **Apply** Africana Studies methods to real-world contexts.
> **Synthesize** scholarly and community-based knowledge into a cohesive narrative.
> **Demonstrate** digital literacy through audio production and content curation.
> **Collaborate** effectively in small teams.
> **Communicate** academic ideas to a non-specialist audience with clarity and cultural sensitivity.

Instructional Context

This approach works best in small- to mid-sized classes (15–30 students) where collaborative projects are feasible. It can function as a semester-long project, a methods course assignment, or a community engagement initiative.

Materials and Equipment

> Recording devices: smartphones, portable recorders, or campus audio labs
> Audio editing software: Audacity, GarageBand, or Adobe Audition
> Recording space: access to ad hoc or dedicated studio spaces
> Equipment: microphones and headphones
> Alternatives: free recording apps and online editing tools (lower sound quality but budget-friendly)

Resources Students Should Review for the Assignment

Morris, Monique W. 2014. *Black Stats: African Americans by the Numbers in the Twenty-First Century*. The New Press.

Zuberi, Tukufu, and Eduardo Bonilla-Silva, eds. 2008. *White Logic, White Methods: Racism and Methodology*. Rowman & Littlefield Publishers.

Example Podcasts: *Code Switch, 1619, Seizing Freedom, Throughline*

Podcasting as Public Scholarship in Africana Studies: A Laboratory Model

Assignment

Overview: Africana Studies Podcast Episode

Students work in production teams to create a 20–30-minute podcast episode integrating scholarly sources, interviews, and reflective commentary. The project emphasizes collaboration, research, production, and public scholarship.

Example Context

In an interdisciplinary Africana Studies research methods course, each group:

> Selects a community-focused topic grounded in Africana Studies.
> Conducts mixed-methods research (quantitative and qualitative).
> Develops a script or discussion schedule and secures guests.
> Manages all aspects of production and post-production, including recording, editing, adding music/sound effects, and preparing for distribution.

All episodes are published on the department website as part of the Roots and Futures Show—a collaborative platform for student and faculty knowledge-sharing and a laboratory for student learning.

Process and Steps

1. **Assign Student Groups**

> Form production teams.
> Teams can remain consistent (for long-term collaboration) or rotate (to strengthen adaptability and communication skills).

2. **Topic Selection**

> Identify a relevant theme grounded in Africana Studies.
> Pare down to a specific episode topic for discussion.

3. ***Research***

> Incorporate at least five scholarly sources.
> Include one community-based interview, ethnography, or piece of archival research to inform episode structure and script development.

4. **Script Development**

> Integrate research findings, personal reflection, interview excerpts, and guest participation.
> Structure the episode: introduction, body, and closing reflection to create a clear script for each episode.

5. **Production**

> Record, edit, and finalize the episode where all team members are satisfied with the final product.
> Add optional elements such as music and sound effects.

6. **Marketing and Distribution**

> Develop a two- to three-minute audio and/or visual promotional trailer for distribution.
> Develop a brief social media campaign (sample post and visual design) to work in tandem with the trailer to publicize your episode to a broader audience.

7. **Reflection**

> As a culminating activity, facilitate an in-class discussion, asking students to analyze their learning journey, intellectually, creatively, and collaboratively.
> Assign students to write a two- to three-page reflection to turn in. This should be presented to students not as an afterthought, but as integral to their long-term learning and creative process. It is an opportunity to name their learning, acknowledge the voices that shaped it, and articulate the broader impact of their public scholarship.

Cross-Disciplinary Adaptation

> **Political Science**: Students might produce podcasts on complex policy issues, using research-based storytelling and interviews to provide evidence-driven discussions accessible to public audiences.
> **Education**: Students could highlight teacher narratives and local school histories to give insight into what shapes the classroom experience, possibly exploring the evolution of the education system in a specific area.
> **History**: Students create narrative episodes tracing local or global historical events using archival materials, oral histories, and primary documents.

Instructor Try-It Activity

Before assigning the project, instructors should experiment with podcasting themselves. Record a three- to five-minute 'mini-episode' reflecting on your own teaching philosophy or a recent classroom experience. Reflect on how speaking changes your relationship to scholarship, what emotions emerge, and how this medium might transform student engagement. Assign the "mini-episode" as a listening and reflection activity to jumpstart thinking about podcast production as experiential learning. Ask students to consider why this medium, how it connects to the discipline, and what they will learn.

Additional Resources/ References

Campbell, Gardner. 2005. "There's Something in Air: Podcasting in Education." *Educause Review* 40 (6): 32-47.

Harris, Jasmine L. 2025. "Rethinking Knowledge and Becoming Podcasters: Three Assignments as Pedagogical Tools to Decolonize College Classrooms," in *Podcast Studies: Practice into Theory*, Lori Beckstead and Dario Llinares, eds. Wilfred Laurier University Press.

By: Ian M. Cook

Discipline: Social Anthropology

Subject: Academic Podcasts

Information Qualities of the Format

Podcasting helps develop critical listening skills. It is often said that when students enter university they haven't been taught how to write, but just as often they haven't been taught how to listen. Given technological advancements, there is less and less reason for students to simply write down everything their instructor says, but it is key that they learn to focus on listening, reflect on what they've heard, and critically apply it to their learning going forward.

Strengths of the Format

> Allows replaying of audio for clarification.
> Communicates meaning through delivery as much as content.
> Strengthens attention and focus through close listening.
> Delivers layered messages through sound, music, and dialogue.
> Fosters connection and understanding between speaker and listener.

Who This Is For

For faculty who want their students to develop deep listening skills and multimodal expression. This lesson plan was written for graduate-level anthropology students but can be used in undergraduate courses across disciplines. Students revisit and repurpose lecture content by **listening to, editing, reframing, and producing** a short podcast-style response.

Learning Outcomes

> **Identify** key segments of lecture content through critical listening.
> **Explain** how podcasting conveys knowledge using voice, sound, and editing.
> **Revise** spoken content for clarity, flow, and audience understanding.
> **Produce** an original audio piece that responds to or reframes academic content.
> **Reflect** on listening as a scholarly skill and its role in learning.

Instructional Context

Each week a ~20-minute lecture is recorded by the instructor and made available to students. Students select one lecture to edit from the several lectures that are provided over the course of the academic year.

Materials and Equipment

> Lecture recordings (provided by the instructor)
> Free Audio editing software: Audacity or GarageBand, or similar service
> Free transcription services: Otter.ai, Deepgram, Riverside, or similar service
> Microphone (can be phone, laptop, headset, or podcast mic)
> Access to the Learning Management System platform for students to upload their podcast recordings; for this assignment, students submit an audio file

Assignment

Student chooses one lecture from the list of topics listed in the syllabus at the start of the academic year.

Process and Steps

1. Select one segment from the lecture.
2. Edit it for clarity and meaning (instructors often want this).
3. Write and record a short script to frame or respond to the lecture (intro, commentary, dialogue, external clips, etc.).
4. Edit response together with the lecture assignment.
5. Use transcription software to clean up automatic transcription.
6. Upload the final version with transcription to the e-learning platform.

Resources Students Should Review for the Assignment

Examples of academic-style podcasts

Material Girls: A scholarly podcast about the zeitgeist, hosted by Hannah McGregor and Marcelle Kosman: https://bit.ly/4hKqcvb

Somatic Podcast hosted by Sam Clevenger and Oliver Rick: https://bit.ly/3LwVRE6

Fishy Work hosted by Ian M. Cook and Alin Kadfak: https://bit.ly/3WImQis

Sound effects for personal, educational, or research purposes

BBC Sound Effects Archive: https://bit.ly/3XcAjPM

Assessment

Comprehension of the lecture

Critical response

> Connect to other relevant topics, theories, or themes.

> Point out inconsistencies in theories ideas discussed.

> Suggest ways to extend the segment.

Production quality

> How clear and listenable the final product is.

Cross-Disciplinary Adaptation

> **STEM**: Respond to a research lecture and clarify jargon for a general audience.

> **Humanities**: Reframe a lecture through dialogue, storytelling, or soundscapes.

> **Social Sciences**: Integrate field recordings or external interview clips to extend the analysis.

Instructor Try-It Activity
Process and Steps

1. Choose a two to three-minute clip from your own lecture.
2. Edit it for clarity.
3. Record a short reflection (as if you were a student) in response to yourself.
4. Combine the two into a five-minute mini-podcast.
5. Share with students as a model of listening, editing, and reframing through audio recordings.
6. Ask students to discuss the pros and cons of in-person lecturing versus listening to the podcast and what they would have done differently with edits and sound.

Additional Resources/ References

Cook, Ian M. 2023. *Scholarly Podcasting: Why, What, How?* Routledge.

Copeland, Stacey, and Hannah McGregor. 2021. *A Guide to Academic Podcasting.* Amplify Podcast Network. https://scholars.wlu.ca/books/2/.

MIDDEN IN PLAIN SIGHT: WHAT OUR TRASH SAYS ABOUT US

By: Mary Kosuth

Discipline: Environmental Science and Public Health

Subject: The Anthropology of Trash

Information Qualities of the Format

In this lesson plan, students learn to "read" material artifacts, building skills in observation, categorization, and interpretation. By treating litter as an information format, students gain a new awareness of how knowledge is embedded in overlooked or stigmatized objects, challenging assumptions about what counts as valuable information.

Students will select a local commons (square, park, plaza, garden, playground, beach, bike/pedestrian corridor) and then collect, inventory, and catalog the litter found in that chosen space. Through this work, something worthless and detested transforms into a valuable artifact or piece of evidence that can inform and educate community members. It will give them an opportunity for reflection on the planned obsolescence of consumer products and the externalized costs of discarded materials, while also empowering them to brainstorm creative ways to communicate findings to the wider community. Students will share the collected data through visual representations such as charts or tables but will also share images of how they arranged trash for categorization. In this way, numbers are anchored by visuals that highlight the material reality of waste, drawing uniquely from public health and environmental science. Together these fields show how gathering, analyzing, and sharing data can drive change.

Who This Is For

For faculty who want to engage students in studying shared spaces to uncover patterns and insights about waste. This activity can be adapted across disciplines. For instance, in Anthropology, students might examine the cultural meaning of trash, create a book or exhibit of photographs that share "trash stories" to reveal what discarded objects can tell us about human behavior in public areas.

Learning Outcomes

> **Identify and quantify** the precise diversity of trash.
> **Classify and organize** data for analysis and interpretation.
> **Evaluate** the values and context of the stakeholder or audience.
> **Design** a means that effectively communicates data-driven insights.

Instructional Context

> One or two sessions, either as a stand-alone project or as preparation for a longer research or community project.
> If collection is done during class, allow time for gathering, sorting, and analyzing materials.
> Workspace is needed for items to be safely spread out and categorized.
> Works well early in the semester to expand students' sense of what counts as information and to encourage curiosity about overlooked everyday artifacts.

Materials and Equipment

> Software to collect, organize data, and communicate data such as Excel
> Phone or camera to take photos of trash

Safety Checklist for the Activity

> **Prioritize safety**: Be cautious with sharp or otherwise hazardous items.
> **Adult supervision**: If children are involved, ensure adults decide what can be handled and by whom.
> **Protective gear**: Provide gloves and bags for all participants.
> **Use tools**: A trash picker with a needle or pincer end is ideal.
> **Sorting space**: Set aside an area to sort the collected trash.
> **Reporting materials**: Gather any supplies needed for the group to share or "report" their findings.

Resources Students Should Review for the Assignment

Connaughty, Sean. 2019. *Lake Hiawatha Anthropocenic Midden Survey: Final Report.* https://bit.ly/497Zavw.

Boonstra, M and Floris van Hest, F., 2017. *The Plastic Bottle Cap Report: Findings of the First Survey of Bottle Cap Pollution on Dutch Beaches.* North Sea Foundation. https://bit.ly/43gIONf.

Frost, Natasha. November 17, 2017. "With Smog Meringues, You Can Taste Your City's Air Pollution Frost." *Atlas Obscura*. https://bit.ly/4p37Bgl.

Yamasaki, Shoji. 2022. "LITTERED MVMNTS | A Dance Film by Shoji Yamasaki." YouTube video, 8:23. https://bit.ly/3YBFlWU.

Assignment

This activity has three major components: gathering materials, organization, and dissemination/communication.

Process and Steps

1. **Gathering Materials**

   Choose a site. Depending on the size of the group and the size of the site, map out an area for participants to pick up trash in pairs.

2. **Organization**

Once everything has been collected, lay a tarp or some kind of cover on an indoor space, or find a large outdoor space (like an empty parking lot) where the items can be spread out.

> Group items based on a taxonomy that makes the most sense.

o For example, they could be categorized based on what they contained, what brands they represent, or what kind of material they are made from. Once they have been grouped in this way, subgroups can be formed. These can be based on size, color, or age/degradation.

> Quantify artifacts in some manner.

o Pie charts, bar graphs, or some sort of visual representation should be discussed and agreed upon by the group. Units such as grams/m2 or items/m2 can be used. Or if two cleanups happen in a known span of time, a unit such as items/hours or items/day can be used.

> Example: 50 grams of litter collected from a 1 m^2 area.

> Example: 12 items of litter collected from a 1 m^2 area.

3. **Dissemination/Communication**

Finally, based on what they found and the site they chose, students decide how they are going to share this information with the larger community.

Ideas:

> Write an op-ed piece in a local newspaper or neighborhood publication, including photos of the arranged trash.

> Present the materials as an installation piece in an art museum or community space.

> Make a series of social media posts, asking for engagement with the images.

> Write letters, either to local lawmakers or to the companies who produce these products. The letters can inform policymakers about

the extent of the problem while letters to CEOs can let them know how many bags or bottles or bits of trash with their brand names were found in the local common.

Teaching Tips

> **Component 1:**
- o Accessible to all; no prior training required.
- o Anyone can participate in this stage.

> **Component 2:**
- o Focuses on analytics, data organization, and presentation.
- o Ideally guided by someone with experience in data analysis.
- o A knowledgeable expert could be invited from a nearby school, college, or community.

> Component 3:
- o Involves identifying a stakeholder or target audience.
- o Requires understanding the audience's motivations, concerns, and interests.
- o Emphasizes crafting a message and selecting a communication medium that resonates.
- o Considers how different audiences (e.g., general public, lawmakers, corporate leaders) may respond differently.
- o If needed, bring in a communication expert to guide the group in message development and outreach strategy.

Assessment

> **Quality of Summarized Data**
- o Does the data accurately and thoroughly represent the items found?
- o Are the data summarized in a thoughtful and compelling way?
- o Is the summarized data accessible to a wide audience?

> **Group Collaboration**
o Were group members respectful of one another's opinions?
o Did group members offer useful, constructive criticism?
o What challenges arose, and how were they addressed or resolved?
> **Internal Evaluation**
o Conducted through an end-of-event survey completed by participants
o Reflects group dynamics, process satisfaction, and self-assessment
> External Evaluation
o Based on engagement from the wider community
o Varies by medium and audience

Examples:
> **Op-ed**: Was it published? Did readers respond in a positive or negative way?
> **Social media education campaign**: How much engagement (likes, shares, comments)?
> **Installation piece**: How many attendees? What feedback did they leave?
> **Letter to lawmakers/corporations**: Were there any meaningful replies or policy actions?

Cross-Disciplinary Adaptation

> **Dance**: Embodied story of discarded trash telling their story within the community.
> **History**: Build a "trash timeline," comparing today's litter to historical waste patterns, illustrating how consumer culture and materials have changed over decades.
> **Creative Writing**: Compose a found-object poem or narrative using brand names, fragments of labels, and packaging language from the trash.

Instructor Try-It Activity

Pick an object in your own discipline and take notes on the following:

1. **Collection**: What would be the equivalent of "trash" in your field (e.g., discarded books, hardware, or prototypes)?
2. **Organization**: How might you group or categorize those items to reveal patterns or insights?
3. **Communication**: How could your students share these insights with an audience outside your discipline (e.g., infographic, short video, installation, social media post)? Ask yourself: *Are these artifacts communicating something about your discipline to others in or outside of the field?*

Examples

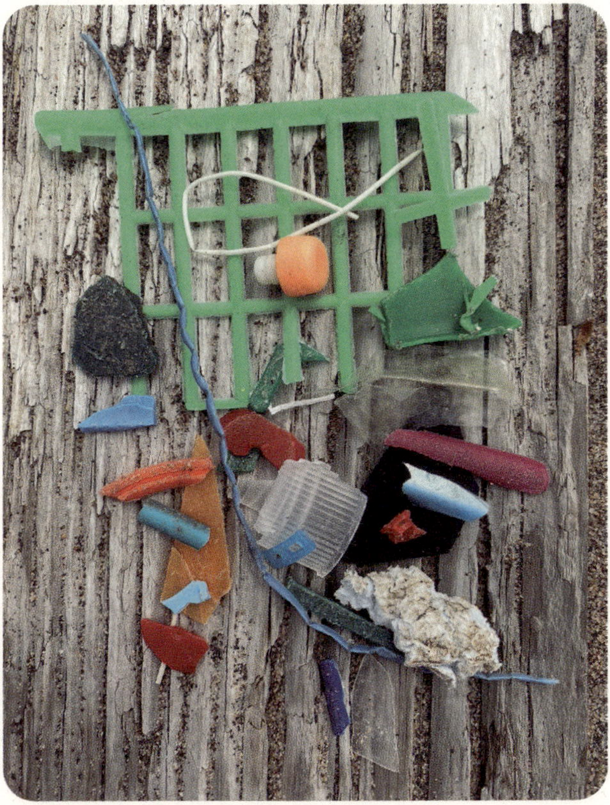

Image 1: Trash arrangement 1
Photo credit: Mary Kosuth

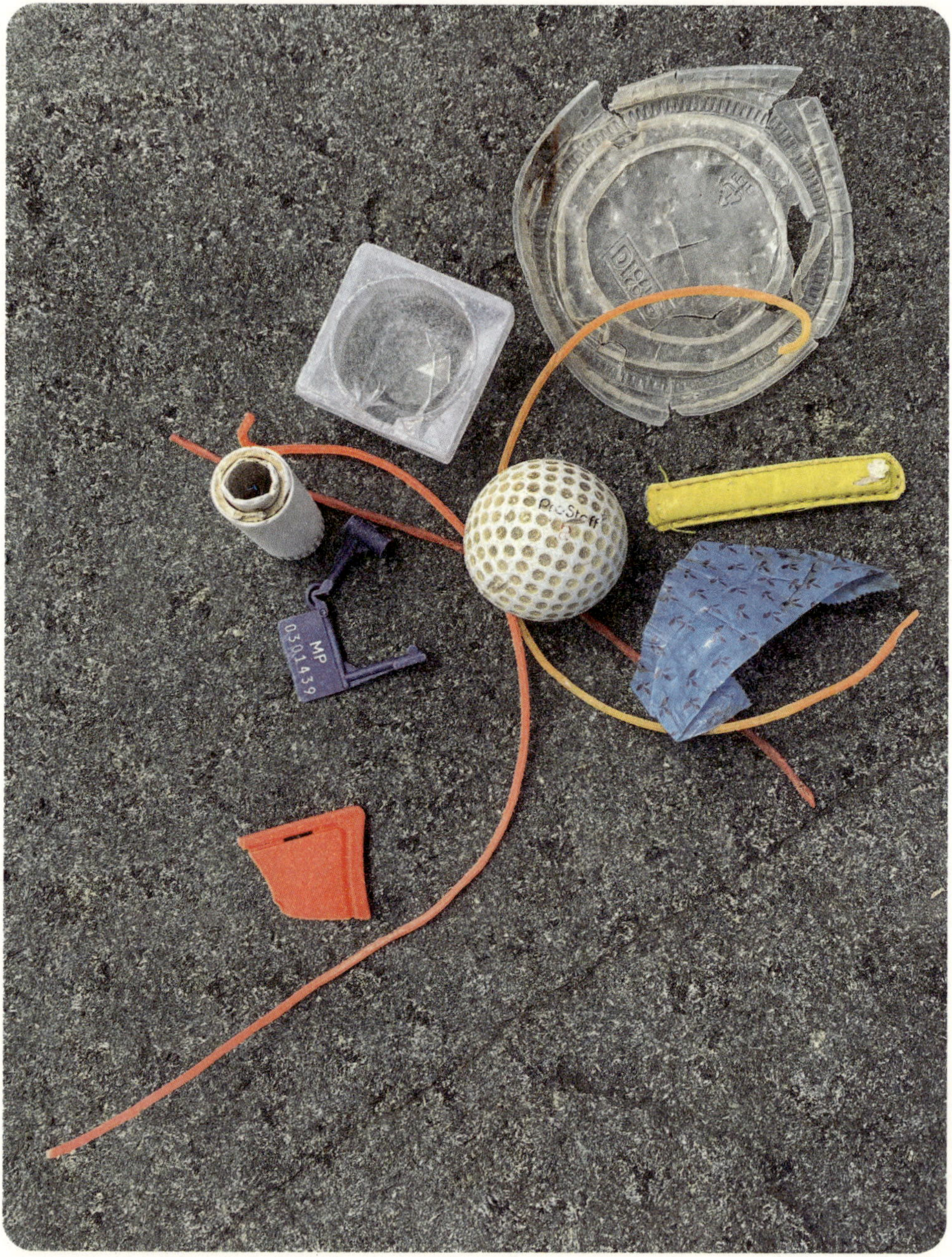

Image 2: Trash arrangement 2
Photo credit: Mary Kosuth

By: Courtney Wittekind

Discipline: Anthropology

Subject: Filmmaking as Social Research

Information Qualities of the Format

This assignment encourages students to experiment with filmmaking techniques from *cinéma vérité*, a French documentary movement of the 1960s that can be translated as "truthful cinema." Breaking from early approaches in nonfiction filmmaking, which created documentaries that were heavily scripted, strove for objectivity, and had a didactic tone, cinema verité embedded filmmakers in daily life, redefining new, lightweight cameras as research instruments that could reveal hidden truths by engaging subjects and provoking reflection. Through this lesson, students will explore the camera as a research tool and a means of collaboration.

Who This Is For

Faculty who would like their students to explore how filmmaking can serve as a research tool to investigate authentic lived experiences.

Learning Outcomes

> **Analyze** cinéma vérité's use of style and ethics to communicate "truth."

> **Investigate** how filmmaking can communicate personal stories, cultures, and social experiences.

> **Explore** how the camera affects people's behavior and what we see as "truth."

> **Practice** observing, interviewing, and analyzing to better under stand and share real-life experiences.

Instructional Context

This assignment is designed for integration into a research methods class in sociology, anthropology, or related social sciences. It is intended for a small, seminar-style class where students create individual films; however, it can be adapted for a larger class by assigning students to teams. This lesson can be completed in three sessions, fifty minutes each.

Materials and Equipment

A phone that can record video is required; an editing program is optional.

Note: Students may choose to edit their films, but this is not required; in all cases, **minimal editing is encouraged given cinéma vérité's commitment to capturing reality as it unfolds with little intervention**.

Resources Students Should Review for the Assignment

Selections from Morin, Morin, Edgar. 1985. "Chronicle of a Film." Studies in Visual Communication 11 (1): 4–29. https://bit.ly/3LkA1nv

o Recommended sections include: "For a New Cinema Vérité" up to the section divider before "In the course of subsequent discussions[...]" (5–7) and "Post-Chronique" (25–29).

Optional: Brody, Richard. 2013. "The Extraordinary Chronicle of a Summer." The New Yorker, February 21, 2013. https://bit.ly/49HvyFf

o This brief 2013 review in The New Yorker situates the film in the historical landscape of 1960s France.

Assignment

Edgar Morin proposes creating not a film, but "an experiment lived by its authors and its actors." Students will craft their own experiments by posing a question of their choice to at least five people they do not know (instructors can choose a plan if exceptions need to be made).

This question should be on a scale appropriate for the "cinematic interrogation" described by Morin and allow for follow-up questions. For example, in the landmark cinema verité film, Jean Rouch and Morin confront passersby with the single question: "Are you happy?" After filming, students will select about three minutes of footage to share in class. This can be unedited clips or a short edited video. Videos should not be shared publicly (e.g., social media) without clear permission and instructor approval.

Session 1
Process and Steps

1. **Introduce** cinéma vérité and historical context.
2. **Watch** *Chronicle of a Summer* (1961, 1 hour 25 minutes) together in class.

Rouch, Jean, and Edgar Morin. 1961. *Chronicle of a Summer*. Directed by Jean Rouch and Edgar Morin. France: Argos Films. In French. https://www.kanopy.com/video/chronicle-summer.

Available to subscribing academic institutions on Kanopy, and for purchase via the Criterion Collection or MUBI.

Session 2
Process and Steps

1. **Collect Reactions**

> Small classes: Students share a moment that stood out to them.
> Large classes: Students share one word (positive, negative, or neutral) that captures their feelings about the film.

2. **Review Ethics of Filming Strangers**

> What do subjects' differing responses to the footage at the end

of the film tell us about the ethics of Morin and Rouch's approach? Remind students that the filmmakers openly discuss whether their project is manipulative.

> Ask:

o Do you think their approach is manipulative?

> Students develop a collective set of rules for ethical filmmaking-as-research.
Include:

o Filmmakers must obtain verbal consent from participants.

o Filmmakers should inform participants what the footage will be used for and who will see it.

o Filmmakers should respect anyone's right to decline participation.

o Filmmakers should be sensitive to concerns about the portrayal of participants.

3. **Compare to Modern Example**

> Show clips from Brett Story's *The Hottest August* (2017), which uses the question "What are your hopes for the future?" to address the contemporary crises facing New York City

> Ask:

o What does *Chronicle of a Summer* reveal about Paris in 1961?

o What does *The Hottest August* reveal about New York City in 2017?

o If you were to make a similar film focusing on West Lafayette, what single question would you ask to prompt participants' reflection?

4. **Workshop: Possible Questions**

> Examples:

o "What is your earliest memory?"

o "What last brought you joy?"

> Students think-pair-share:

o Do these questions align with Morin's ideal of a "cinematic interrogation" that encompasses both the basic, everyday aspects of life and the nature of humanity itself?

o How would they answer these questions; what challenges could they face in constructing an answer; and what revisions to each question might improve their ability to answer?

5. **Assignment Review**

> Read the assignment together.

Ask:

o What does Morin's proposition of "an experiment lived by its authors and its actors" mean?

o Morin sketches a "cinematic interrogation" that encompasses both everyday life and individuals' reflections on humanity, in general. Why was this his ideal? What might it achieve?

> Discuss requirements:

o Interview at least 5 strangers

> Film length = (maximum three minutes). Note that limited editing is expected. If anyone chooses not to edit, they need to provide timestamps for viewing.

Session 3
Film Screening and Reflection

1. **Watch Student Films**

> After each student film screening, the filmmaker gives a **two-minute reflection** on their process and what they learned from their experiment.

2. **Group Feedback and Class Discussion**

> In small classes: Have a short group discussion after each film.

Ask:

o What worked well?

o What could be improved?

o What does this film communicate about society?

> In larger classes: Pair students. Each student gives feedback on their partner's film using the same questions.

3. **Full-Class Reflection Questions**

> Post these prompts for whole-class discussion:

o What did you learn about your community or environment?
o How did this shape your idea of "truthful cinema"?
o Did it feel more like art or research—or both?
o What surprised you most about your footage?

Assessment

Students are evaluated on the following points:

> Film's engagement with the assignment
> Thoughtfulness of question selection
> Clarity and relevance of footage to social research
> Meaningful reflection on their own filmmaking practice
> Participation in discussion

Cross-Disciplinary Adaptation

> **Urban Studies or Engineering (Human-Centered Design)**: Students could explore how people interact with specific spaces or technologies by asking questions like, *"What challenges do you experience using this space or technology?"*

> **Public Health**: Students might interview community members about their personal definitions of health, using prompts like, *"What does being healthy mean to you?"*

> **Key Value of Filmmaking Across Use**: Filmmaking captures vivid, authentic insights that written surveys may miss.

Instructor Try-It Activity

Process and Steps

1. **Pick a Question or Theme:**

Choose a simple, open-ended question to ask people around you (e.g., "What inspires you?", "What worries you about the future?", or "What makes this place unique?").

2. **Film (3–5 minutes)**:
   Let things happen naturally. Don't direct or script. Edit as little as possible—only trim if necessary.
3. **Review Your Video**:
   Ask yourself:

o What did I capture that I didn't expect?
o How did the camera change the situation?

Reflection and Planning Prompts (for Instructors)

> **Could your students explore a broad topic (like "belief") through this method?**

o How does cinéma vérité offer something different from surveys, interviews, or focus groups?

> **If students treat the camera as a research tool**:

o Where else in their field or future jobs could they apply this method?

> **What might feel intimidating to students?**

o How could you support them with:
- In-class prep activities?
- A practice round before filming?

Additional Resources/ References

Story, Brett, dir. 2019. *The Hottest August*. Grasshopper Film. https://www.thehottestaugust.com/

In *The Hottest August*, a 2017 film inspired by Morin and Rouch, Brett Story and her crew travel around New York City, approaching strangers to ask the question: "What are your hopes for the future?" The film is a portrait of collective anxiety, revolving around contemporary issues of climate change, economic precarity, and political polarization. Including clips or screening this contemporary film shows the continued relevance of *Chronicle of a Summer* and its approach.

"Man on the Street" interviews are increasingly featured in media as varied as late-night television and TikTok. In classes with longer sessions, I often ask students to bring examples of this format, and we discuss how these differ from Morin and Rouch's vision.

SMARTPHONE DATA: COMMUNICATING HIDDEN PATTERNS CREATIVELY

By: Shannon McMullen and Sarah Huber

Discipline: Media and Communication / Visual Arts/ Library and Information Science

Subject: Creative Dataset Design and Data Visualization Basics

Information Qualities of the Format

Data from everyday technologies, including smartphones, are at the heart of countless contemporary new media artworks. As Ian Bogost might argue, smartphones are a "mature medium": we use them constantly for a whole host of purposes and activities, from the creative to the mundane. What data stories can smartphones tell? Visualizing the data from them can provide a shared anchor for meaningful comparison, a more critical understanding of everyday new media use, and awareness of data-archiving capabilities of smartphones. Inspired by artist Anna Ridler's work that investigates the hidden patterns of data observed in nature and the hand-drawn data measured and quantified through the daily lives of Giorgia Lupi and Stephanie Posave, this assignment asks students to visualize a small, original dataset based on the hidden patterns of their smartphone use. It is an introductory assignment that highlights key aspects of visualization: defining purpose (exploratory, story-driven, or artistic expression), visual hierarchy, and data representation. By focusing on "little data" rather than big data, it invites exploration and creative insight at a human scale.

Who This Is For

Faculty interested in combining creative, collaborative assignments with introductory principles of data visualization.

Designed for students in media, communication, data science, information design, anthropology, visual art, industrial design, or interdisciplinary courses who wish to explore how data is shaped, visualized, and communicated.

Learning Outcomes

> **Collect** and organize a small dataset based on smartphone use.
> **Analyze** patterns in the data to identify potential insights or stories.
> **Evaluate** visualization types based on audience needs and context.
> **Apply** design principles using visual hierarchy.
> **Create** an original, hand-drawn, physical, or digital data visualization that allows for meaningful interpretations to be made by viewers.

Instructional Context

Three sessions (50 minutes each) are recommended. It can be conducted in classrooms with limited tech (for handmade visualizations) or in computer labs (for digital visualizations). Students are invited to use existing skills (e.g. drawing, graphic design, creative computing, sewing, etc.) in their approach visualizing data.

Materials and Equipment

> Laptops or tablets with Excel/Google Sheets
> Access to Canva, Illustrator, or data viz platforms (optional: D3.js, p5.js)
> Physical materials for handmade or 3D visualizations (paper, fabric, needles/thread, cardboard, etc.)
> Large sheets of paper and drawing tools

Resources Students Should Review for the Assignment

Artist References

The Museum of Modern Art. December 4, 2024. *How Giorgia Lupi Visualizes Through Data*. YouTube. https://bit.ly/43SAUd9.

Ridler, Anna. 2023. "Synthetic Iris Dataset." annaridler.com. https://bit.ly/46jR8gH..

Data as Art

Freeman, Julie, Geraint Wiggins, Gavin Starks, and Mark Sandler. 2018. "A Concise Taxonomy for Describing Data as an Art Material." *Leonardo* 51 (1): 75–79.

Assignment

Session 1

What is Data? An Instructor-Facilitated Presentation and Discussion

Data is anything that can be observed and measured—people, plants, actions, or events.

> "Every plant, every person, and every interaction we take part in can be mapped, counted, and measured, and these measurements are what we call data"
> (Lupi and Posavec 2018, introduction).

Instructors can tailor the discussion of data to focus on discipline-specific discussion of uses and significance.

Working with a Partner

Decide how you and your partner will collect and visualize your data using one of the approaches below:

> **Comparative Approach**: Each of you collects your own data on the same topic and compares results.

o *Example*: Lupi, Giorgia, and Stefanie Posavec. 2015. Dear Data: A Year-Long Analog Data Drawing Project. https://www.dear-data.com/theproject.

> **Shared Approach**: Collect one dataset together and create a single visualization.
o *Example*: Ridler, Anna. 2018. "Myriad (Tulips)." Installation of Hand-Labeled Tulip Images. annaridler.com. https://bit.ly/4sjsOnE.

Data Requirements

> Focus: smartphone use or content (photos, apps, health tracking, text messages, etc.)
> Must show variation in:
o Time (hour/day/week)
o Space (location)
o Or type (e.g., people, apps, species)
> Collect 100–200 data points
> Create a legend or labeling system

Visualization Format Options

Choose a presentation format that fits your interests and your existing skills or a new skill you would like to practice. A few ideas:

> Quilt: Combine stitching and custom quilt shapes to represent each day's steps over a month.
> Photos: Group a selection of photos by subject, dominant color, or dominant shape (e.g., face=circle, building= rectangle) to create a physical installation or a digital poster.
> Postcards: Hand-draw or collage a set of postcards that show which emojis you use most and how often over a month, or year.
> Digital Graphs: Use a program like Illustrator or Excel to show through a creative graph how you spend time on your phone.

Deliverables

The following should be completed before the second session:

1. **Project Description**

> Title
> Topic description
> Guiding question driving data collection
> Time period covered
> Spatial scope (if relevant—e.g., mapped locations)
> Intended audience
> Format of interest (this can change)

2. **Data Collection Plan**

> How will you and your partner split the work?
> How will you record the data?
> Where will you securely store the data?
> Define an *if/then rule* for what counts as a data point:
o Example: If I unlock my phone, then I record the time and app used.

Class time will be provided to find partners and plan your data collection together.

Session 2

Mini-Lecture

Identify Audience

> Have students identify audience and decide whether their visualization will be exploratory, communicative, or expressive:
o **Exploratory**: Presents all data equally for open-ended exploration. Examples range from a simple spreadsheet to a bar chart. The title signals that the purpose is to explore rather than argue a point.
o **Communicative**: Shows all data but emphasizes a specific insight or story the creator wants to convey. The title highlights that

message.

o **Expressive**: Interprets data poetically, prioritizing mood, narrative, or ambiguity. Titles can reflect conceptual or aesthetic framing rather than a strict summary.

Note: The exploratory versus communicative categories adapt Cole Nussbaumer Knaflic's terms, while the expressive is drawn from the IEEE VIS Arts Program (VISAP).

Mini-Lecture
What is Visual Hierarchy?

(See Design Basics section to prepare presentation and/or cater the "Hands-on Hierarchy: Designing a Concert Poster" lesson plan to support this activity.) Create examples that show visual hierarchy being both used and not used to illustrate how hierarchy serves as a visual navigation map for the viewer. Discuss how the following contributes to visual hierarchy:

> Titles and subtitles
> Font size and type
> Color and contrast
> Spacing and alignment
> Accessibility (e.g., colorblind-safe palettes, font size)

Draw Graphs

Provide students with paper and drawing tools to experiment with which graph best communicates their data as well as the above visual hierarchy principles. Depending on their format choice, like grouping images, a chart may not be appropriate, but it can still help them think through how they will categorize, organize, and present data:

> The Data Visualization Catalogue: https://datavizcatalogue.com/
> Depict Data Studio's Chart Selector: https://depictdatastudio.com/charts/

Deliverables

The following should be completed by the third session:

> Completed visualization
> A 100–150-word reflective memo on what you found most valuable in this assignment and how you plan to build on it, as well as which areas remain unclear and need further study.

Session 3

In this final session, students share their work in a 7-10 minute presentation. Possible items to include in the presentation:

> Question that guided data collection
> Data collection parameters
> Documentation and discussion of collection process
> One to three influences on the data visualization approach (drawn from course materials)
> Presentation and discussion of the completed visualization

The assessment below guides peer feedback and discussion for each group.

Assessment

> Guiding question
> A title that reflects your visualization's content
> Timeframe and scope defined
> Use of exploratory, communicative, or expressive approach is clear
> Use of appropriate graph forms
> Effective use of visual hierarchy
> Effective use of legend or labeling system
> Thoughtful connection to readings and influences
> Collaborative reflection and process documentation

Cross-Disciplinary Adaptation

> **Public Health**: Visualize phone data to talk about wellness.
> **Environmental Science**: Chart usage as it corresponds to carbon emissions and environmental damage.
> **Literature/ Writing**: Record text patterns—texts sent, words used, emojis used to create a data visual poem or data narrative structure.

Example

The following example is taken from students Caitlin Kao and Anthony Vivio (New Media Art, Culture, and Technology, Department of Art & Design, Purdue University) who said they were visually influenced by Rafael Lozano-Hemmer's Pulse Topology, equalizer displays, and drone shows. It is an example of exploratory and expressive combined.

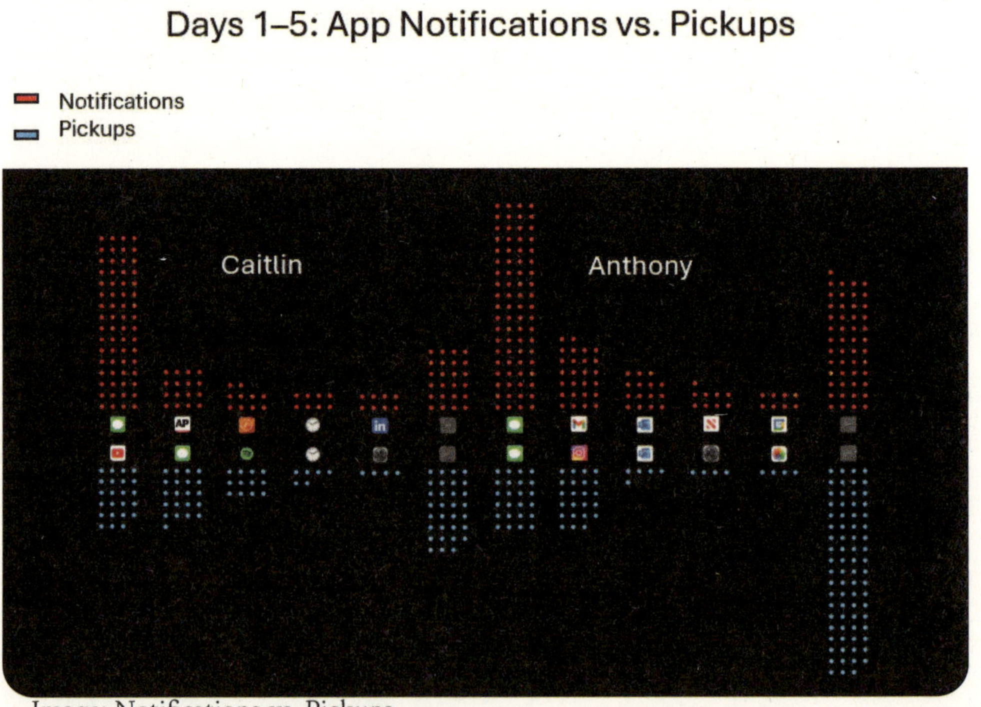

Image: Notifications vs. Pickups
Image credit: Screen capture from Kao and Vivio's work

Instructor Try-It Activity

Choose your own guiding question related to smartphone usage and collect data for one day. Think about an artist's work or any visual approach you think would display data well. Visualize the data using either a handmade or digital format. Bring this to class to share as a model or talking point, asking students their thoughts on how creativity is used. Ask if it is apparent what the purpose is of the visualization, their thoughts on how it is organized, and if they can locate a visual hierarchy. Take notes on their response and use them to help develop a lesson plan.

Additional Resources/ References

Knaflic, Cole Nussbaumer. 2015. *Storytelling with Data: A Data Visualization Guide for Business Professionals*. Wiley.

Lupi, Giorgia, and Stefanie Posavec. 2018. *Observe, Collect, Draw! A Visual Journal: Discover the Patterns in Your Everyday Life*. Princeton Architectural Press.

Tufte, Edward. 2001. *The Visual Display of Quantitative Information*. 2nd ed. Graphics Press

By: Sarah Huber

Discipline: Visual Literacy, Library and Information Science

Subject: Material Data Practice

Information Qualities of the Format

The African American quilters of Gee's Bend began quilting in the nineteenth century in a remote Alabama community. Using what they had—flour sacks and used clothing—they created abstract, improvisational designs that expressed "their own compositional language" (Simpson 2021), an approach they called quilting "my way" (Souls Grown Deep, n.d.). Their collaboration and innovation inspire this lesson plan. Though simpler, it invites participants to use fabric and stitches with personal meaning. A patch from worn jeans may convey more than a cell in Excel. Can material form combined with group collaboration reveal insights digital formats can't?

This lesson offers a tactile approach for students to conceptualize research project components. Each stitch represents a unit of data—one cup of a chosen drink—transforming quantitative information into a visual and textural artifact. By sewing individual felt squares into a collective quilt, students visualize group patterns, informing next steps in their research process. This activity engages both mind and body in collecting, organizing, and interpreting data, making research methods more approachable and fostering fresh insights through collaborative discussion and hands-on making—without opening a computer or spreadsheet. It draws on a long-standing tradition of using textiles to record experience and meaning.

Who This Is For

This lesson helps instructors combine creative making with data literacy in visually and multimodally-focused courses. It encourages students to explore, experiment, and discover insights from a different perspective. It's beginner-friendly and adaptable for:

> Introductory data visualization courses
> STEM communication workshops
> Interdisciplinary art/science projects

Learning Outcomes

> **Perform** basic stitches by hand.
> **Use** fabric and thread materials safely and effectively.
> **Create** a small, embroidered data representation.
> **Collaborate** to assemble a quilt using sewing machines.
> **Reflect** on how tactile, physical artifacts communicate information.

Instructional Context

> Makerspace or classroom with sewing machines, tables, and cutting mats
> 10–20 students
> Duration:
o Week 1: Learn stitching basics, prepare felt squares (50 minutes).
o Week 2: Collect data (one week outside of class).
o Week 3: Sew squares into a collaborative quilt and discussion (50 minutes).

Materials and Equipment

> Felt squares (one per student, 6" × 4")—colors represent drink type (e.g., brown = coffee, red = soda)
> Embroidery floss or Sashiko thread in white or various colors (color can indicate drink type)
> Embroidery or Sashiko needles, scissors, and threaders
> Fabric markers or fabric-safe pens
> Sewing machine(s) for quilt assembly
> Pins, pin cushions, and seam rippers
> Rulers and cutting mats
> Optional: Rotary cutter, iron

Accessibility Notes:

> Provide pre-threaded needles and needle threaders for students with limited dexterity.
> Offer larger felt squares or thicker needles for easier handling.
> Include both written and video instructions with large, clear visuals.
> Allow students to work in pairs if additional support is needed.
> If color contrast or small details limit readability, include a written key or description of the final piece.
> A unique benefit of this project is its tactile quality—stitches can be felt and even "read" by touch to discern titles and data counts.

Resources Students Should Review for the Assignment

Bravo, Liz. 2021. "Data and Technique: Reflections on Visualizing by Hand." *Nightingale: The Journal of the Data Visualization Society.* https://bit.ly/4osgQXp.

Assignment
Session 1: Intro to Sewing and Material Exploration Process and Steps

1. Bring sample fabrics—jeans, felt, cotton, polyester, fleece, linen—for students to compare weight, texture, and stretch.
2. Demonstrate a basic running stitch.
3. Practice threading, knotting, and stitching on sample felt.
4. Let students test a few stitches on different fabrics to see how each performs. Use a ruler and fabric marker to show how straight lines can be followed.

o *Note*: Keeping straight lines helps viewers read the data rather than notice irregularities.

5. Group discussion:

o Which fabric was easiest or most enjoyable to work with?
o What might fabric choice communicate in a final visualization?
o Decide on one material type for the project.

Planning Data Visualization

1. Students bring (or are provided) a square of the chosen fabric.
2. Begin with a research question. Each student tracks one variable (e.g., drink type, music, or social media use) for five days to collect data that answers it.
3. Choose fabric color, stitch color, or style to represent data categories (e.g., coffee vs. soda, hot vs. cold, caffeinated vs. decaf).
4. Encourage students to personalize their square with a small stitched symbol or image representing themselves (e.g., one student sewed a kitten to reflect their nine cats).

Session 2: Data Collection (Outside Class)

Over one week, students record each cup of their chosen drink with one stitch. For accuracy, encourage daily stitching rather than bulk stitching at the end.

Session 3: Quilt Assembly and Discussion
Process and Steps

1. Bring stitched squares to class.
2. Pin, sew, and assemble squares into a collective quilt.
3. Create a legend: In the example below, the square where the participant didn't follow the directions became the legend on the left, showing each line as Monday-Friday.
4. Step back to observe patterns—what trends appear?
5. Reflect as a group:
> What worked or didn't?
> Did color or fabric choices communicate meaning?
> How could the process improve or scale into a larger project?
6. Create a title:
While not done in the example below, you can stitch with thicker thread into fabric at the top of the quilt.
7. Identify the type of data visualization it is:
> In "SmartPhone Data: Communicating Hidden Patterns Creatively" there are definitions of different types of data visualizations. This would be an exploratory data viz because all the data is shown for the viewer to investigate as is. There is no story being told. It could also be expressive.
8. Discuss: How does this tactile visualization differ from digital charts?
9. Photograph the finished quilt for documentation or portfolios.

Assessment
> **Sewing Technique**: Even stitches, easily read
> **Data Accuracy**: Data recorded daily
> **Creativity and Design**: Clear, easily read
> **Collaboration**: Active contributor
> **Reflection**: Insightful process reflection

Cross-Disciplinary Adaptation

> **Environmental Science**: Stitch a square for each water bottle or reusable cup used in a week.
> **Public Health**: Visualize caffeine, sugar, or hydration habits through stitched patterns.
> **Sociology**: Examine collective habits through stitched data storytelling.
> **Art and Design**: Explore color theory and textile design alongside data collection.

Example

This project began as a small test run with friends before teaching it in a visual literacy course. During a week of national stress, I tracked our caffeine intake to answer: Does caffeine consumption increase on difficult days? The data showed no clear pattern, but the process revealed what I would do differently at a larger scale. What struck me most was the individuality expressed through the data that wouldn't surface in an Excel sheet. Everyone stitched differently and added their own signatures—a data-driven compositional language emerged, reminiscent of the Gee's Bend quilters stitching "my way." This lighthearted project fostered conversation and suggestions on alternative approaches, supporting the idea that hands-on interaction with data and group collaboration can prompt deeper, more personal reflection than working on a screen.

Example (next page)

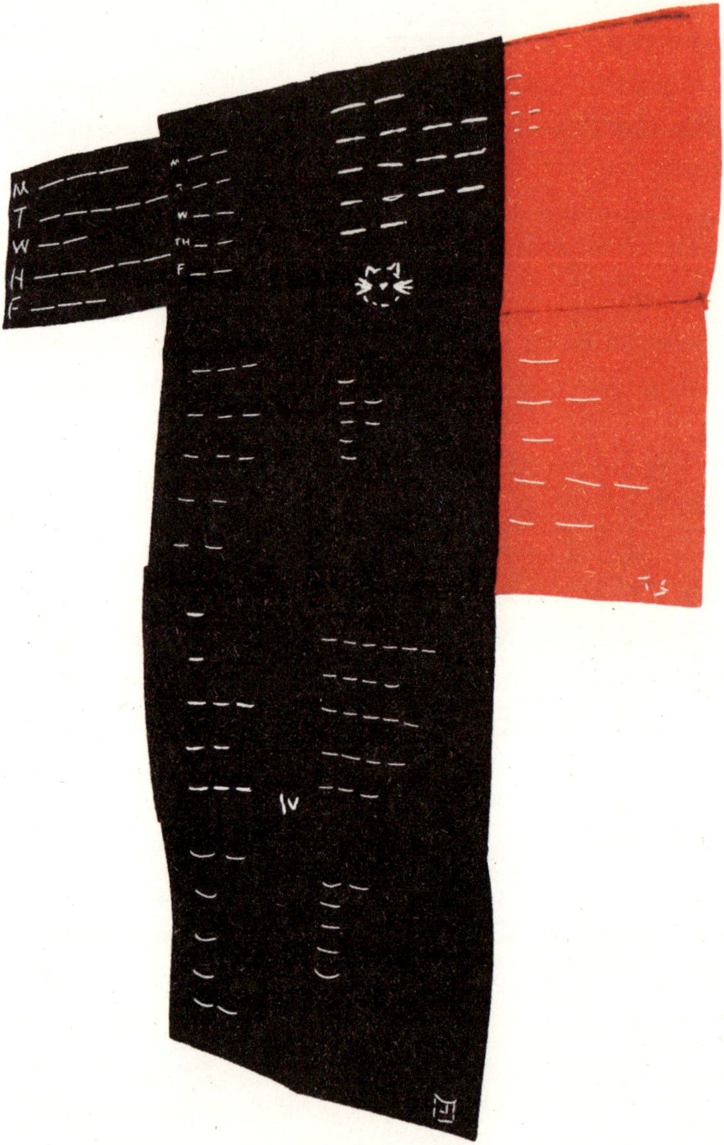

Image 1: Quilted data
Photo credit: Sarah Huber

Instructor Try-It Activity
Process and Steps

1. Choose a drink (or behavior of choice) and track for five days.
2. Stitch a felt square using a running stitch for each behavior, each day.
3. Practice pinning and sewing two squares together on a machine.
4. Reflect: Did the data offer any insight? What will you do differently next time?
5. Bring your stitched square as a demo sample to class and discuss how the activity could be used to inform a larger study.

Additional Resources/ References

Simpson, Veronica. January 25, 2021. "The Gee's Bend Quiltmakers." *Studio International*. https://bit.ly/49Fem3e.

Souls Grown Deep. (n.d.). "Gee's Bend Quiltmakers." https://bit.ly/3LA1Qbj.

DATA MADE PRACTICAL: QUILTING TEMPERATURE POTHOLDERS

By: Alison Roth

Discipline: Medical Physics

Subject: Fiber Arts Representation of Climate Data

Information Qualities of the Format

The visual representation of data can be a powerful storytelling device. By engaging with a tactile color scale, students reflect on how color, texture, and material together convey meaning—how temperature, intensity, or frequency can be felt as well as seen. Information becomes both visual and sensory, inviting interpretation through touch as well as sight.

Who This is For

Developed through a Purdue Libraries makerspace workshop, this project teaches data visualization through quilting. It was open to all Purdue students, postdoctoral fellows, faculty, and staff, and can be adapted to other fiber arts—such as crochet, knitting, or felting—or even non-fiber media like construction paper.

Learning Outcomes

> **Interpret** temperature data by selecting and justifying corresponding colors and fabrics.

> **Create** a tactile representation of data using quilting techniques that communicate meaning through color, texture, and composition.

> **Evaluate** the effectiveness and readability of the finished piece in conveying information to viewers.

Instructional Context

This project was developed as part of a Purdue Libraries makerspace workshop to teach students about visual representation of data and quilting skills. As such, it is not fully developed for instructional implementation and assessment. This specific project was to represent the monthly average temperature in West Lafayette, IN in 2024 via a quilted potholder.

Materials and Equipment

> Cotton quilting fabric in a variety of colors
> Thread for either a sewing machine or hand sewing
> Insul-Bright Insulated Thermal Lining
> ½" bias tape maker
> Sewing machine or hand-sewing needles

Assignment

Process and Steps

> Provide students with the mean daily temperature for each month in your area for the current or previous year.
> Have students select a color scale to represent the temperature data. *Tip*: Esri's "Creating a meaningful temperature palette" can help students choose colors: https://bit.ly/4hKzcQJ
> Once colors are chosen, students choose fabrics to match that color scale.
> Instruct students to **create a quilted potholder** following the steps below:

1. Select a fabric to represent each month's temperature and press flat.
2. Cut twelve 1.5" x 7.5" strips, one from each piece of fabric.
3. Cut one 7.5" x 12.5" rectangle of thermal lining.
4. Cut one 7.5" x 12.5" rectangle of backing fabric.
5. Piece the monthly strips together with a ¼" seam allowance.

6. Press seam allowances to one side, lengthwise, pressing toward the dark fabric rather than the light.
7. Join the strips in order of months, sewing lengthwise until all are connected.
8. Layer the quilt: Place the backing fabric (right side down), thermal lining (center), and quilt top (right side up). Pin to hold in place.
9. Quilt the layers together using the "stitch in the ditch" method (sew directly along the seam lines) by hand or with a sewing machine.
10. Trim edges and square corners so all layers are even.
11. Cut a 2⅛" wide strip of binding fabric on the bias (approx. 43" long).
12. Make the bias tape: Feed the strip through the bias tape maker, pressing the sides toward the center as it exits. Press in half length wise to form double-fold bias tape.
13. Attach the bias tape: lay it flat along the quilt edge, right sides together, with raw edges aligned. Pin or clip in place.
14. Start sewing midway along one side, leaving a 6–8" tail free for joining later.
15. Sew the binding to the quilt with a ¼" seam allowance.

> Remember to sew backstitch at the beginning and end to secure seams.

16. Mitered corners:

> Stop stitching ¼" from each corner and backstitch.

> Fold the binding up at a 45° angle, then fold it down so the raw edges align with the next side.

> Resume stitching from the edge of the new side.

17. Join the binding ends with a diagonal seam, trim excess, and finish sewing the final section.
18. Finishing the binding:

> Fold the binding over to the back side of the potholder, enclosing the raw edge.

> Press and clip or pin the folded edge in place.

19. Finish the binding:

> For a machine finish, topstitch close to the binding edge (about ⅛") on the front, catching the back fold as you sew.

> For a hand finish, secure the folded edge on the back with small, nearly invisible whip stitches or ladder stitches.

20. Press the entire potholder flat for a polished, professional appearance.

Assessment

As this activity was not developed within a formal class, no assessment criteria were originally defined. For classroom use, include a brief written reflection in which students describe their chosen temperature (or data) scale and how it is visually represented. Assessment should emphasize the appropriateness of the scale, the clarity and readability of the finished piece, and its effectiveness in communicating meaning to viewers. Attention to craftsmanship—clean lines, secure threads, and a clear color legend—enhances readability and prevents distraction.

Cross-Disciplinary Adaptation

> **History**: Students create "data quilts" that reinterpret historical weather logs, diaries, or ship records as visual fabric narratives.

> **Communication, Media Studies, and Humanities**: Students narrate the human experience of climate change, using each fabric strip as a chapter or emotional cue.

> **Atmospheric and Environmental Science**: Students replace temperature data with daily air-quality or humidity readings to explore relationships among variables.

> **Gender Studies:** Discuss gendered histories of textile work and the intersection of domestic craft with scientific and political storytell ing.

Example

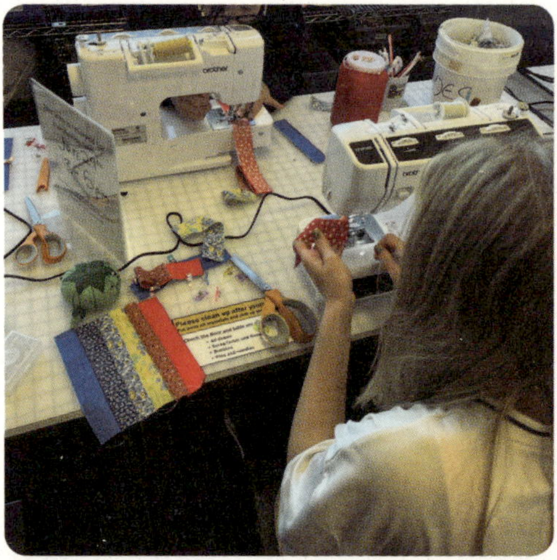

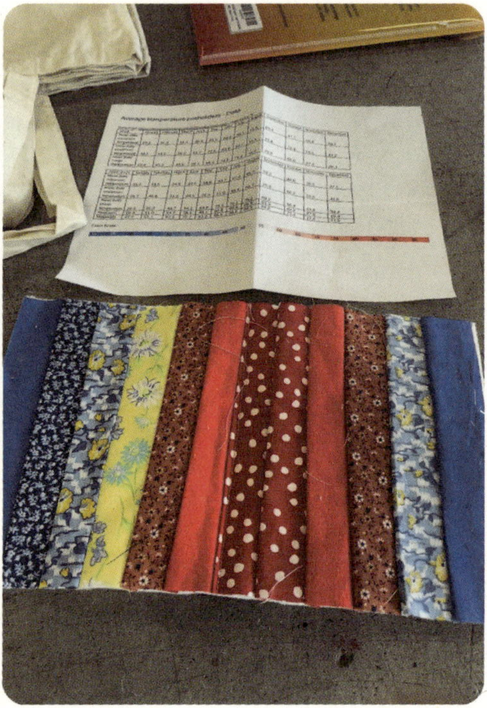

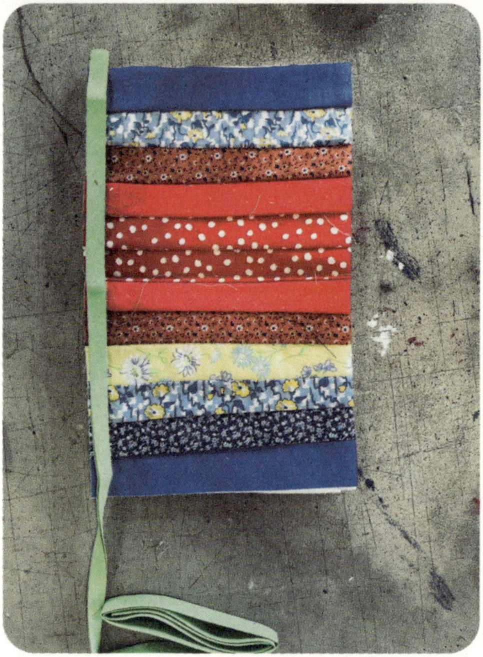

Images 1–3: Quilted data visualization
Photo credit: Patricia Swanson

Instructor Try-It Activity

In your field, are there default conventions around data representation that students could explore? What are the strengths and weaknesses of that scale? How can it lead to misinterpretations? What could be another scale?

Process and Steps

Try translating a small dataset into a stitched format.

1. Select a simple dataset (e.g., daily steps, weather for the week).
2. Assign meaning to data through color.
3. Sew a small 5 x 7 sample to test your design.
4. Reflect:

o What does sewing reveal or obscure about the data?

o How readable is it to others?

o What legend or labeling might improve clarity?

o How might this help students think about data in a new way?

By: Patricia Swanson

Discipline: Libraries and Makerspaces

Subject: Button Making

Information Qualities of the Format

Buttons have historically been a format used to carry political messages in both subversive and creative ways that can engage the like-minded as well as passersby. People wear buttons as a public symbol to say, "I'm a part of this group" or "I believe in this cause, movement, or ideology" or simply "I like this person, place, or thing." It's an innate human desire to share a part of ourselves with the world around us and this medium provides a small and simple avenue for that mode of self-expression.

The surface of a button is limited, so students must carefully consider the visual elements they use (color, font, shapes, images) when crafting a message. This assignment introduces creative message-sharing and offers guidance while allowing exploration. It's not a full design unit—see "Design Basics" in the Practical Skills Index section for resources.

Who This Is For

This lesson is for instructors interested in having their students create wearable graphics to communicate concise ideas or messages. This button-making assignment could be a stand-alone assignment or the first

step in helping students refine research topics or project ideas.

Learning Outcomes

> **Summarize** complex ideas by condensing a message into 1–3 impactful words.
> **Experiment** with color and font choices to convey meaning.
> **Reflect** on the connection between format and meaning, recognizing how mode of delivery influences audience perception.
> **Constructively critique** visual messages of peers.
> **Refine** visual messaging through structured peer feedback.

Instructional Context

> Two 50-minute sessions
> Works best for small groups due to the guidance needed for button making.
> Big tables and room to spread out materials is needed

Materials and equipment

> Materials for students to hand-draw their designs
o Paper
o Pencils
o Erasers
o Colored pencils
o Permanent markers
o Recommended pen: Pilot Precise V5 extra fine
o Stencils and shape templates for those intimated by drawing
> Digital mockups can be the alternative to buttons if students want to create an original digital design or for students who physically cannot use a button press.
o Canva (or digital platform of choice)
> For sourcing images:

- o University archives for topic-specific images
- o Library of Congress for public domain images
- o Creative Commons for images with creator permission
- > Button Maker

  Recommendation: Buy a metal button maker if budget allows (plastic ones break easily). Size depends on content: Students often prefer smaller buttons. Larger buttons allow for more detail and drawing. We use American Button Machines: https://bit.ly/4nIn6Jl Many university makerspaces will also lend out button makers.
- > Button Parts:
- o Shell
- o Clear mylar
- o Collet
- o Spring pin or regular pin
- > Templates:
- o Print button templates for students or share digitally.
- o Templates help ensure visuals remain visible after pressing.
- o Free templates are available from American Button Machines and online.

Resources Students Should Review for the Assignment

- > Review resources on the use of color and fonts from the "Design Basics" section.
- > Review Harvard Kennedy School's Button Collection and History: "Decades of Resistance: Political Movements and Protest Pins Since 1960." Students should take note of how these artifacts document resistance, activism, or identity. https://bit.ly/482Cn32
- > Review the online Busy Beaver Button Museum, which features over nine thousand buttons, themed categories, historical articles, and a digital exhibit of fan-submitted buttons. Students may also submit their own buttons as part of the assignment. https://buttonmuseum.org/

Assignment
Session 1
Process and Steps

1. Lead a discussion on assignment pre-work.
   Ask:

> How do these collections change your view of everyday objects in public discourse?
> Which buttons stood out to you, and why?
> What stood out about color and font choices?
> What details did you notice in the images (framing, simplicity, or complexity)?

2. Provide discipline-specific prompts that help students choose a topic of interest. To simplify the activity and avoid copyright concerns, students will create original visuals rather than sourcing images online.

Example (Library Topic): Public library programming and resources (e.g., Drag Queen Story Hour, social workers in libraries, OER, privacy, AI ethics).

Prompts:

> What library topic interests you most right now?
> Why does it interest you?
> What aspect would you most like to share?
> Summarize its importance in one to three words.
> Combine two or three visual elements to represent it (color and shape).

Activity and Reflection

> Provide drawing supplies and button templates.
> Students use this time to make buttons based on the prompts.

> At the end of class, each student shares their topic and chosen visuals.
> Students refine their buttons before the next session (e.g., trying different photos, improving drawings, or collaging ideas to brain storm).

Session 2

Students are given additional time to work on buttons during the first part of class.

Process and Steps

Peer Critique

1. Have all students place their buttons on a table.
o Give students time to look at each design and take notes on the intended message.
o Discuss one design at a time:
2. Classmates share what they think the design communicates (through color, text, image choice, etc.) and ask questions.
3. After all comments, the creator explains their intended message.
4. Allow students the opportunity to refine buttons after feedback and reflect on how peer feedback informed their changes.

Cross-Disciplinary Adaptation

> **Education**: Create buttons to list class rules.
> **Health Sciences**: Create public health button for a wellness campaign.
> **STEM**: Create awareness buttons for sustainability.
> **Humanities:** Condense an historical moment into a symbol for an exhibition.

Example

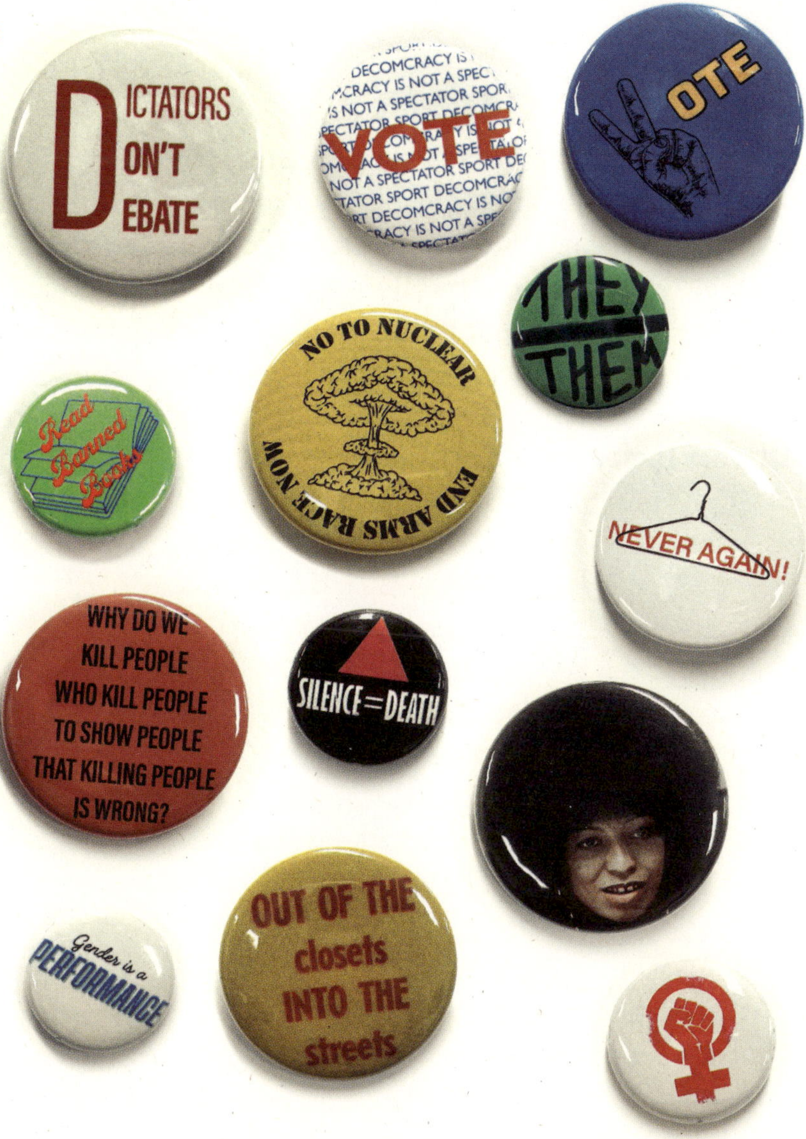

Image: Visual discourse buttons
Photo credit: Patricia Swanson

Angela Davis photo: Library of Congress. (n.d.). *Angela Davis, half-length portrait, with "x" markings that indicate the photographer's or editor's selection of a photo for printing*
[Photograph]. Prints & Photographs Online Catalog.

Instructor Try-It Activity

Choose an upcoming event—a department gathering, rally, or party—and design a button to convey a message. Wear it at the event without explanation, inviting friends or colleagues to guess its meaning. Gather feedback, note reactions (if it leads to laughs and/or deep discussions – success!), and reflect on what worked. Use these insights to determine how this activity could enhance your course curriculum.

Additional Resources/ References

Carter, Christian and Ted Hake. 2020. *Button Power: 125 Years of Saying It with Buttons*. Princeton Architectural Press.

THE INFORMATION OF RITUAL: UNDERSTANDING FOOD AND AGING ACROSS THE LIFE COURSE

By: Sherylyn Briller and Erika Carrillo

Discipline: Anthropology and Gerontology

Subject: Anthropology of Aging

Information Qualities of the Format

Getting food is more than just a functional act. It carries biological, social, and symbolic meaning. The cultural, physical, and sensory components of obtaining and preparing food—and the ways we assemble it into something that matters symbolically—are central to this ritual activity. Students are invited to think like anthropologists as they explore how rituals around food shape meaning across the life course. It emphasizes that everyday practices—like cooking, sharing, or gathering food—are as significant as formal ceremonies. Through a chosen food-related ritual, students will connect ordinary and special moments, examining how such acts help make life understandable and meaningful over time.

Food rituals are an embodied, lived practice that can anchor us to time, place, and to one another.

Documenting rituals transforms these meaningful acts into a communicable form of information—turning lived experience into something that can be shared, studied, and interpreted. This can be done through writing, photography, list making, or even recreating the act itself.

The Information of Ritual: Understanding Food and Aging Across the Life Course

Who This Is For

This lesson is designed for faculty interested in helping their students explore the significance and power of ritual, aging, and food over the life course. While many people think that studying aging is all about older adults, it is in fact a lifelong process shaped by both personal and cultural factors. Many daily practices—including those related to eating—make us who we are. Ritual helps structure our everyday lives and gives meaning to key life transitions.

In this activity, students are encouraged to see ritual itself, and the act of documenting it, as information formats. This is done in the ways of capturing, organizing, and communicating meaning through embodied, social, and sensory forms. By studying and representing food rituals, students learn how information is created not only through text or data, but through lived experience, repetition, and shared cultural expression.

Learning Outcomes

> **Describe** how the life course is culturally constructed and experi enced across food contexts.

> **Explain** the value and meanings of ritual in shaping identity and community.

> **Analyze** how food rituals reflect both ordinary and extraordinary moments in people's lives.

> **Evaluate** how information formats, such as documentation, per formance, or representation, shape the ways rituals are shared, understood, and preserved.

Instructional Context

This lesson is intended for students to explore their own food rituals but can bring an interesting layer of meaning in group settings such as senior centers, lifelong learning communities, or intergenerational programs that bring together college students and older adults to share traditions and experiences.

This is a three-part activity:
> **Session 1**: Plan and Prepare for the Food Ritual
> **Session 2**: Conduct the Food Ritual
> **Session 3**: Reflect on Lessons Learned

The size, scale, and timing of the ritual can be adjusted to fit the goals and context of the participants.

Materials and Equipment

This activity involves some form of food procurement or symbolic food representation. Participants can choose from a range of approaches depending on resources, accessibility, and creative intent:
> Grocery shopping for ingredients
> Picking food from a garden or foraging
> Cooking, baking, or assembling dishes
> Cutting images from food magazines
> Printing pictures from the internet to create a collage
> Drawing, sculpting, or otherwise representing food symbolically

Note:
> Food items do not need to be literal—the goal can be to symbolically represent food and its meanings.
> The activity can be adapted for different budgets, effort levels, and accessibility needs.
> Participants are encouraged to be creative, use available materials, and select an approach that best supports their process and context.

Resource Students Should Review Before the Assignment

If your institution has access, have students read the following article:

Briller, Sherylyn and Andrea Sankar. 2011. "The Changing Roles of Ritual in Later Life." *In Special Issue on Ritual in Later Life: Its Role, Significance, and Power.* Edited by Sherylyn Briller and Andrea Sankar. *Generations: Journal of the American Society on Aging* 35 (3): 6–10.

Assignment

Students can share their ritual experience in their final product as an individual or in a group presentation, paper, or performance. Nontraditional approaches are encouraged, such as creating a comic book, a series of memes, or silhouette storytelling. Whatever the chosen format, the goal is for students to come together around it and discuss everyone's experiences. In this case, it would be in an anthropology or a gerontology class.

Session 1: Preparing and Planning the Food Ritual

Guide students step-by-step as they plan their own food ritual.

1. **Choose Your Focus**
> Select a life-course event or moment to represent in your food ritual.

2. **Plan Your Approach**
> Decide on the theme (birthdays, dinner, morning coffee and breakfast routine) and format to communicate experience—writing, performance, comic book, or visual project.

3. **Gather Inspiration**
> Review the example project, A Star is Born: Food Rituals to Celebrate, to help imagine what your own creation might look like. A birthday example works well since it's a familiar and accessible type of ritual.

4. **Collaborate and Refine**
> Work with peers to plan your ritual. You might:

o Outline the sequence of events.
o Create a simple materials or food list (a grocery list works as a start).
o Sketch, storyboard, photograph, or collect symbols, colors, or shapes that represent your chosen moment or event.

Warm-up Prompts

What occasion are you considering for your ritual?

> Why does this event matter to you?
> What do you want to communicate or share with others?
> In one to three sentences, describe what a successful version of this ritual would look or feel like. What are the most important elements of the ritual?

Session 2: Conducting the Food Ritual

In this session, participants organize and carry out their food ritual—either by performing it in real life (e.g., hosting a birthday celebration) or by simulating it through creative means such as storyboarding, photography, or illustration.

As the ritual unfolds, encourage students to notice where information is developing, emphasizing that the process itself is a form of information creation, and that it is happening in the planning, gestures, interactions, and choices made during the activity. Participants should also think about how documentation will occur. This might include:

> Taking photos or short videos
> Writing reflections or field notes
> Collecting objects, menus, or recipes
> Creating sketches or visual records

These materials will later serve as evidence and interpretation of how meaning was made through the ritual. Students can share their documentation during class through their final product.

Session 3: Reflecting on the Learning

Students present their final product along with the documentation gathered throughout the process. They reflect on each stage—planning, conducting, and documenting—to identify where information was created and how meaning developed. From an anthropological perspective, observing how meaning emerges and how it is recorded is essential. The documentation—photos, notes, drawings, or collected materials—serves as data revealing values, relationships, and cultural patterns. In doing so, students begin to think like anthropologists: Recognizing what counts as information, where it appears, and how it can be interpreted. Information they gathered from the process may answer the following:

> Did they learn something new about themselves or those they collaborated with?
> Was anything surprising?
> Will they examine this aspect of their life going forward as they age?

Emphasize that this is not a critique but a personal reflection supporting lifelong learning and curiosity about everyday rituals. Over time, instructors may, with permission, collect examples for future classes to illustrate how documentation transforms lived experience into shared knowledge.

Social Justice Extension

An important consideration for this activity is the recognition that food is a reflection of socio-political forces that influence our everyday lives. This activity serves as an opportunity to explore these linkages and learn how food can be viewed through a social justice lens. Invite students to consider who has access to food and ritual opportunities—and who may not. Also, what resources (e.g. money, ingredients, time, etc.) can they put toward these activities? Food rituals can expose inequalities as well as creativity in times of scarcity. Discuss how people adapt their traditions during hardship and how such stories connect to issues of hunger, sustainability, and food insecurity. Reflection here can promote empathy and awareness, linking personal experience to broader social realities.

Example: A Star Is Born—Food Rituals to Celebrate

Overview

This example illustrates how an ordinary celebration—a birthday—can be understood as a ritual. It traces the evolution of one person's relationship with theatrical performance through food-centered gatherings over time. Each stage uses food memories as a format to connect aspects of their identities and how they evolved over time

Part 1: A Star Is Born (Childhood Beginnings)

This part tells of your early life growing up in "Name of American Midwestern Town". It covers annually celebrating your July 4th birthday at the family cabin on the lake. Every summer you would organize all the local kids—your siblings, cousins and neighbors--to put on a play. It was not a coincidence that you starred in the production all the time. And during the school year, you would audition for and perform in every school show. Your family and friends would turn out to see you and recognize your talent as a triple threat—singing, dancing and acting!

Ritual Elements

> Gathering family and friends at a lakeside cabin.
> Hosting a small play or skit as part of the celebration.
> Sharing familiar summer foods that anchor memory and tradition.

Food Components

Burgers, s'mores, and red-white-and-blue desserts act as edible symbols of childhood times, community, and seasonal rhythm.

Documentation Ideas

Family photos, a recreated birthday menu, or a short storyboard illustrating the sequence of the day.

Part 2: Dreams of Broadway (Young Adulthood)

For many aspiring actors, it is a rite of passage to journey to New York City and try to break into show business. Even with talent, hard work, and luck, you learn that very few people are ultimately Broadway bound. But you have lots of company—other actors like you waiting tables and hoping for their "Big Break." You make some good friendships that last even after you all leave New York. While you are disappointed that chasing the big dream does not work out the way you wanted it too, you move on to your next act.

Ritual Elements

> Informal gatherings with fellow actors and friends.
> Shared meals in diners or delis symbolizing creative struggle and support.

Food Components

Bagels, pizza slices, and deli sandwiches evoke urban life and shared career pursuit.

Documentation Ideas

A visual collage of receipts, menus, and sketches of city spaces; a playlist of show tunes representing aspiration and persistence.

Part 3: Starring in a New Role (Adulthood and Return)

This section is about your life now. After your time in New York, you returned to where you grew up and are "Back Home in Indiana" as the famous song goes. In this phase of your life, you discovered a vocation that aligns with your lifelong love of theater. You are a high school music teacher and direct the school plays. While you did not make it on Broadway, you are using your skills and talents every day—it turns out, this is your calling. Importantly, the students look up to you and feel inspired by their creative teacher. They love to hear your stories about life in the Big City and look at your pictures, too. A few say that they are going to try it out themselves and see what happens. You are a star in community theatre now. Although you did not become a "legend" on Broadway—you are a local legend!

Ritual Elements

> Community or family gathering that mirrors the childhood celebrations.
> Shared meal that connects past and present through familiar dishes.

Food Components

Regional favorites such as tenderloin sandwiches, sweet corn, and sugar cream pie ground the ritual in place and memory.

Documentation Ideas

Photographs of teaching moments, students' reflections, or a recreated "program" celebrating the person's local legacy.

Assessment

In this instance, self-evaluation may be appropriate for letting students consider how things turned out, what they learned, and its value for them.

Cross-Disciplinary Adaptation

> **Health Sciences**: Ritualized health behaviors, including taking medication, exercising, and preparing certain foods, are embodied practices that involve biological, social and behavioral information. When documented through logs, visuals, or narratives, these rituals can reveal patterns of health, access, and care across individuals and groups.

> **Education**: Classroom rituals, including warm-up activities for the day, icebreakers, and group discussion circles, are embodied acts that produce and communicate information about learning and belonging. Documentation through lesson plans or reflective writing transforms daily educational practice into shared pedagogical insights and knowledge production.

Instructor Try-It Activity

Choose a recurring practice in your field that feels ritual-like—something patterned, symbolic, or community-building, such as rounds, meetings, or performances. Observe and reflect on how information is produced through actions, tools, or interactions, and document it using a format of your choice (notes, photos, sketches, or recordings). Afterwards, review what your documentation reveals: how the ritual communicates meaning, and how this process might help students in your field recognize and share information in similar ways.

Additional Resources/ References

Here are some other materials that can serve as "food for thought" to accompany the activity.

Films

Baijnauth, Rock, dir. 2014. Barista. Samuel Goldwyn Films.

Shigeno, Koki, dir. 2017. Ramen Heads. Kino Lorber.

Writings

On Aging, Ritual, and Life Course Studies

Briller, Sherylyn, and Erika Carrillo. 2020. "Applying Anthropological Insight in an Aging World." In Oxford Research Encyclopedia of Anthropology. October 27. https://bit.ly/3JQ51ev.

Keating, Elizabeth. 2022. Th*e Essential Questions: Interview Your Family to Uncover Stories and Bridge Generations*. Tarcher Perigee.

On Food and Food Ritual

Nahum-Claudel, Chloe. 2023 [2016]. "Feasting." In *The Open Encyclopedia of Anthropology*. Edited by Felix Stein. https://bit.ly/47vI5u4.

Sutton, David E. 2001. *Remembrance of Repasts: An Anthropology of Food and Memory*. Berg Publishers.

BOILING IT DOWN: PLAIN TALK AND EFFECTIVE VISUALS TO INFORM AUDIENCES

By: Professor Alexandria Johnson

Discipline: Atmospheric and Planetary Sciences

Subject: Atmospheric Thermodynamics

Information Qualities of the Format

This assignment combines text with images to explain complex scientific concepts. By simplifying thermodynamics into plain language and reinforcing it with visuals, students learn they can communicate beyond their discipline, potentially affecting change. Visual explanation enables audiences without technical training to understand concepts that could otherwise remain inaccessible.

Who This Is For

Students in higher education, particularly graduate students, often work at great depth within narrow areas of study. This introductory-level activity is designed for STEM majors to develop effective interdisciplinary communication skills both across fields where thermodynamics concepts apply, including atmospheric science, planetary science, physics, astronomy, and mechanical engineering, and with audiences outside these disciplines, such as homeowners, elementary school children, and city planners. In math or physics-heavy courses, the activity provides a valuable opportunity to reframe complex material in simple language and support it with visuals, ensuring clarity without sacrificing accuracy.

Learning Outcomes

> **Explain** a scientific topic in language nonexperts can understand.
> **Apply** visual design principles to guide viewers through complex ideas.
> **Design** an infographic that communicates complex concepts clearly to nonexperts.
> **Evaluate** peer-created infographics by providing structured feed back.

Instructional Context

> Small group collaboration
> Class Time: Two sessions (50 minutes each) for brainstorming, sketching, and instructor and peer feedback. (Students are expected to work on projects outside of class as well.)
> Environment: Digital lab or classroom

Materials and Equipment

> Computers or tablets
> Infographic creation tools:
o Digital: Canva, Piktochart, Microsoft PowerPoint, Adobe Illustrator, Microsoft Paint, Microsoft Create
o Analog: Poster board, markers, cut-outs, printouts
> Access to course materials
> Drawing materials for sketching ideas in Session 1

Pre-Class Homework

Ask students to complete the following before Session 1:

> Read associated chapter(s) from the course text.
> Choose at least one concept they find interesting or challenging.
> Bring a sample science infographic (print or digital) for critique.
> Answer a mini-reflection prompt:

- Choose a thermodynamics concept and explain how you would teach it to someone with no science background. How would you describe your topic using everyday language? What visuals might assist your explanation?

Resources Students Should Review for the Assignment

Language

- AGU: Advancing Earth and Space Sciences: Essential Topic and Tools for Communicating Your Science: https://bit.ly/4qS7rtY
- The Up-Goer Five Text Editor: A Tool to help communicate scientific information to a non-scientific audience: https://splasho.com/upgoer5/

Design (links not provided can be found in the Practical Skills Index section)

- Canva: The Ultimate Guide to Visual Hierarchy https://bit.ly/4oVhRHd
- Canva: How to Choose the Perfect Font Palettes
- W3 Schools Color Schemes
- W3 Schools Color Accessibility
- WebAIM: Typefaces and Fonts
- Graphics: The Noun Project: https://thenounproject.com

Assignment

Session 1: Introduction to Infographics and Brainstorming Session

Process and Steps

1. **Warm-up Discussion**

   Students choose a partner to Think, Pair, Share their chosen infographics with and prompt answer:

> What makes the infographic work visually and conceptually?

> What confused or distracted you?
> Share the answer to the assigned prompt with partner.
> Share the infographic and prompt answer with the class.

2. **Mini-Lecture** (referring to the provided resource)
> Identifying the audience. This can be another discipline, such as planetary science or physics, or populations outside of academia, including agricultural workers, siblings, or policymakers.
> Use of plain language. The instructor could role-play explaining a topic to a nonexpert or provide examples for how discipline-specific jargon can be replaced with commonly used words.
> Use of visual hierarchy to navigate viewers through a concept.
> Accessibility in visuals and text.
> Discussion on copyright and image use:
o When creating infographics, students must respect copyright: use original visuals or visuals/images with permission (e.g., Noun Project).
Even with government or public domain images, attribution is the best practice. Always credit sources.

3. **Brainstorming and Team Formation**
> Students form small groups (two to four people).
> Each group chooses one thermodynamics concept to explain with an infographic.
> Ask:
o Who is your audience?
o What's the core concept?
o What knowledge does your audience already have about this concept?
o What images, data, or even analogies might you use?
o In what ways will your team specifically customize your message, tone, and visuals to engage your target audience?

4. **Exit Ticket**

   Each group submits a short plan:

> Working title
> Target audience
> Main message
> Initial sketch that includes:
o Three colors chosen with readability and accessibility in mind.
o At least four blocks of information (which will be 50 words max) that each have at least one graphic/image.
o Four separate take-aways or pieces of information
o Technical terms that will be included with definitions.
o Choice of fonts (limit to two or three with readability in mind).

Session 2: Workshop and Peer Review Process and Steps

1. **Peer Review Rotation**

   Post draft infographics either digitally or physically around the room. Each student gives feedback to at least three groups using this peer critique format:

> Describe what you see.
> Ask for any needed clarification.
> Say what you think works.
> Offer any helpful suggestions.

2. **Class Debrief**

   Whole class discussion (this may be an opportunity to reach out to the Graphic Design or Communications department to see if students would be willing to participate in the Debrief):

> What trends or pitfalls did you see across the drafts?
> What makes a science infographic successful?
> How did your perspective change from seeing others' work?

3. **Wrap-Up**

> Individual group members discuss changes they need to make to their infographic before submitting for a final grade.
> If time permits, students can work on revising their projects.

Assessment

Reflection

Since elements of this assignment may have been new to students, such as visual hierarchy, rather than a strict rubric, students submit a reflection on how their language use and design choices affected the clarity and effectiveness of their infographic along with their final product. The following topics are included:

> Audience awareness
> Accessibility
> Visual hierarchy
> Effective use of graphics
> Citation and attribution

Cross-Disciplinary Adaptation

> **Public Health**: Students create infographics to explain processes like fever, heat stroke, wind chill, frostbite, or sweating. For audiences such as school communities, community organizations, or families, images communicate what text alone would take too long to explain.
> **Architecture**: Students create infographics to emphasize insulation, passive heating, and material choices, enabling audiences such as clients, stakeholders, or policy makers to see how buildings handle heat without needing detailed descriptions.
> **Environmental Studies**: Students create infographics to show climate change, greenhouse gases, and urban heat islands, helping city planners, policymakers, and the public understand complex systems when they lack time for detailed explanations.

Instructor Try-It Activity

Before assigning the activity to students, test it yourself with paper, markers, and glue.

Process and Steps

1. **Pick a Concept**
   Choose a simple thermodynamics idea (e.g., "Why ice melts in your drink").

2. **Make a Mini-Infographic**

> Include:
o A clear title
o Two or three short text blocks (under 20 words)
o At least one simple visual (drawn or cut-out)
o Readable fonts and colors
o Make note of how you used visual hierarchy to guide the viewer.

3. **Share and Reflect**

Show a colleague and ask:
> Is the message clear?
> Do visuals add meaning?
> Is the layout easy to follow?

4. **Take Notes**

Record what worked, what didn't, and how you'd improve it for students.

Additional Resources/ References

DK. 2018. *How Science Works: The Facts Visually Explained.* DK Publishing.

Examples

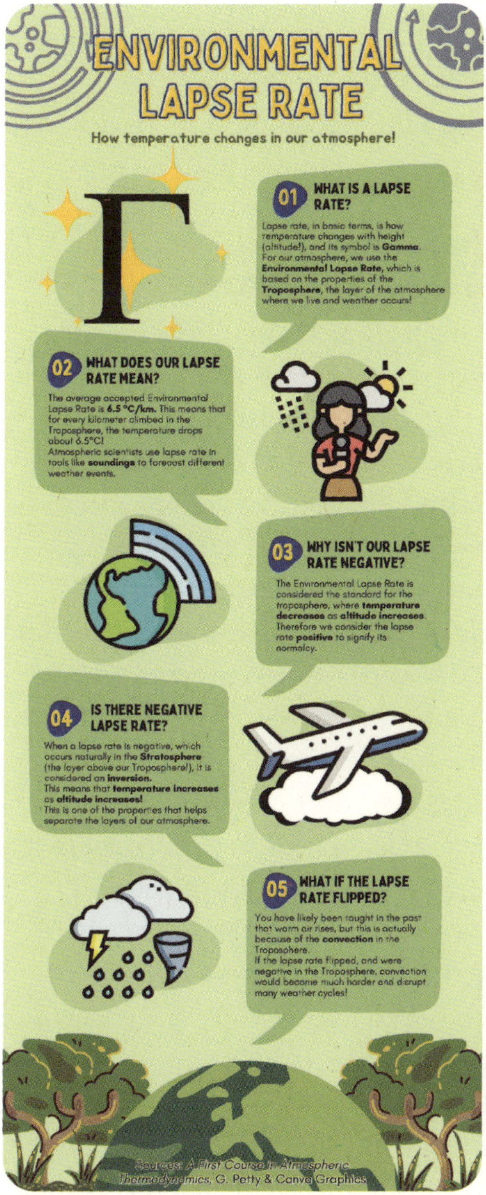

Image 1 : Environmental Lapse Rate

Photo credit: Screen capture of student created work.

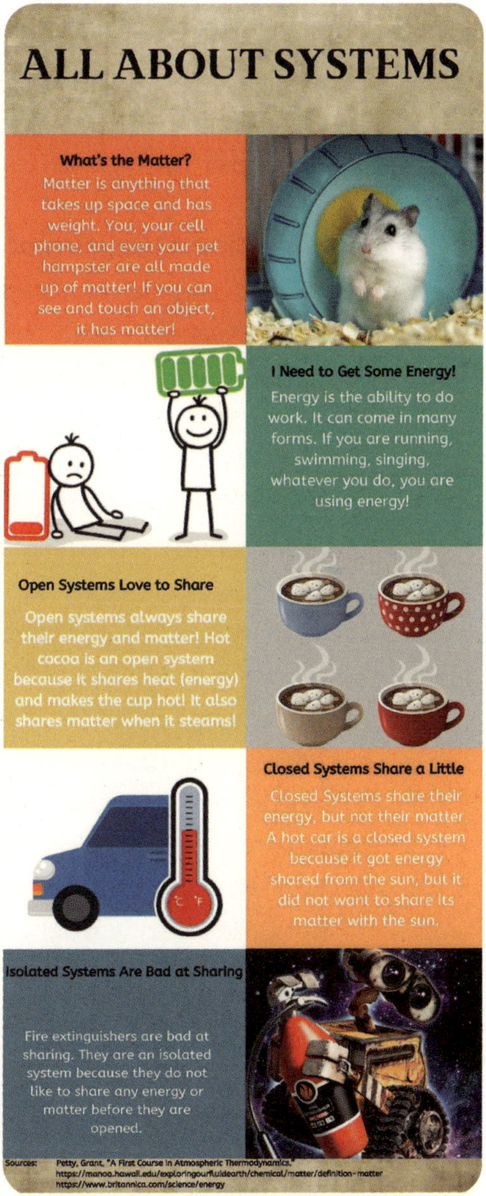

Image 2: All About Systems Image

Photo credit: Screen capture of student-created work.

LANDSCAPES AS LIVING DOCUMENTS: PHOTOS AND STORIES AS TOOLS TO FIND PLACE

By: Hui-Hui Wang

Discipline: Agricultural Sciences Education and Communication

Subject: Community Engagement

Information Qualities of the Format

Historical and contemporary photos paired with community interviews convey rich, multidimensional insights into landscape change. Comparing past and present images reveals shifts in land use, farming practices, rural infrastructure, and community growth, sharpening critical observation and analysis. Interviews add firsthand context that deepen understanding of agricultural, environmental, and social impacts. Together, these visual and narrative data do more than record change—they communicate layered stories of place and invite students to read landscapes as active texts where environment and human experience intersect. Framing these methods as tools within agricultural education—combining visual documentation, oral histories, and community knowledge—helps students connect local agricultural heritage with present challenges and envision their own future roles in farming, land stewardship, or rural development. This activity treats the area as a living document, with students writing their role in its future.

Who This Is For

Designed for undergraduates in community engagement, this lesson suits many fields: environmental science and geography (land use, sustainability), sociology, anthropology, and history (cultural heritage), and urban planning or design (development, preservation). It is intended to help students envision a future role and place within the evolving landscape.

Learning Outcomes

> **Analyze** visual evidence of landscape and community change by comparing historical and contemporary photographs.
> **Interpret** environmental and social transformations through the integration of visual data and oral histories.
> **Demonstrate** critical observation skills by identifying and articulating patterns of change in land use, architecture, vegetation, and community infrastructure.
> **Formulate** a future role(s) within the evolving landscape.

Instructional Context

Students may work individually or in pairs/small groups.

Resources Students Should Review for the Assignment

To support their photo documentation and community interviews, students should review:

> Visual and historical context, such as local archives or historical societies for old photographs and maps, or community newsletters or newspapers for historical events and changes.
> Ethical guidelines for engaging with community members, including informed consent and respectful listening.

Assignment

Photo Documentation

Students will take one or two local landscape photographs that highlight areas of interest or change. They may also gather older photos from family, friends, or community sources to enrich their perspective. Possible guiding themes include:

> Economic development (e.g., job opportunities, industry shifts)
> Urbanization and land use (e.g., rural-to-urban transformation)
> Environmental change (e.g., conservation efforts, loss of green space)
> Cultural or historical preservation (e.g., maintaining cultural identity)
> Education and public services (e.g., schools, community centers)

In class, students present and discuss their images to build a shared visual timeline of landscape change and develop questions for community interviews.

1. Explain their choice of location and its significance.
2. Suggest possible stories behind the site.
3. Identify questions or curiosities the photos raise.
4. Describe what they hope to learn and why, including how their choice connects to where they might fit within the future landscape.
5. Contribute their images to a collective display that sparks discussion, critical thinking, and the development of interview questions.

Community Interviews

Building on the photo discussion, students will conduct an interview with a community member—such as an elder, local historian, or other knowledgeable individual—to gather personal stories, historical context, and perspectives related to their chosen sites and themes. These interviews deepen understanding of the visual evidence and connect observed changes to lived experiences.

Interview Plan Outline

Before conducting interviews, students must provide:

> The name or role of the person they plan to interview

> The reason for selecting this individual (e.g., expertise, personal connection to the site)
> A list of proposed interview questions informed by their photo analysis and class discussion

This process ensures students approach interviews thoughtfully, respect community knowledge, and use the gathered narratives to enrich their understanding of the landscape's evolving story.

Presentation

Formal Assessments

Students structure presentations around:

> Why they chose the location
> Possible stories behind it
> Questions or curiosities the photos raised
> What they hoped to learn and key insights gained from the interview
> How the community member's perspective confirmed, expanded, or challenged their initial ideas
> How they now see themselves fitting into the future landscape

Final Reflection

Summative Assessment

Students submit a final reflection (one page, double-spaced) that:

> Explains how visual and narrative data were synthesized
> Describes key lessons learned from the process
> Highlights community insights gained through the interviews
> Reflects on where they could see themselves fitting into the landscape's future

Cross-Disciplinary Adaptation

> **Clothing and Fashion Design** (Landscape-Inspired Wearables):

Students photograph local sites or use archival images to inspire garment shapes, textures, and color palettes. Pair these with community interviews to inform design choices. Deliverables might include a design board, a prototype garment or accessory, and an artist statement connecting visual and narrative research to their creative decisions. Display pieces with photos or interview excerpts for a mini-gallery or pop-up fashion show.

> **Art, Media, and Communication** (Visual Storytelling Projects): Use the photo/interview pairing as inspiration for a zine, short video essay, or mixed-media installation. Emphasize sequencing, pacing, and emotional impact to communicate place-based stories. Display finished works with excerpts or images for a small exhibit or online showcase.

> **Computer Science** (Digital Landscape Analysis): Students use historical and contemporary photos as datasets for basic image processing, GIS mapping, or change-detection algorithms. Pair these visual findings with community interviews to add narrative context and ethical considerations. Deliverables could include a simple program or visualization that highlights detected changes alongside quotes or stories, prompting discussion of technology's role in documenting and shaping communities. This approach connects technical skills to real-world, place-based problem solving and shows students how their expertise can contribute to understanding and preserving evolving landscapes.

Examples

The Horse Barn (Image 1) was built in 1919 and replaced by the Ray W. Herrick Laboratories (Image 2) in 1957–1958, with renovations in 2013. Today, it supports mechanical engineering research on heating, cooling, and air quality; engine and fuel testing; sound and vibration; and indoor environmental experiences like temperature, light, and sound. Students in agriculture can now collaborate with mechanical engineers on projects such as animal housing, grain storage, and agricultural machinery.

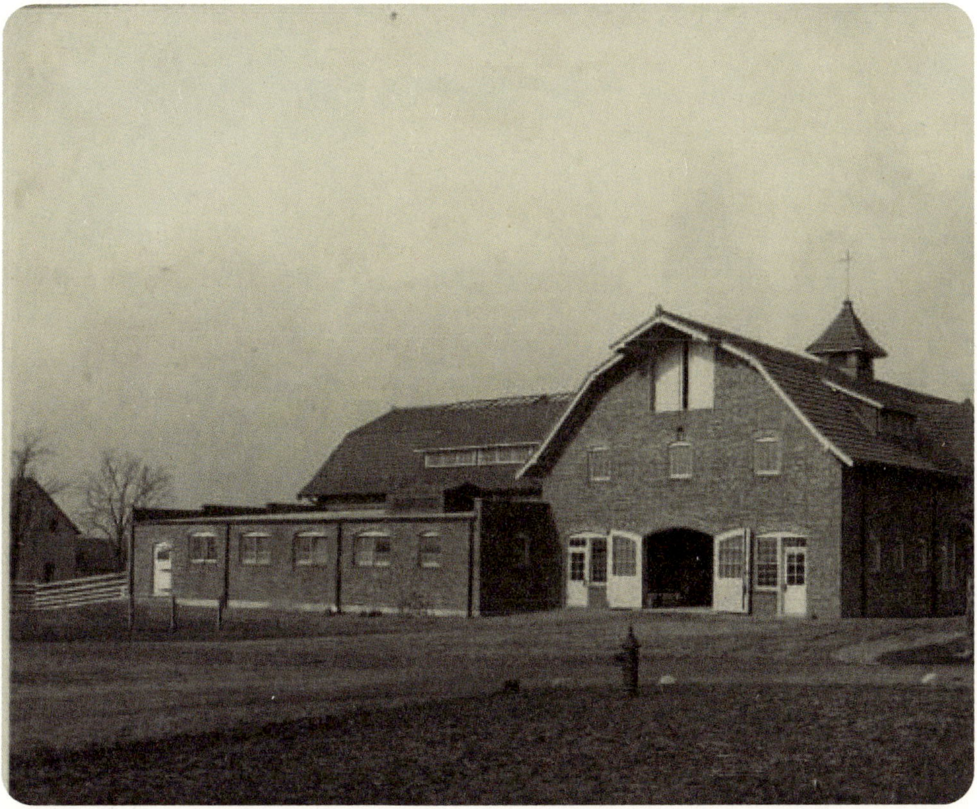

Image: Horse Barn
Photo credit: Image and information about the Horse Barn are courtesy of Purue University Libraries, Archives and Special Collections.

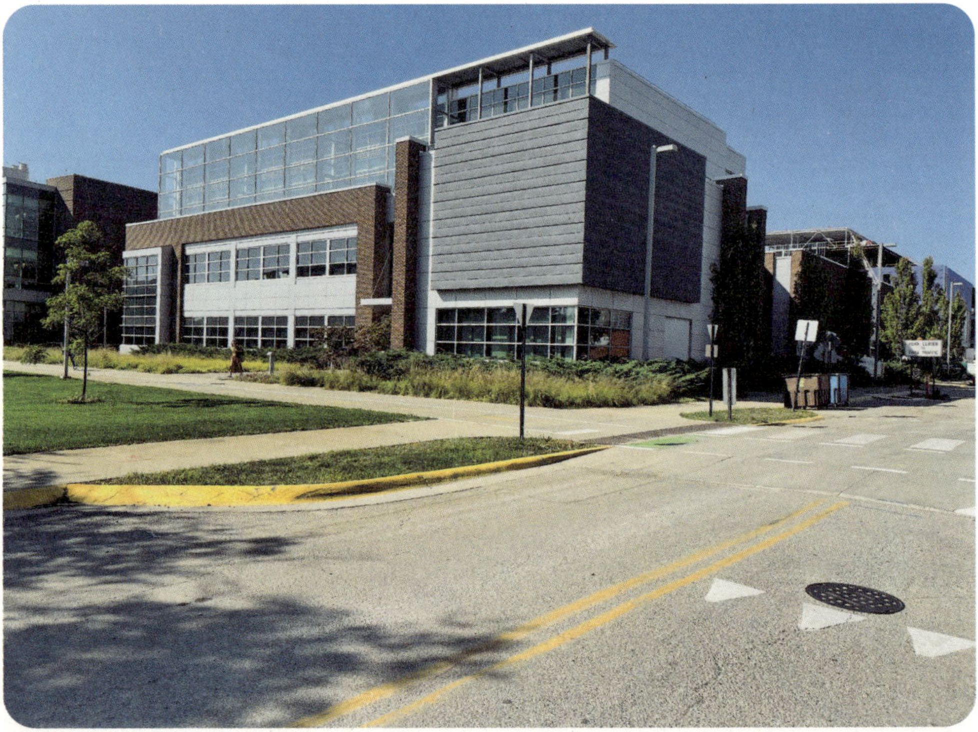

Image 2: The Ray W. Herrick Laboratories, Purdue University.
Photo credit: Sarah Huber

Instructor Try-It Activity
Process and Steps

1. **Choose** a site that is essential to your discipline, a specific gathering place, library, lab, outdoor space, etc.
2. **Capture and Compare**

> Take a current photo and find or imagine an older image to reveal change.

3. **Add Narrative Context**

> Note whose stories or memories would deepen these visuals and what future stories could emerge.

4. **Link to Your Course**

> In two or three sentences, describe how combining visual and narrative data could help students see both the subject and their place within its ongoing story. Specifically, what current and future roles could your students see contributing to the discipline or field.

Additional Resources/ References

Knapp, Clifford E. 2014. "Place-Based Curricular and Pedagogical Models: My Adventures in Teaching through Community Contexts." In *Place-Based Education in the Global Age*, 29–52. New York: Routledge.

Vander Ark, Tom, Emily Liebtag, and Nate McClennen. 2020. *The Power of Place: Authentic Learning through Place-Based Education*. Alexandria, VA: ASCD.

SHAPED BY FORMAT: EXPLORING RADIATION THERAPY THROUGH DIFFERENT FORMS OF ENGAGEMENT

By: Alison Roth

Discipline: Medical Physics

Subject: Fiber Arts Representation of Climate Data

Information Qualities of the Format

This assignment invites students to explore an advanced radiation therapy modality or theory (e.g., FLASH, MR-guided adaptive RT, proton arc, carbon-ion, spatially fractionated RT, radiomics-guided planning) through one of three formats—song, podcast, or paper—encouraging them to consider how each of the format's qualities will shape their perspective and engagement with the materials.

The following qualities can guide discussion on how format choice will influence their experience:

> **Songs** could aid memorization through repetition, as well as help students find personal meaning through word choice and instrumentation that resonates with them.

> **Podcasts** could help students listen more deeply, finding meaning through voice, sound, and story.

> **Point-Counterpoint Papers** could foster the reflection needed to build evidence-based reasoning through structured argument.

Who This is For

Students in graduate courses in medical physics. Also suitable for advanced undergraduates and graduate students from the disciplines related to medical physics, biomedical engineering, nuclear engineering, and physics. Adaptable to other disciplines where scientific reasoning, evidence synthesis, and communication format are central.

Learning Outcomes

> **Research** and **synthesize** advanced topics in radiation therapy using primary and secondary literature.
> **Translate** scientific information into an alternative format that requires new structural strategies.
> **Reflect** on how format alters understanding and communication of knowledge.
> **Demonstrate** accuracy and clarity in their chosen format.

Instructional Context

This serves as a final project for the course Radiation Therapy Physics. Students research a topic not covered in lecture and present it in a format that demonstrates both scientific mastery and communication awareness.

> For small classes, presentations or performances may be held in class.
> For large classes, submissions may be digital, with optional peer listening or reading.

Materials and Equipment

> Song: Optional instruments or background tracks (can be per formed live or pre-recorded)
> Podcast: Recording device (phone, laptop, or microphone)
> Paper: Standard text editor or word processor
> All Formats: Access to journal databases, recording/editing software (e.g., Audacity)

Resources students should review for the assignment

> Purdue Podcasting Guide: https://bit.ly/4939cOp
> Audacity Tutorials: https://bit.ly/4oYtoaq
> Point-Counterpoint Examples: https://bit.ly/43XEliF

Assignment

Students will:

1. Select an advanced radiation therapy topic not covered in class.
2. Decide if this will be an individual or group project.
3. Research the topic using at least five scholarly sources, including two or more original research articles.
4. Identify five key points central to understanding their topic (physics, instrumentation, clinical/preclinical relevance, or theoretical debate).
5. Translate those key points into one of the three formats described below. Specify expectations for tone (e.g., serious vs. playful; allowance for humor or parody).
6. Turn in a reflective memo using the prompts below.

Option 1: Song

> Rewrite lyrics of an existing song to communicate the five key points of their chosen topic.
> Ensure syllable counts fit the original rhythm.
> Length: Two to five minutes.
> Submission: Original lyrics, new lyrics, five key points, citations, and (optional) audio recording.
> In-class performance or playback optional.

Option 2: Podcast

> Record a seven to nine minute (individual) or 12–15 minute (group)

episode that clearly presents the selected topic.

> Format options: Conversational, narrative, interview, panel, or solo.
> Must include flow (smooth transitions) and five key points.
> Submission: Audio file, citations, list of key points, contribution ratings.
> In-class component: Brief (two to three minute) summary or live playback excerpt.

Option 3: Point-Counterpoint Paper

> Write a three to five page (two students) or four to six page (three students) paper structured like a professional debate article:

o Overview
o Opening for the Proposition (supporting implementation)
o Opening against the Proposition (cautioning limitations)
o Rebuttal (for)
o Rebuttal (against)
o Summary/Conclusion
o Submission: Paper, citations, group contribution ratings

> In-class component: Two to three minute informal summary of findings

Reflective Memo Prompts

> How did the format you chose (song, podcast, paper) shape your understanding of your topic?
> What aspects of your topic were easier or harder to express in this format?
> How do you think your audience's understanding changes depending on format?
> How did the quality of your and your peers' formats affect under standing?
> If you could redo this project in a different format, what would change?

In-Class Presentations

> Students share their chosen format briefly in class (2–3 minutes).
> Optionally, a short discussion follows:

o How did the medium affect what you learned, and how you expressed it?

Example

Flash Me Maybe (Parody of "Call Me Maybe" by Carly Rae Jepsen)
By Ethan Mahaffey

[Verse 1]
I tossed a wish in the beam,
High dose per second—extreme,
Oxygen drops in the scene,
Protects the normal, maybe!
Conventional's too slow,
Tissues take too much blow,
But FLASH is stealing the show—
It's kinda crazy, maybe!

[Pre-Chorus]
Tumors get
stressed, But not all
the rest, ROS spikes,
I think FLASH just saved me maybe!

[Chorus 1]
Hey, I just FLASHed you, and this is crazy,
40 Gray/sec, so heal up, maybe!
One ultra-fast dose to you baby,
But here's your doctor, so heal up,
maybe!

Hey, I just FLASHed you, and this is crazy,
Millisecond hit, so heal up, maybe!
Hypoxia shields up, tumor's gettin' lazy,
Here's your FLASH beam, so heal up, maybe!

[Verse 2]
Dose dumped in less than a blink,
Linear Energy—wink,
Tumor cells starting to shrink,
While healthy tissue's waving!
Short pulses end the bad days,
Less damage, fast relays,
Vessels and lungs can replace,
It's FLASH, it's crazy, baby!

[Pre-Chorus]
Tumors get wrecked,
But we protect,
Normal response,
I think FLASH just saved me maybe!

[Chorus 2]
Hey, I just FLASHed you, and this is crazy,
40 Gray/sec, so heal up, maybe!
FLASH-enabled LINAC, upgraded daily,
Here's your FLASH beam, so heal up,
maybe! Single-shot dosing, trials lookin'
crazy,
Here's your FLASH beam, so heal up, maybe!
And all the other modes, drive me crazy.
They take too long now, so FLASH me maybe!

[Post-Chorus]
Before you FLASHed into my lab, it was so bad,
It was just so bad, it was just so so bad.
No more endless fractionation—it's just one blast,
Now the tumors dead, it was just so so bad!

[Bridge]
It's hard to treat all, these tumors baby,
But there's the LINAC, so FLASH me, maybe!

[Chrous]
Hey, I just FLASHed you, and this is crazy,
One pulsed-up treatment, so heal up, maybe!
And all the other modes, drive me crazy,
They take too long now, so FLASH me maybe!

[Post-Chorus]
Before you FLASHed into my lab, it was so bad,
It was just so bad, it was just so so bad.
Before you FLASHed into my lab, it was so bad,
Now the tumors dead So FLASH me, maybe!

Assessment

Key Points: Student clearly explains and connects five main ideas about their topic. Creativity and Engagement (10 pts): Format (song, podcast, or paper) feels intentional, flows naturally, and there are added elements (use of sound, use of narrative, etc.) that draws the audience into the material.

Quality: The final product is polished and professional: clear audio for podcasts or songs, strong writing and formatting for papers.

Group Contribution: Everyone pulls their weight; peers agree contributions were fair.

Reflection: A short (100–150 word) reflection explaining how your chosen format shaped what you learned and how you communicated it.

Cross-Disciplinary Adaptation

> Biology: Students rewrite a popular song to explain mRNA technology. Reflective memo focuses on how repetition, rhythm, and rhyme reinforced scientific vocabulary and process.
> Business/Marketing: Students produce a panel-style podcast about an emerging industry trend. Reflective memo focuses on how voice and pacing establish credibility and persuasion.
> Political Science/Law: Students argue opposing positions on a proposed policy or law through a point-counterpoint paper. Reflective memo focuses on how structuring logical, evidence-based argumentation through text helped them reflect and explain.

Instructor Try-It Activity
Process and Steps

1. **Pick a Concept**

> Choose an advanced topic you teach (e.g., adaptive planning, image guidance, dose optimization).

2. **Try Two Formats**

> Write a 100-word summary as a research abstract.
> Then explain the same concept in a different format—record a one-minute podcast or write four lines of lyrics.

3. **Reflect** (5 min)

> Which version helped you think differently?
> What was easier or harder to express?
> How might each format change what students notice or remember?

Conclusion

Toward a Community of Practice

By Sarah Huber

Working on this project with contributors across disciplines deepened my understanding of how information and knowledge are created differently across fields. My own background—an AAS in Audio-Video Digital Media, a BA in English, an apprenticeship with a clothing designer, and an MLIS—has shaped how I see connections among these varied approaches to making and communicating meaning. While faculty and students in art and design disciplines often recognize how form shapes meaning, I have consistently seen those in STEM fields treat form and content as separate concerns. This divide has persisted across my work in K–12 education, a trade school, and a research university, where efforts to integrate art into STEM rarely took hold in sustained or systematic ways. Yet this gap represents an opportunity rather than a limitation. When disciplines work together, material and format choices can be understood as integral to knowledge-making rather than as surface-level additions. *Creating Formats Across Media and Disciplines: Assignments Beyond the Essay* offers a practical, accessible entry point for instructors and students working in unfamiliar material territory. Rather than focusing on discipline-specific content, the book centers the qualities of information formats themselves—how they are constructed, what they communicate, and how foundational art and design principles shape meaning.

When the Knowledge Lab opened, I expected it to attract primarily liberal arts students. Instead, it drew a strong mix of STEM students, many of whom said the same thing: "I hate the term STEM; it makes it sound like we aren't creative." When asked how the personal projects they created in the Lab might demonstrate understanding in their coursework, their responses were immediate and enthusiastic. Students want to express ideas in ways that feel natural to them—ways they already communicate outside academia—but they need shared language, practical tools, and consistent expectations to do so effectively. In practice, this often means basic art and design skills: color theory, visual hierarchy, the rule of thirds, timing, and composition.

This book was written to meet that interest and to support instructors who want to make space for diverse forms of expression without requiring design expertise. Positioned in the library—a neutral space across campus—this work helps bridge fields where format diversity is readily embraced and those where form and content remain separate concerns. Format knowledge alongside foundational art and design skills helps students make informed judgments about generated and mediated outputs rather than treating them as authoritative or complete. My hope is that it fosters more integrative approaches to knowledge-making that validate multiple ways of thinking, communicating, and sharing work. We already have strong models to learn from; what is needed now is the willingness to experiment, reflect on what works, and build a community of practice grounded in shared principles and practical strategies across disciplines.

Practical Skills Index

Design Basics

Color and Contrast

WebAIM: Color Contrast Checker. WebAIM (Web Accessibility in Mind)

> Offers tools and guidance for creating color palettes that meet accessibility standards. https://bit.ly/49oV7Rz

W3 Schools: Color Schemes

> Provides resources on all things color – schemes, palettes, theory, and more. https://bit.ly/3Jndvtv

Font and Typography

Google Fonts Knowledge: Typography Essentials

> Explains font pairing, readability, and typographic hierarchy. https://bit.ly/4qJsazX

Canva: How to Choose the Perfect Font Palettes

> Offers the basics in creating effective and easy to read graphics. https://bit.ly/47qkoVx

YorkU: Principles of Print Accessible Design

> Details 10 rules to make print accessible. https://bit.ly/4poQM5H

Layout and Hierarchy (Visual Balance, Alignment, Spacing)

Canva: Design Elements and Principles

> Provides an approachable resource for a broad range of design skills.

https://bit.ly/4nZz5Tb

Accessible Design (Color Contrast, Alt-Text, Captions, Screen-Reader Compatibility)

W3C Web Accessibility Initiative (WAI): Accessibility Principles.

> Details the industry standards for inclusive and accessible digital content.
https://bit.ly/4nIBSjn

Inclusive Design

These resources provide diverse approaches to design, emphasizing inclusion, equity, and social justice.

Gilbert, Regine M. 2019. *Inclusive Design for a Digital World: Designing with Accessibility in Mind.* Apress. https://doi.org/10.1007/978-1-4842-5016-7.

Lupton, Elizabeth, Fahrah Kafei, Jennifer Tobias, Josh A. Halstead, Kaleena Sales, Leslie Xia, and Valentina Vergara. 2021. Extra Bold: *A Feminist, Inclusive, Anti-Racist, Nonbinary Field Guide for Graphic Designers.* Princeton Architectural Press.

Moses, Terresa and Omari Souza, eds. 2023. *An Anthology of Blackness: The State of Black Design.* The MIT Press.

Place, Alison, ed. 2023. *Feminist Designer: On the Personal and the Political in Design.* The MIT Press.

Tunstall, Elizabeth (Dori) and Eni Agi. 2023. *Decolonizing Design: A Cultural Justice Guidebook.* The MIT Press.

Walters, Kelly. 2021. *Black, Brown + Latinx Design Educators: Conversations on Design and Race.* Princeton Architectural Press.

Data Visualization

How-To Guides

Evergreen Data: 5 Data Viz Mistakes & How to Fix Them

> Offers practical tips for making clearer, more effective charts.
https://bit.ly/4tO45cy

Evergreen Data: How to Build Data Visualizations in Excel

> Offers instructions, tips, and examples for users to create unique and effective data visulizations in Excel.
https://bit.ly/4kMoWWT

Dávila P. 2025. *Diagrams of Power. Visualizing, Mapping, and Performing Resistance* 4th Ed. Set Margins' publications

Stephanie D. H. Evergreen. 2017. *Effective Data Visualization: The Right Chart for the Right Data*. 2nd ed. SAGE Publications.

Photography and Video

Rule of Thirds and Visual Balance

Adobe: Photography Composition Basics

> Explains how to apply the rule of thirds to create visual balance.
https://bit.ly/49zoiLG

Leading Lines

Photography Life: Creating and Using Leading Lines

> Explains how to spot and utilize compositional lines.
https://bit.ly/43VqF7P

Framing and Perspective Choices

BBC Maestro: What is Framing in Photography

> Discusses framing as a key compositional technique.
https://bit.ly/3LhV7mq

Alt-Text Image Description

WebAIM: Alternative Text

> Gives directions on how to write alternative text across a variety of visuals.
https://bit.ly/43WpTYe

Cooper Hewitt Guidelines for Image Descriptions

> Provides guidelines for image descriptions, including describing people.
https://bit.ly/4qICYOz

Filming and Editing

Below are older resources but both offer very relevant tips presented through easy to follow videos.

BBC Academy: Filming with a Smartphone

> Provides simple tips on how to optimize filming with your phone.
https://bit.ly/4hNYAW3

YouTube Creator Academy: Total Beginner's Guide to Video Editing (by Google)

> Offers a simple and clear process pipeline for editing.
https://bit.ly/4ojxNmK

Podcasting

General Advice

NPR Training: Starting Your Podcast: A Guide for Students.

> Offers tips on everything from equipment and software to brain storming your podcast.
https://bit.ly/3WD3YS3

Academic Podcasting

> Amplify Podcast Network
A curated list of podcasting guides and tools for learning how to make podcasts.
https://bit.ly/45EgEgr

>An open educational resource for how to approach academic pod casting.
https://bit.ly/3NMOEkC

Accessible Podcasting

ADA Site Compliance: Making Podcasts Accessible: Tips for Engaging a Diverse Listener Base.

> Provides a comprehensive guide on the why and how of making your podcast accessible.
https://bit.ly/3WGoIby

Contributors

Dr. Jennifer Bay is a professor of English at Purdue University where she specializes in technical and professional Communication. Her research focuses on community engagement and experiential learning, internships, digital rhetorics, and rhetorical theory.

Dr. Sherylyn Briller is a professor of anthropology at Purdue University. Her work focuses on aging, care, and life course studies. She is interested in how ritual is infused in people's everyday lives and is intertwined with aging and meaning making.

Dr. Ian M. Cook is a Marie Sklodowska-Curie Postdoctoral Fellow at Dublin City University, a member of the Allegra Lab editorial collective, and a volunteer at Budapest's Open Learning Initiative (OLIve). He researches urban India, scholarly podcasting, environmental justice and university education initiatives for displaced people in Europe.

Dr. Erika Carrillo is an assistant professor of anthropology at San Jose State University, specializing in care and aging. She researches care and food, food politics, and food heritage. She enjoys teaching applied anthropology and working in multidisciplinary teams.

Eli Craven is an associate professor of photography at Purdue University. His research begins with acts of looking and collecting, then progresses to a critical investigation of the image and its relationship to ideologies of masculinity, desire, and death.

Liz Evans is a lecturer of media and mass communication at Purdue

University, where she teaches courses focused on multiplatform storytelling, video production, and broadcast journalism. Prior to teaching, she worked in media and public relations for more than 10 years. She is passionate about coaching and mentoring students, encouraging them to focus on their individual strengths and to embrace their own unique creative style.

Dr. Daniel Guberman is assistant director for student-centered pedagogy in the Center for Instructional Excellence at Purdue University. He is co-author of Designing Impactful College Courses to be released in 2026 by Routledge Press.

Dr. Jasmine L. Harris is professor and department chair of Africana Studies at Metropolitan State University of Denver. Her research examines institutional racism in higher education.

Kathleen Hickey is a choreographer, dancer, and teacher. She is an Essential Level–certified teacher of Molly Shanahan's Spiral Body Techniques® and teaches in the dance program in the Department of Theatre and Dance at Purdue University.

Brian Hitselberger is a senior lecturer in the Department of Art + Design at Purdue University, where he works as Design Foundations coordinator and teaches courses in the MFA department. He is also the founder of Two Steps Press, an independent publishing imprint.

Dr. Alexandria Johnson is an assistant professor of atmospheric and planetary sciences at Purdue University, where she studies the formation of clouds in planetary atmospheres both near and far. She sees every question as a powerful opportunity to grow and learn.

Dr. Mary Kosuth is a postdoctoral fellow at the University of Minnesota's Institute on the Environment. She is a researcher, systems thinker, and social change enthusiast. She secretly delights in the irreverence of wild, unkempt lawns and the smell of freshly sharpened pencils.

Dr. Shannon McMullen is an associate professor of electronic and time-based art at Purdue University with a collaborative creative practice at the intersection of nature, new media art, and emerging technologies.

Sammie L. Morris is Giustina Director of Special Collections and University Archives at the University of Oregon, where she researches teaching with primary sources. She is coauthor of two books and is dedicated to providing transformative learning experiences with rare collections.

Renee Murray is a senior lecturer of dance at Purdue University, where she teaches modern dance, choreography, dance for the camera, and intermedia dance technology. Her teaching objectives are to heighten each student's knowledge of their own body, expand movement possibilities, and explore opportunities for self-expression.

Alyssa Nez is a graduate assistant at Purdue University's Native American Educational and Cultural Center, where she works with the Indigenous Endangered Languages Lab in the Department of Linguistics. She focuses on Indigenous languages and is deeply committed to planning and hosting educational and cultural events that promote understanding of Indigenous Peoples and cultures within the Purdue community.

Matt Olson has an "open practice" and works with art and design through gardening, community, research, teaching and learning. He's founder of OOIEE (Office Of Interior Establishing Exterior), a studio based in St Paul, MN.

Dr. Sara Veglahn is a writer, editor, and educator. She has taught literature and writing since 2008, most recently serving as Chair of Writing and Poetics at Naropa University. Her latest novel, The Ladies, was published by Noemi Press.

Dr. Alison Roth coordinates Purdue's Radiation and Environmental Health Program. She is passionate about advancing health sciences education through teaching, experiential learning, student mentorship, career counseling. Her research focuses on using medical imaging to identify biomarkers and optimize treatment strategies.

Patricia Swanson is the manager of the Knowledge Lab makerspace at Purdue University, where she specializes in helping students explore multimodal forms of scholarship. She's passionate about hands-on learning and enabling students to creatively problem solve and try new things.

Dr. Hui-Hui Wang is an associate professor at Purdue University, with expertise in agricultural sciences education, communication, and curriculum and instruction. Her research focuses on integrated STEM education through agriculture and natural resources. She is passionate about creating engaging, student-driven learning environments.

Courtney T. Wittekind is an Assistant Professor of Anthropology at Purdue University. She teaches courses on ethnographic methods, technology, and media, and is passionate about interdisciplinary approaches to social science research.

Acknowledgments

I thank my colleagues at Purdue University Libraries for supporting the Knowledge Lab as a space for work that extends beyond traditional academic forms. I am especially grateful to the staff who volunteered their time to develop early programming and workshops, helping shape the ideas that led to the Lab, as well as to the staff who now run and sustain the Knowledge Lab through their ongoing care, expertise, and commitment. I also thank collaborators across campus and beyond who trusted unconventional assignments and helped demonstrate how multimodal work can deepen the learning experience across disciplines.

I am sincerely grateful to the designers, artists, educators, and scholars whose work appears throughout these pages and whose ideas about form, materiality, and communication continue to influence how I teach and learn. Their contributions made it possible to situate classroom practice within a wider landscape of making and meaning.

About the Editor

Sarah Huber is an associate professor of Library Science at Purdue University Libraries and director of the Knowledge Lab, a makerspace that supports low-stakes experimentation with multimodal forms of assignments and scholarship. Her teaching and research focus on visual literacy and on how information formats shape ideation, meaning-making, and scholarly communication across disciplines.
Her creative practice—including textile art, creative writing, and painting—has shaped this work, emphasizing the value of moving across formats to explore and communicate ideas. She approaches both scholarly and creative projects through shared frameworks grounded in principles of composition, language, color, and design, holding each to the same expectations of clarity, rigor, and purpose. Whether using traditional or AI-assisted tools, she treats format as a deliberate means of exploring and expressing ideas with intention.

Colophon

Set Margins' #105
Creating Formats Across Media and Disciplines: Assignments Beyond the Essay
Sarah Huber

ISBN: 978-90-836575-2-3
Contributors: Dr. Jennifer Bay, Dr. Sherylyn Briller, Dr. Ian M. Cook, Dr. Erika Carrillo, Eli Craven, Liz Evans, Dr. Daniel Guberman, Dr. Jasmine L. Harris, Kathleen Hickey, Brian Hitselberger, Dr. Alexandria Johnson, Dr. Mary Kosuth, Dr. Shannon McMullen, Sammie L. Morris, Renee Murray, Alyssa Nez, Matt Olson, Dr. Sara Veglahn, Dr. Alison Roth, Patricia Swanson, Dr. Hui-Hui Wang, Courtney T. Wittekind

Graphic design: Freek Lomme / Set Margins'

Text editor: Dr. Sara Veglahn

Printer: Balto, Vilius (LT)

Fonts: Almost Gothic by Poem Editions and Quieta by Zetafonts

Made possible thanks to Purdue University, Set Margins' publications and Sarah Huber.

Special thanks to the Purdue University Book Initiative

This publication is licensed under a Creative Commons Attribution-NonCommercial-ShareAlike 4.0 International Licence (CC BY-NC-SA 4.0). To view a copy of this license, visit https://creativecommons.org/licenses/by-nc-sa/4.0/

First edition, 2026

Set Margins'
www.setmargins.press